John Edward Bunch II
Black Dragon
Lifer
East Coast Regional President
Former National President
Mighty Black Sabbath Motorcycle Club Nation
A Breed Apart
Since 1974 and Still Strong………..///
www.bikerliberty.com
Host Black Dragon Biker TV YouTube
Host Black Dragon Biker Facebook
Host BlackDragonBikerTV Instagram
Host BlackDragonBikerTV TikTok
Host The Dragon's Lair Motorcycle Chaos Podcast – Spreaker.com
Sales/Advertising 404.692.0336
blackdragon@blacksabbathmc.com
Bunch Media Group
P.O. 931792
Norcross, Ga 30003

85,664 words.

Lifting As We Climb!

Edited by

- Christin Chapman

Cover design by

- Holly Joseph

Project Management, Outline

- Holly Joseph

First Edition, First Printing December 2023

Social Clubs Bible
Revival of the Women's Social Club Movement
"Lifting As We Climb!"

By, John Edward Bunch II 'Black Dragon' BSFFBS

Social Clubs Bible "Revival of the Women's Social Club Movement" is the sixth book in the Motorcycle Club Bible series. This manual teaches hang-arounds, prospects, and full patch sisters of women's social clubs the history, protocols, rules, and principles of the Black MC set - thus, empowering them to successfully navigate its social and political climate. It also revisits the historical Black woman's clubs movement; focusing today's social clubs toward improving the African American MC set, communities, and social construct.

Bunch Media Group
Motorcycle Club Education Division
**Copyright © 2023 by John E. Bunch II/Bunch Publishing/
Bunch Media Group**

All rights reserved, including the right to reproduce this book or portions thereof in any form whatsoever without expressed written authorization from the author. For information, address Bunch Media Group P.O. 931792, Norcross Georgia 30003.

Written and printed in the United States of America utilizing American ingenuity, pride, and workmanship.

Library of Congress Control Number: **2023922965**
International Standard Book Number: **978-0-9974322-7-5**

◊◊◊

For information about special discounts for bulk purchases or club purchases please contact Bunch Media Group at 404.692.0336 or blackdragon@blacksabbathmc.com.

Black Dragon can speak at your live events, host your annual, teach at your MC protocol training sessions, or host your life events. For more information or to book an event contact Bunch Media Group at 404.692.0336 or blackdragon@blacksabbathmc.com.
BlackDragonBikerTV - Instagram
Black Dragon Biker TV - YouTube
Black Dragon Biker - Facebook
BlackDragonBikerTV - TikTok
The Dragon's Lair Motorcycle Chaos Podcast
www.bikerliberty.com

◊◊◊

Acknowledgements:

Above all, I thank God. To Him be the glory.
To my love and my rock Tahmehrah 'Tia' Purdue.
To my editor Christin Chapman, thanks for sticking with me for two years on this one. We've done it again.
To my project manager Holly Joseph. Next time we pack in the beginning.
To my beloved mother Anese Yvonne Bunch 1942 – 1997.

I would like to give a special thank you to my subject matter experts (SMEs):

"Coffy" Vice President Eye Catchaz MC; Georgia Council Secretary
"2 Extra" President of Dominant Beautiz SC
"T. Solo" Founder/President of Simply Divas and Dames SC

I would like to send an honorable mention to:

"Voluptuous 10" Goddess Black Sabbath MC Nation Atlanta, GA
"Lady Tazz" First Lady Black Sabbath MC Nation Beaufort, SC
"Heavenly" First Lady Black Sabbath MC Nation Atlanta, GA
"Lady Chi" Head Goddess Black Sabbath MC Nation Houston, TX
"Brown Sugar" First Lady Black Sabbath MC Nation Houston, TX
"T Baby" First Lady Black Sabbath MC Nation Spring, TX
"Lovable" Head Goddess Black Sabbath MC Nation Spring, TX
"Southern Belle" First Lady Black Sabbath MC Nation Fort Worth, TX
"Pink" First Lady Black Sabbath MC Nation North Shore, LA
"Kut-N-Up" First Lady Black Sabbath MC Wichita, KS
"WyldKard" Head Goddess Black Sabbath MC Nation Topeka, KS
"Spider Woman" Godmother Black Sabbath MC Nation Macon, GA
"Sunshine" Vice President Simply Divas and Dames SC
"Foxy" Business Manager Simply Divas and Dames SC
"Sunny D Lite" Lady Voice Black Sabbath MC Nation I.E., CA
"Miss Never" Lady Vice Voice Black Sabbath MC Nation I.E., CA
"Ride R Die" Lady Voice SAA Black Sabbath MC Nation I.E., CA
"Essence" Founder Simply Divas and Dames SC Mother Chapter
"Secret" Founder Tosic Kisses
"Hottie" Sgt-at-Arms Tosic Kisses

The Social Clubs Bible

Figure 1 Father Paul Pep Perry (left) Advising John E. 'Black Dragon' Bunch II (circa 2015)

I have always felt privileged to have the counsel of the Original 7 Founder of the Mighty Black Sabbath MC Nation Father Paul 'Pep' Perry. As a young man who did not have a dad, I searched for many years for someone I could just make proud of me and give me somewhere to belong. Where there are those who will not believe in me there is always one who does. He was the man who told everyone that there was nothing I couldn't do. He instilled in me a sense of purpose and always demanded that I considered the club first where it was appropriate. He constantly admonished me to stop saying, "I, I, I, me, me, me, mine, mine, mine, and to start saying We!" This was his litany he repeated like a piece of software stuck in an endless loop. In 2008 he assigned me the mission of building our brotherhood into a mighty MC nation with chapters from coast to coast across the United States. I accepted that challenge knowing that I would finally get a chance to make him proud for taking the time to care about and believe in me. For me this was a good reason to be a national president. For him, for it is from him that I learned how to be WE!   #WeMC

Figure 2: Master Chief (SS) Tommy Hog Man Lewis (L) & Black Dragon (R) Circa 2011

Every man must know his strengths, weaknesses, and limitations. When I set out to build the Black Sabbath MC into a national club, I realized I lacked command experience. I could not let my pride get in the way by convincing myself that I could do it all when such was not the case. I enlisted former Mother Chapter President, Submarine Command Master Chief (C.O.B.) Tommy 'Hog Man' Lewis to come out of Black Sabbath retirement and help me lead the buildup of the nation. Master Chief Lewis had Submarine Navy experience in leadership at the highest level. He was a living legend and became a fire battalion chief after he retired. I called daily for nearly a year asking him to come back out of retirement. At first, he would laugh at me with big guffaws. He would say, "I'm glad to hear from you John, let's talk about something else." And we would talk. But I would always come back to saying, "You know we have your home for you right here whenever you are ready to come back." He would laugh again and say, "Goodbye John." Then, one day to my surprise he said, "Okay, I'll do it." Without Hog Man I could never have built the Black Sabbath MC into a national club. A president must never be too proud to seek help and guidance. The Master Chief was glad to lead from behind while I was the face out front.

The Social Clubs Bible

Foreword

The incredible strength, class, and beauty of the Black woman has been on full display in everything that she has accomplished since landing upon these shores against her will. She has refused to accept the place in life this society has designed for her, but rather has defined Her place to which she soars. She stands as one of the most educated and accomplished citizens the United States has ever seen as she has advanced herself by sheer will and determination. Today I have lived to see Black women serve as Secretary of State of the United States, Justice of the United States Supreme Court, and Vice President of the United States. These are accomplishments a sixty-year-old African American man thought he would never witness. So, I must tell you that I am honored to write this the first book of its kind that will help to guide my sisters to reaching new heights and accomplishing even greater things in this chosen passion of theirs, I shall lovingly dub "the modern social clubs' movement of the Black motorcycle club set!" I will watch with pride as our Black women continue to lift as they climb.

The Social Clubs Bible

"Good instincts are earned by making a few mistakes."

Who Should Read this Book?

It should be read by SC members, officers, prospects, hang-arounds, and women who are interested in learning about the history and purpose of Black women's SCs in the United States from slavery until present, the purpose of SCs on the Black biker set, and the intricacies of motorcycle club protocol, politics, and the biker set social construct. It will enhance your knowledge about the secretive societies of biker club nations and their associated communities. Biker club brothers can read this book to learn about SCs and how to interact with them respectfully.

- Social Club Presidents
- Social Club Vice Presidents
- Social Club Secretaries
- Social Club Business Managers
- Social Club Sgt at Arms
- Social Club Founders
- Social Club Members
- Motorcycle Clubs

Young woman know this, you are not a groupie! On the contrary without you the African American MC set would be nothing. Recognize!

◊◊◊

When to Use this Book

Use this book as a reference manual to help you develop your knowledge and experience. In these chapters you will find valuable information that will prepare you to operate on the biker set smoothly and effectively! Learn well and be wise. Good luck!

The Social Clubs Bible
The first love is self-love. The first respect is self-respect... Everything else is secondary!

JB11

Table of Contents

CHAPTER ONE Social Clubs on the Black Motorcycle Club Set 11

CHAPTER TWO Black Women, Strong Since Slavery 15

CHAPTER THREE The Progressive Movement and how it led to the establishment of The Woman's Social Clubs Movement in the United States.. 18

CHAPTER FOUR General Federation of Women's Clubs and the "Ruffin Incident" 20

CHAPTER FIVE The Black Woman's Club Movement 24

    Decline of woman's clubs 28

CHAPTER SIX Understanding the Motorcycle, Motorcycle Clubs, The Biker Club Sets 31

    The History of the Motorcycle in the United States 32

    The History of Motorcycle Clubs in the United States................. 33

        Early 1900s: 34

        1910s: 40

        1920s: 43

        1930s-1940s: 49

        Emergence of Outlaw Motorcycle Clubs 51

        1950s-1960s: 53

        1970s-1980s: 58

        Chopper Subculture 61

        1990s-Present 63

        MCs Growth and Diversification 65

CHAPTER 7 *How Do MCs Operate* 69

The Makeup of the MC 69
   National Officers 70
   What Is a National MC 73
   Summary of Motorcycle Club Operations 115
CHAPTER EIGHT *The Social Club, Biker Club's, Sets, Relationships, Protocol, & Moving Around* 116
   A Deeper Explanation and Look at the "Set" 116
   MC Protocol 117
      Inner-club MC Protocol 118
      Club Colors and Patches 118
      Respect for Club Hierarchy 118
      Club Meetings and Communication: 118
      Riding Formation and Etiquette 119
      Club Events and Activities 119
      Loyalty and Brotherhood/Sisterhood 119
      External Club Interactions 119
      Internal MC Protocol Summary 119
   Intraclub MC Protocol 120
      Respect for Club Colors and Patches 120
      Permission and Courtesy 120
      Greeting and Acknowledgment 120
      Communication and Diplomacy 121
      Non-Interference 121
      Protocol at Events 121
      Avoidance of Territory Disputes 121

- Protocol for Riding Together 122
- Intraclub MC Protocol Summary 122
- Hierarchy of Clubs on the Set 122
  - 1% Outlaw Motorcycle Clubs (OMCs) 124
  - Outlaw or Diamond MCs 125
  - Riding Clubs 125
  - Law Enforcement MC (LEMCs) 125
- Traditional MCs 127
- Veteran's MC 129
  - Christian MCs (CMCs) 130
  - Faith-based Focus 131
- Masonic MCs 132
- First Responder MCs 134
- Sober MCs 136
- Coed MCs 137
  - Charity MCs 140
  - Vintage Motorcycle Clubs: 140
  - BACA and Anti Child Abuse MCs 140
  - Female MCs 142
  - Motorsports Clubs (MSCs) 144
  - Riding Clubs: 145
- Patriot Guard and Specialty Biker Groups 145
- Motorcycle Organizations 147
- Motorcycle Rights Organizations (MROs) 148

CHAPTER NINE Overcoming Challenges Facing Black Women in SCs On the Biker Set 151

Overcoming the Basic Bullshit and Succeeding 151

Gender Dynamics and Patriarchy 151

Exclusion and marginalization 152

Objectification and Hyper-sexualization 154

Start Out Like You Can Hold Out 155

The Surprising Effect of the MC Set 155

Bikers On the MC Set Gossip More Than Women 156

All New Women are New Meat on the Set 157

My Club Brother Train and the Big, Sexy Girls 158

Limited Support Networks 158

Catty Petty Women 158

Safety concerns 159

Don't Just Be Jumping on Just Anyone's Motorcycles 160

Hard Head Not Hard Enough to Withstand the Fall 161

Brittany Morrow: The Queen of Road Rash 162

All of the Gear All of the Time 163

True Support Means Knowing It All, or as Much as You Can . 163

Learn the Signs of Trouble on the Set 164

CHAPTER TEN DEALING WITH THE 1%, DOMINANTS, DIAMONDS, OUTLAWS, OMGS, AND THE LIKE 166

A Quick Overview to Bring You Up-to-Speed 167

What are they called 167

One-Piece, Two-Piece, Three-Piece, and 5 Piece Patches 171

Hierarchy Among the 1% 174

How Do 1% Control the MC Set 176

What is a Blessing 177

Sponsoring MC (Brother Club) 178

Colors 179

Should I Sleep with a 1% President to Get my Club Blessed .. 181

The 1% Clubhouse 182

CHAPTER ELEVEN The Prospect's List of 45 Do's and Don'ts to Gain Entry into the SC 191

1 Prospecting is Getting into The Habit of Prospecting 192

Everyone Goes Through It 192

Your Pride May Take a Few Hits 192

Never Compromise Your Values 193

Sexual Harassment 193

Not Every Sister Who Wears the Patch Will Be Your Sister ... 194

No Means No! Rape is Rape! Punish a Rapist with the Law! . 196

Give Prospecting Your Best Effort 197

2 Conduct Yourself Responsibly 197

3 Always Display a Positive Attitude 197

4 Participate as Much as You Think is Acceptable then Participate More 198

5 If You See a Club Sister You Haven't Met Take the Initiative to Introduce Yourself 199

6 Ask to Circulate and Greet Every Patch Holder 199

7 Anticipate Needs, Don't Wait to be Told 200

Anticipatory Observation Skills 200

8 Don't Get Overly Friendly with Any Non-Regular Acquaintance of the Club 201

9 Sisters' Information Stays in the SC 202

"Loose Lips Sink Ships" 204

10 SC's Information Stays in the SC 205

11 Stay Alert 205

11B. Listen to Your Somethings 206

12 Conduct Yourself with the SC in Mind 206

13 Sisters Never Travel Alone on the Set 207

14 Alert the SAA or Senior Sister to Negative Vibes 208

15 Keep your Eyes and Ears Open 208

16 You are a Prospect 24/7 208

17 You Are Every Sister's Prospect 209

18 Never Wear Your Colors Out of Your Area Without Your Sponsor's Approval and Never Out of State Unless You are with Your SC 209

19 Private Conversations Among Sisters 210

20 "Outlaw Club" Should Never Be Uttered on the Set 211

21 Never Lie to a Member of Another Club 211

22 Show Equal Respect to Full Patch Sisters of Any Club 212

23 Always Carry Pen, Paper, Watch, and Calendar 212

24 Frequently Ask Full Patch Sisters How You Are Doing and if there's anything you Should be Doing Differently 212

25 Never Ask When You may be getting Your Full Patch 213

26 Never Call a Full Patch Your Sister 213

27 Never Call a Full Patch or Prospect of another SC Sister 213

28 Patches are Earned Not Given 214

29 Never Bring a Personal Friend or a Stranger into the Presence of your Prospective Sisterhood without asking Permission 215

30 Never Turn your Back on a Patch Holder of Another MC 215

31 Always Show Respect and Courtesy to Patch Holders of Other Clubs 215

32 Keep Away from Men Associating with other SCs due to Pillow Talk 216

   "Me No Date Butterfly" 216

33 Prospects Never Partake in Consuming Alcoholic Beverages at any Open Function 217

34 Prospects Never Partake in any Unnatural Drug 217

35 Never Acknowledge a Prospective Sister's Husband or Boyfriend especially upon First Meeting Him 218

36 Do not Touch or Sit on a Patch Holder's Motorcycle Unless Invited 218

   Turning Your Cut Inside Out 218

37 It's Not an Insult Not to be Acknowledged on the Set.......... 219

38 Learn Your Patch Parts and Colors 220

   Knowing Other Club's Patches and Meanings 221

39 A Prospect must do Anything a Prospective Club Sister may ask 221

40 Don't Touch another Club's Colors 221

41 Prospects must show a Sincere Interest in the Club 222

42 Stealing is Not an Option 222

43 Do Not Sleep Around with Members of the Sponsor MC or Multiple Men on the Set 222

44. Your Colors Should Never Touch the Ground 223

45 For Now, Just Follow the Rules 223

BEST OF LUCK PROSPECT! 224

CHAPTER Twelve An SC Founder/Prez Speaks 225

I Keep my Prospects Quiet 225

When the So-Called Experts and Bros Talk to Your Prospects ... 226

A President Educates Her Girls 227

Some SC Presidents and Founders will Sell Their Girls Out 228

If SC Presidents and Founders Knew Protocol 228

SC Presidents and Founders Don't Know What to Ask an MC ... 229

Some MCs Don't Want to Play Fair If not, Don't Play 229

MCs Pitting One SC Against Another 229

Why are Women Competing against Women 230

Division Amongst SCs Because of Outside Influences 230

We are Not Fuck Buckets 231

A Few Rules Prospects Should Know About Dealing with MCs .. 231

This is Why We Keep our Prospects Quiet 231

Problems Associated with Having the Wrong Brother MC 232

You May Support the MC but does the MC Support You 232

MCs want to Govern SCs Bank Accounts 232

Pimping is Alive on the Set 233

Finding a Good MC is Nearly Impossible 233

Dropping an MC can be a Problem 233

Having a Controlled SC gets it Labeled as "Trouble" 233

A Circle of Ladies who Define Themselves Empower Themselves 234

The SC is Responsible for its Members to their Families 234

"BE" Mindful of these Niggas 235

Creeper Niggas 235

Don't be Foolish Treat "Brothers" in Clubs with Caution 236

Learn to Cover Your Ass when dealing with the MC 236

Know what Questions to Ask Everybody before joining an SC .. 237

CHAPTER Thirteen The Way Forward 238

Black Men Don't Understand Your Purpose 238

TikTok Influencer DarkMatterGoddess 239

A Broken Clock is Right Twice Per Day 239

Why They Assault and Violate Black Women 240

These Men are Jealously Obsessed with our Beauty 240

Follow Yourselves Not Unfit Men 240

How can the Broken Clock be Right 241

Stand in Your Own Devine Power 241

Love the MC but Keep it in its Place 241

Message to the Broken Clocks 242

Do You Require a Clearer Message 242

Appendix A: 244

Bibliography 244

Recommended Sources for further Research 255

Appendix B Ida B Wells 257

Appendix C: Alabama Colored Women's Clubs 260

Appendix D: Margaret James Murry Washington 262

    Black Women Rising to Power 263

    Activist for Anti-lynching 272

Appendix E: Association of Deans of Women and Advisers to Girls in Negro Schools 274

Appendix F: California State Federation of Colored Women's Clubs 276

Appendix G: Joesphine Silone Yates 277

Appendix H: Georgia Mabel DeBaptiste 279

Appendix I: Benefit Societies 281

Appendix J: 4 African American Women's Clubs That Helped Write History 285

Appendix K: Biker Set Readiness Test 292

Appendix L: Brief History of the Mighty Black Sabbath Motorcycle Club Nation 302

Glossary 317

If anyone is writing a book and you need professional coaching, oversight, and project management, I highly recommend my friend of nearly 20 years, Holly Joseph. hjoseph.works@gmail.com 333

CHAPTER ONE
Social Clubs on the Black Motorcycle Club Set

The Black motorcycle club (MC) set is blessed to align with sister social clubs – a remarkable experience not known in other MC sets within the United States, which continue to be racially, and gender segregated. Social clubs (SCs) are unique to the African American biker club experience. Black MC SCs consist of women (mostly African American) who operate independent clubs within the Black biker club set in support of Black MCs, while simultaneously supporting their communities at large through their charitable works. As such, they have etched themselves into a place of existence among Black biker clubs not customary for women on any other MC set no matter the race. Women are rarely included in today's male dominated world of biker clubs and their voices are consequently muted. SCs on the Black MC circuit have flourished on the MC set because they have embraced the culture and standards of the MCs they support, thereby enriching the MC set with their beautiful presence.

Many SCs are administratively set up much like the MCs they support. Some even have the same officer positions, ranking structure, operational standards, and traditions as MCs—including prospecting their sisters before allowing them to become members. SCs have even been known to attend some MC coalition meetings to have their grievances addressed – an opportunity they never would have been allowed a few years ago.

Despite these advances, they continue to face the long and arduous task to be recognized as full contributors to the set. SC members continue to endure sexual harassment, intimidation, and gaslighting at the hands of male members of MCs on the Black biker set. Sisters are regarded as "raw meat," treated as sexual objects and playthings to be hunted and objectified. Seemingly, many Black MCs are on a mission to marginalize Black women forcing many SC members to wage an uphill battle for recognition. Because SCs are not "Property Of" nor are they the wives or girlfriends of MC members, there is little protection afforded them to guard against sexual harassment or exploitation.

Unfortunately, some MCs have even bought forth the slave-era stereotypes that the Black women of the SC are "devoid of morality, sexually wanton and incapable of upholding marital and family responsibilities," and feel justified to treat them as such. These attitudes and behaviors have negatively impacted the growth and success of many SCs on the MC set. MC efforts to exert control over their Black sisters rather than embracing them for their contributions to the MC and the MC set, retards the growth potential of the SCs, which they rightfully deserve. It has come to be a self-loathing, self-fulfilling prophecy targeted at destroying the SCs for self-aggrandizement, male testosterone, and sexist superiority on the MC set.

Many MCs have pushed to establish barriers and rules to "regulate" SCs – especially when the SCs have greater success than the MCs they support. These rules seek to control everything from the colors of the vests they are allowed to wear, to declaring what days they can throw their annuals, social mixers, charitable events, and fund-raising operations. In some jurisdictions SCs are not allowed to operate without being assigned a so-called "brother club" which often is really just a group of insecure, sexually immature males looking to lord over the SC, negatively impacting their positive influence, and attempt to sexually exploit every sister that will entertain their advances and tolerate their company.

All of this to maintain the "purity" of the "men's club" imperatives that are represented as MC protocol, but new rules seem to be made up as they go. And thus the "men" can enjoy the role of overlords over the women's SCs.

When I observe SCs, I see so much more than a competing group upon which to prey! I have had the illustrious opportunity to spend a great deal of time studying their inception, growth and social movement within the MC set and the greater African American community. I have come to admire and love them for all they have given and continue to give to... US! I am aware of the importance of releasing their shackles, standing back, and watching them roar. I have come to admire and love the SCs for all they have given and continue to give to ... US! I am aware of the significance of releasing their shackles, standing back, and watching them soar. I have come to appreciate their renowned history within the foundation of this country and seek to inform all about what they can do to advance Black society if left unchecked.

When you look at the charitable contributions of SCs in our communities, you should ask yourself "Where does that come from?" Black women's participation in socially conscious philanthropic SCs building and uplifting Black communities and societies is nothing new in the United States. It may be new on the biker set—about 60 years for some of the oldest SCs—but in the communities of need across the country African American women's SCs (Woman's Clubs) have been well established for centuries!

It is my belief that if more bikers actually knew the history of these esteemed woman's clubs and how closely connected today's modern SCs are to their original missions, they would drop the chauvinistic bullshit and sexist prejudices when dealing with SCs on the MC set. These women are the great granddaughters of a social movement of Black women that changed the course and direction of Black people on these shores and uplifted our condition. Their DNA beats with the blood, objectives, sacrifices, and goals of those women leaders of the past. They march stubbornly on the exact path with the same trajectory and sense of purpose of their foremothers as though programmed by some prehistoric, ancestral genome sequencing routine. They don't need to be shown the way the mapping is already in their heads and their every action is in lock step with their sisters from a time before theirs. I believe if MCs knew this they would truly understand and appreciate the terrific history backing these mighty sisters and demonstrate an awed respect for the remarkable contributions these women make daily to our communities in the United States. In fact, I call upon MCs to learn and acknowledge them and cease the negative behavior displayed towards our great sisters. These fine Black women should be seen as more than sexual objects and profane conquests upon which to embark and instead endeavor to worship them for the queens they have been and continue to be to the African American race and the benefit they are to our society. MCs need to treat Black SC members as sisters to be uplifted by their brothers and get away from the nonsense so that these women can be further empowered to continue their long history of building up their race, their children, and their neighborhoods. But have no fear and do not worry, for I will get you there. Just keep reading.

CHAPTER TWO
Black Women, Strong Since Slavery

Black women have been a pivotal force in fighting for their race since landing upon England's mainland American colonies' shores against their will in late August 1619 at Point Comfort, today's Fort Monroe in Hampton, Va., aboard the English privateer ship White Lion (Hampton.gov/3580/the-1619-landing-report). Their dedication and strength of purpose while fighting the double setbacks of racism and sexism along with the dehumanization of chattel slavery (from the 16th to the 18th century) illustrates the remarkable heroism of African American women, the mothers of Black culture, in this society. During slavery in the United States, when Black men were powerless to improve their condition, Black women often established and navigated the paths and systems that ensured the survival of African Americans and ultimately led to their emancipation and upward mobility that continues to this day.

The uplifting began with the few wealthy sisters of the time, who were free and chose not to forget their impoverished sisters who were still in bondage. Instead of abandoning them to their plight and living their lives of freedom and opportunity they formed groups and committees that performed much needed social services on slave plantations; acts that often put their own safety and freedom in jeopardy. They organized feeding programs for enslaved Black children to nourish them beyond their starvation rations and provided them with blankets, medicines, and clothing. They taught classes in hygiene, cooking, washing, sewing, tailoring, and other domestics to better equip their sisters with new skills that could improve their work status on the plantation and move them up to better jobs such as working as house maids instead of field hands. A domestic-skilled slave woman could be rented out to cook, clean, and wash, enabling her to escape the back-breaking labor in the fields and bless her with more free time to rear her children. They taught slave women how to operate the China cabinet and manage the serving table. These skills empowered them to move from rented out washing and cleaning women to trusted servants in the big house thus further improving their lot in life and giving them access to better food, hygiene, clothing, medicines, and shelter. This in turn helped them to provide better nourishment for their children and families with more protein-rich scraps from the masters' tables such as chitterlings, hog-maws, pig's feet, and other table cast-offs. By today's standards, these small successes might seem paltry, but it was by those small infusions, inch-by-inch, that the Black salve family would find ways to survive. They slowly progressed, then eventually, centuries later thrived! Black women helping Black women initially began as an effort of the upper class, with less wealthy sisters eventually adding with their own contributions. In fact, some were barely better off than the sisters they were helping, and at great risk to their own safety with the threat of being kidnapped back into slavery an ever-present reality. Undaunted, they lifted the life condition of their sisters, brothers, and communities one small victory at a time often enduring horrible setbacks in between but never giving up, instead they forged on.

As Black men toiled tirelessly in the slave killing fields under the domineering shadow of the whip, Black women were looking for ways to improve the lot of Black people. Refusing to be annihilated under genocidal practices Black women pulled themselves up and made improvements in their lives and in the lives of those less fortunate. They did this through their newly formed social networks where they combined their resources to empower themselves to elevate their own social condition and the circumstances of those around them. They created the motto, "Lifting as We Rise" to remind themselves to never forget where they had come from. And to never forget their responsibility to improve the life circumstance of every Black person that they could possibly reach.

It is to the history of these pioneering SC women that I pay homage. It is my greatest hope that by spreading the facts and information about who they were and detailing their contributions to our great diaspora that I will inspire my beautiful African American sisters to continue to move forward with their chins held high in pride— expecting nothing other than absolute respect, acceptance, and honor from any MC they should encounter or support. And it is also my greatest hope that they will continue to lift as they rise!

So, let us go back to the beginning and examine the history of Black Woman's social clubs in the United States of America. This history began way before motorcycle clubs ever existed. This is what I call the beginning of the movement we now see as SCs on the Black biker set. This is the history of where today's SCs originate.

CHAPTER THREE
The Progressive Movement and how it led to the establishment of The Woman's Social Clubs Movement in the United States

The Progressive Movement came to the United States in 1890 as an intellectual rebellion against the political philosophy of Constitutionalism (Waluchow) but has its roots in early 1800s Europe.

Immanuel Kant identified progress as being a movement away from barbarism toward civilization. 18th century philosopher and political scientist Marquis de Condorcet predicted that political progress would involve the disappearance of slavery, the rise of literacy, the lessening of sex inequality, prison reforms, and the decline of poverty (Appleby and Jacob) (Kant and Reiss). In the 19th and 20th centuries, modernization was seen as the key requisite for progress, with a push to remove traditional hinderances to free markets and the free movement of people, thus encouraging rapid modernization of the economy and society (Appleby and Jacob). In the late 19th century, a political view in the western world implied that progress was being stifled by vast economic inequality between the rich and the poor, minimally regulated laissez-faire capitalism with out-of-control monopolistic corporations, intense and often violent conflict between capitalist and workers, and identified a need for measures to address these problems (Nugent).

Progressives held that it was possible to improve human societies through political action. As a political movement, progressivism sought to advance the human condition through social reform based on advancements in science, technology, economic development, and social organization (Oxford). Adherents to progressivism held that it had universal application and endeavored to spread the idea to human societies everywhere (Mah).

What began in the 1890s in the United States as a social movement grew into a popular political movement referred to as the "Progressive Era." During this era, progressives believed that the problems society faced, such as class warfare, greed, poverty, racism, and violence, could best be addressed by providing a good education, a safe environment, and an efficient workplace to the masses and that the government could be used as a tool for change (Roosevelt).

It is this progressive mindset that became the basis for the Woman's Social Club movement, which established the idea that women had a moral duty and responsibility to transform public policy. While women's organizations have always been a part of the United States history, it was not until the Progressive Era that it came to be considered a movement, consisting primarily of white, middle class, protestant women (Appleby, Chang and Goodwin, Encyclopedia of Women in American History).

Black women initially thought they would be allowed to participate in such women's clubs that espoused the desire to elevate society, but race was to play an all too important role in holding them back from their desire to participate and contribute. The reality of "For Whites Only" soon took hold of these organizations, causing them to turn a blind eye to the political, social, economic, anti-lynching and anti-slavery concerns of Black women. Consequently, those woman's clubs were simply out of reach for Black women.

CHAPTER FOUR
General Federation of Women's Clubs and the "Ruffin Incident"

In 1868, a leading New York Journalist, Jane Cunningham Croly founded "Sorosis", a professional woman's club that was to be the model for the nationwide General Federation of Women's Clubs (GFWC), founded in 1890. In 1889 Jane Croly organized a conference to bring together delegates from 61 women's clubs in New York. The women eventually formed the GFWC with Charlotte Emerson Brown elected as the first president (National Women's History Museum). In 1901, the GFWC was granted a charter by Congress, wherein then president, Ella Dietz Clymer proclaimed, "We look for unity, but unity in diversity", which became the motto for the GFWC. Black women thought surely that they would be able to participate in organizations such as the GFWC that espoused such lofty and glorious intent. Unfortunately, southern white women played a central role in the early year, bringing with them the vestiges of racism that would proliferate their organizations (Flanagan).

Local women's clubs initially joined the GFWC directly, but later came into membership through state federations that began forming in 1892. In 1900, the GFWC invited Josephine Ruffin, a Black journalist to attend the GFWC conference in Milwaukee as a representative of three Boston organizations —the New Era Club, the New England Woman's Club, and the New England Woman's Press Club. Southern white women, led by President Rebecca Douglas Lowe, a Georgia native, told Ruffin that she could be seated as an honorary representative of the two white clubs but would not seat a Black club. Ruffin refused on principle and was excluded from the proceedings. These events became known as "The Ruffin Incident" and were widely covered in newspapers around the country, most of whom supported Ruffin (Flanagan 1048, 1050).

Figure 3: Josephine St. Pierre Ruffin 1852-1924 Image Public Domain

Born in Boston, Massachusetts in 1852 Josephine St. Pierre Ruffin was a committed suffragist, civil rights activist, and acclaimed publisher. Her father was a leader of Boston's Black community in the years before the Civil War. At sixteen, she married John Ruffin, the first African American graduate of Harvard Law School, first African American elected to the Boston City Council, and first African American municipal judge in Massachusetts in 1868.

The Ruffins moved to England to protest the 1857 Dred Scott decision, which bolstered the system of slavery in the United States and ruled that Congress could not prohibit slavery in U.S. territories. After returning to Boston to advocate for abolition,

Ruffin and her husband recruited Black soldiers for Massachusetts regiments of the Union Army during the Civil War, including the much-lauded Massachusetts 54th. In 1879, she founded the Boston Kansas Relief Association, which raised money to help African Americans who had migrated to Kansas.

Ruffin was a charter member of the Massachusetts School Suffrage Association, which pushed for women to be able to vote in school board elections, as well as run for school board positions. Her work with school suffrage brought her into contact with suffragists Julia Ward Howe and Lucy Stone, who invited her to join the New England Women's Club; she was the group's first African American member. Ruffin worked as a writer for the Black newspaper The Courant and was a member of the New England Women's Press Association.

In 1893, she co-founded the Woman's Era Club, the first club founded and managed by Black women in Boston. The club published the Woman's Era newspaper, which was the first newspaper in America published for and by Black women. It is also known for publishing the early writings of activist Ida B. Wells-Barnett.

In 1895, Ruffin organized the first national conference of Black women's clubs, which resulted in the formation of the National Federation of Afro-American Women which eventually merged with the National Association of Colored Women (NACW) in 1896, wherein Ruffin served as the first vice president.

Ruffin was a consistent critic of all-white national women's clubs like the Women's Christian Temperance Union and spoke out about the dual burden faced by Black women. When she attempted to attend the Milwaukee conference of the GFWC in 1900 when southern white women from Georgia discovered that the Woman's Era Club was a Black organization, she was told she would only be able to sit as a member of the predominantly white clubs to which she belonged. A white conference attendee even attempted to grab her badge from her and caused the national scandal known as the "Ruffin incident."

In 1910, Ruffin helped to found the Boston chapter of the **National Association for the Advancement of Colored People (NAACP).**

She died in Boston in 1924 (Black Weomen's Suffrage) (National Women's Hall of Fame) (Britannica) (Boston Lieterary District) (AAREG) (Massachusetts Hall of Black Achievement Josephine St. Pierre Ruffin) (Above The law) (Mount Auburn Cemetery) (History.com) (Constitution Daily) (The Woman's Era) (Massachusetts Secretary of State).

◊◊◊

CHAPTER FIVE
The Black Woman's Club Movement

The Black woman's club movement began in the 1890s as an alternative to the white woman's club movement which began in the mid-1800s. While white women's clubs were initially established as social, cultural, and educational gatherings for middle-class women, Black women's clubs had a more pressing interest in social and political reform. Although white women's clubs did eventually shift their activities to social reform, they were often segregated not allowing Black women to join.

It is important to note that long before the 1890s, Black women came together to look after their community's welfare (Scott). Many of those organizations stemmed from the Black church with their roots in Christianity, missionary service, and church outreach projects. Black women were very quick to "organize themselves for self-help" (Scott). One of the first African American women's clubs was the Female Benevolent Society of St. Thomas, in Philadelphia, which was started in 1793 (Scott). At the time, Philadelphia had numerous Black organizations (Hall). After the African Benevolent Society in Newport, Rhode Island, would not allow women to be officers or vote, women created their own group (Scott). Another group, the Colored Female Religious and Moral Society in Salem, Massachusetts was created in 1818 (Scott). Black women's clubs helped raise money for the anti-slavery newspaper The North Star (Scott). Many Black churches owed their existence to the dedicated work of African American women organizing in their communities (Mjagkij). Black women's literary clubs began to show up as early as 1831, with the Female Literary Society of Philadelphia (Dunbar).

When slavery ended with the ratification of the 13th Amendment in 1865 (National Geographic Society), Black women continued to organize and often worked with churches to ensure their communities were taken care of (Shaw, Mink and Navarro) (Scott). In 1868, Black women's clubs were formed in Harris County, Texas (Timeline). Between 1880 and 1920, Black women in Indianapolis, Indiana had created more than 500 clubs addressing various issues (Mjagkij).

During the Progressive era, many Black women migrated to the Northern United States and into more urban areas (National Women's History Museum). The club movement for Black women in the 1890s began to focus on "social and political reform" (Movement) and were more secular (Scott). Black women had to face the same issues as white women during this period but were often excluded from services and help that benefited whites only (Scott). Black women were not only excluded from white clubs but also from clubs created by Black men (Rabaka). In addition, many Black women felt as though they were defying stereotypes for their community (Scott). Woman's clubs allowed Black women to combat the period's stereotypes which "portrayed African American women as devoid of morality, sexually wanton and incapable of upholding marital and family responsibilities" (Mjagkij). Being a member of a woman's club also helped give Black women greater social standing in their communities (Lerner).

Black colleges helped the creation of African American women's clubs (Scott). Ida B. Wells was an important figure in the growth of these clubs during the Progressive Era (African American Reform Ethics. National Women's History Museum) (Hendricks). A number of clubs, named after her, were created in large cities across the country (Mjagkij). In Chicago, the wealthy former abolitionist Mary Jane Richardson Jones supported the development of several clubs, serving as the first chair of Wells's (Smith and Phelps). Other influential woman's club organizers were Josephine St. Pierre Ruffin and Mary Church Terrell (Lerner). In 1896, the National Association of Colored Women (NACW) was founded (Encyclopedia Britannica). The NACW grew out of anti-lynching campaigns spearheaded by Wells (Movement). Her anti-lynching campaign provoked the president of the Missouri Press Association who viciously attacked Black women in a letter that was widely circulated among women's clubs by Ruffin. Ruffin eventually helped bring together the NACW, using the letter as a "call to action" (Zackodnik).

Figure 4: First Convention of the Montana Federation of Negro Women's Clubs, Butte, Montana, August 3, 1921, Image Public Domain

By 1900, almost every Black community had a women's club (Scott). By 1910, in proportion to population size, African American women's clubs outpaced white women's clubs in the number of clubs created (Scott). By 1914, the NACW had fifty-thousand members and over a thousand clubs participating in the umbrella organization (Scott).

The NACW raised more than $5 million in war bonds during World War I (Wada). The Woman's Club of Norfolk wrote letters and sent care packages to the segregated Black units sent to fight overseas (Watson). During the Great Depression, Black women's clubs began to move towards "structural change and electoral politics". The National Council of Negro Women (NCNW) became a dominant group in the women's club movement in African American circles (Movement). After World War II, working class and poor Black women took the place of upper-class Black women in organizing communities (Wright).

The hundreds of Black women's clubs across the country were eventually organized into the National Association of Colored Women in 1896, in response to the anti-lynching campaign of Ida B. Wells and the need for a more powerful national group. Through the NACW, thousands of clubwomen across the country devoted their efforts to a range of political, social, and economic reforms, including housing, education, health care, childcare, job training, wage equity, voter registration, and the anti-lynching campaign.

According to legal scholar Dorothy Roberts, the Black women's club movement's approach to child welfare differed tremendously from the mainstream approach this country has adopted. Instead of the "punitive approach of the modern child welfare system," the Black Women's Club Movement had an entirely different understanding of how to build a social support system for children. "These women understood the relationship between the well-being of individual children and their group identity and social surroundings; they focused on improving the general welfare of children rather than responding to particular cases of child maltreatment; and they promoted children's welfare by supporting, rather than punishing, mothers."

The majority of the Black clubwomen were civil rights and women's rights activists, and the clubs became a crucial vehicle for organizing around both issues. Some of the most famous women in U.S. history were clubwomen, including Harriet Tubman, Anna Julia Cooper, and Mary McLeod Bethune.

When the NACW's formed in 1896, their first president was Mary Church Terrell, and their motto, which remains to this day, was "Lifting As We Climb. (Yahn)." There keynote speaker was Harriet Tubman "Mother Moses" herself.

Figure 5: The Phylls Weatley Club of Buffalo circa 1905

Decline of woman's clubs

African American women's clubs began to decline in the 1920s as they had more opportunities to socialize, many clubs found their members were aging and were unable to recruit newer members (Bowles).

Woman's clubs began to turn over their work to city entities and became less influential (Kent State) (University of Washington). In addition, more women began to enter the workforce during the

1960s and had less spare time to devote to club work (Emporia State University).

Many women today are working long hours or spending time with their children's extracurricular activities (Ball State University). By 2010, the number of women's clubs had significantly decreased across the country (Gates). This reflects a trend in all club memberships in the United States: most clubs are losing members because there is a lack of leisure time for younger people (Comas).

Although there has been a decline in the number of women's clubs since the 1920s, there has been an increase in the presence of Black women's SCs associated with the Black MC set over the past two decades. Though not as organized or documented, Black women's SCs have blossomed by the thousands if not tens of thousands across the United States! They have coalesced around their love of motorcycle club culture and support of the Black biker club set. Though not as politically active as in previous decades, their social contributions to the African American communities in which they live is as prolific as ever.

This is why I have dubbed this book the "revival of the women's social club movement." Just look at how many of you there are that have risen from the ashes over the last fifteen to twenty years! Even though you may be challenged with many obstacles—like your sisters of yesteryear— you continue to persevere and thrive. My deepest honor and respect go out to all my MC set SCs.

Now that you have seen the strength and legacy from which you came, I challenge you to accept zero nonsense, subjugation, intimidation, or retardation of your movement. I encourage you to continually move forward, uniting, recruiting, organizing, and fighting for social and political change—just as those before you. Remembering always to be "Lifting as you climb!"

Black Dragon

Figure 6: **Black Dragon**

◊◊◊

CHAPTER SIX
Understanding the Motorcycle, Motorcycle Clubs, The Biker Club Sets

We are going to start by discussing the biker club sets because it is important to understand the functions, traditions, history, and protocols that govern all biker sets. But it is also important to realize that biker sets individually are still largely divided by race in this country. So, yes there is a Black biker set, white biker set, Hispanic biker set, Asian biker set, so forth and so on. And racism can run rampant on any or all of these sets. Still all the sets can and do interact often with great respect. Knowing how these sets operate allows you to matriculate your SC safely and by protocol around them if need be. And if you are operating according to protocol, you can have lots of fun as well. As I've said before SCs are unique to the Black biker set and you will seldom find them operating on other sets independently. So, for this reason even though I will be explaining all biker sets initially (Black, White, other) I will concentrate on explaining the Black biker set primarily since that is where your social club will most likely be.

We will start with a general overall look at motorcycle club history in the United States and how all clubs interconnect on every set before we get more granular to covering protocol. Another point to consider is that when we are talking about the history of the first clubs there isn't much written about the Black clubs and others that existed back then. Remember that they were there.

Now, since none of this would have been possible without the iron horse itself, I believe it is appropriate to start with the history motorcycle in the United States.

The Social Clubs Bible
The History of the Motorcycle in the United States

A motorcycle, motorbike, bike, or trike (if 3-wheeled) is a two or three-wheeled motor vehicle steered by a handlebar from a saddle styled seat (Merriam-Webster) (Foale) (BMV) (Cossalter) (Britannica) (GovInfo). Motorcycle means a motor vehicle with motive power having a seat or saddle for the use of the rider and designed to travel on not more than three wheels in contact with the ground).

Motorcycles first appeared in the United States in 1866 following the invention of the bicycle in 1817. The first motorcycle was driven by steam invented by Pierre Michaux in Paris. He called his motorcycle the Michaux-Perreaux steam velocipede (Burgess Wise). In 1866 one of his employees, Pierre Lallement, brought the design to the United States (Fiedler).

Gottlieb Daimler and Wilhelm Maybach in Germany are widely credited with inventing the first internal combustion, petroleum fueled motorcycle in 1885. It was called the Daimler Reitwagen. In 1894, Hildebrand & Wolfmuller became the first series production motorcycle (Motorcycles).

The Orient-Astor became the first production motorcycle in the United States of America built by Charles Metz in 1898 at his factory in Waltham MA.

By 1901 two of the biggest motorcycle brands in United States history were born. Indian Motorcycle Manufacturing born in Springfield, Massachusetts, and Harley Davidson Inc., born in Milwaukee, Wisconsin. Both motorcycle companies survived the Great Depression even though most others did not. Both companies are viable and operating today even though Indian went out of business in 1953. In 2011 The name was purchased by Polaris and the Indian motorcycle was back up and running. Harley, on the other hand, went on to enjoy one of the strongest name brands in U.S. history and is the brand of choice mandated by thousands of motorcycle clubs across the country.

The Japanese motorcycle is a popular bike in the United States that rose in popularity in the late 60s. The term Universal Japanese Motorcycle, or UJM was coined in the mid-70s because all major brands—Honda, Kawasaki, Yamaha, and Suzuki made similar bikes following the same form, function and quality. In the 1980s the manufacturers began to diversify building incredible street legal racing platforms, dirt bikes, enduros, and adventure travel bikes that have been wildly successful. They revolutionized the industry by creating motorcycles with better performance, reliability and equipment packages with a much cheaper price than the American and British manufacturers. In 1974 Honda introduced what was then coined as the world's biggest motorcycle," with the introduction of the Goldwing. It has dominated the motorcycle touring industry for decades. In the mid-90s Japanese manufacturers went directly after the Harley market by creating cruisers that closely resembled and sounded like Harleys. Following their pattern of creating better performance, reliability, and equipment packages at a cheaper price caused those bikes to be wildly popular as well.

The History of Motorcycle Clubs in the United States

Once motorcycles became commercially available, they instantly drew the reckless, thrill seekers, and adventurists of the day. These types of individuals (men and women alike) saw them as daredevil machines to race, test the limits of their skills, express their freedoms, chase their passions for adventure and for some they even became the vehicle upon which they experienced death. Another thing is for certain; where two or more kindred spirits are gathered to experience the lifestyle of motorcycling and share the passions of the love of the two-wheeled-life obsession, interests were sparked in forming closer bonds that quickly became riding groups, then MC extended families. These bonds were sealed by the shared love of life clinging to the backs of speeding steel as folks found that they wanted to share time exclusively in members' only organizations that became the first MCs. And interestingly enough many MCs of yesteryear consisted of both male and female members.

Let's take a look at the progression of MCs in the United States:

Early 1900s:

Riding Enthusiasts

In the early 1900s, informal groups of motorcycle riders began to form as the popularity of motorcycles grew and enthusiasts sought opportunities to connect and ride together. These groups were often comprised individuals who shared a passion for motorcycles and enjoyed riding together, exploring the countryside or participating in early motorcycle races. They laid the foundation for the development of more structured motorcycle clubs that were soon to follow. As mentioned before, most often these groups were segregated by race and the practices of racism and later Jim Crow laws and policies. The White biker sets were formed for the benefit of white Americans. However, Black men and women undeterred formed their own groups and learned to MC on their own accord, by their own standards, expectations, and policies. Their groups would also lead to more formalized biker clubs that became known as the "Black Biker Clubs Set" or simply the "Black MC Set" that went largely unknown, undocumented, and unrecognized until about 2002 when we filmed the movie Biker Boyz with Director Reggie Rock Bythewood.

Exploratory Excursions

Many early riders saw their machines as a means of exploration and adventure. Groups would gather to explore the countryside, rural areas, and scenic routes. These excursions allowed riders to share the joy of discovery and experience the thrill of riding together. Riders would often exchange information about roads, routes, and places of interest, fostering a sense of camaraderie and knowledge-sharing among participants.

Motorcycle Racing

Motorcycle racing played a significant role in the formation of informal riding groups. Early motorcycle enthusiasts were drawn to the thrill of competition and would come together to watch or participate in races. Racing events provided opportunities for riders to connect, exchange technical knowledge, and share their experiences. These gatherings often served as informal meeting points, laying the groundwork for future collaborations and the formation of more structured MCs.

Community-Based Groups

Communities and neighborhoods often contributed to the formation of many informal groups as riders who lived in the same area would organize rides, social events, or simply come together to enjoy the thrill of riding. These community-based groups promoted a sense of belonging as riders shared a common bond over their love for motorcycles and local ties.

Shared Mechanical Knowledge

Early motorcycles required regular maintenance and repairs, which provided a platform for riders to exchange technical knowledge and expertise in maintaining their machines. Members of these groups would gather to share tips, troubleshoot mechanical issues, and help one another with repairs. In the days before social media, these training opportunities had to occur in-person. These personal interactions facilitated the exchange of skills within the community and strengthened the bonds between riders.

Motorcycle Manufacturers and their Contribution to Establishing and Supporting MCs in the United States

It was actually motorcycle manufacturers who played the first significant roles in aiding the establishment and growth of the early motorcycle clubs in the United States. During the early 20th century, when motorcycles became increasingly popular, manufacturers recognized the potential for creating brand loyalty and fostering a sense of community among riders. They also knew that their strong support of the sport of bike riding would directly result in more motorcycles being sold. They began sponsoring motorcycle riders and motorcycle clubs to stimulate, grow, and encourage the new passion that was taking place across America. They fostered the beginning of biker MC life in the following ways:

Product Development

Motorcycle manufacturers focused on creating dependable, powerful, and affordable machines that appealed to a wide range of riders. By making motorcycles more accessible to the general public, manufacturers helped to popularize the sport and laid the foundation for, and encouraged the formation of, riding groups and clubs.

Sponsorship and Support

Motorcycle manufacturers recognized the importance of promoting racing events to foster the competitive spirit among the riding community, intertwining the sport with their brand. By sponsoring races and racers, they were further establishing their brand with supporters and fans. These racing events not only showcased the capabilities of their motorcycles, but also brought riders together, providing the catalyst that led to the formation of the legendary racing motorcycle clubs of the twenties, thirties, and forties.

Promotion and Advertising

Early on, manufacturers used strategic marketing tactics to promote their motorcycles by depicting riders in groups to emphasize the sense of belonging and community that came with owning a motorcycle. By associating their brand with the idea of riding as a social activity, manufacturers helped popularize the concept of motorcycle clubs.

Dealer Networks

With the establishment of extensive dealer networks, motorcycle manufacturers were able to provide community hubs. Dealerships became gathering places where riders could socialize, share stories, and exchange information further facilitating connections. By supporting dealer-sponsored events, such as group rides and rallies, manufacturers further strengthened the sense of community.

Technical Support

Manufacturers recognized the importance of rider skill and safety in promoting their motorcycles. To support riders, they offered technical assistance, training programs, and educational materials. They conducted workshops and training sessions to help riders improve their riding skills, understand motorcycle maintenance, and promote safe riding practices. This support encouraged the obsession of most organized clubs to focus on safety, proper maintenance, and skill development of their riders. This led MCs to initiate the roles of Road Captain, Sergeant at Arms, and other specialist positions designed to ensure the club had officers responsible for the safe conduct of the club on the road.

Community Engagement

Motorcycle manufacturers organized rallies, events, and gatherings that brought riders together from various regions. These events provided opportunities for riders to network, socialize, and bond over their shared passion for motorcycles. Manufacturers often sponsored or participated in these events, further solidifying their connection to the motorcycle community and the pulse that drove their direction. The celebrated awards distributed at these events, including "Longest Distance Riders," "Best Dressed MC," "Most Attended MC," and "Best Looking Motorcycle" are still awarded in many MC annuals and cabarets today.

Motorcycle manufacturers are instrumental in the development of the first motorcycle clubs. By designing and promoting motorcycles for a wide range of riders, hosting community-focused events, encouraging and emphasizing safety, knowledge, and skills, sponsoring racing events, developing dealer networks, and organizing community-focused events, manufacturers created a sense of identity and belonging among riders, laying the foundation for the formation and need for MCs.

Manufacturers Helped Define the Roles of Women in MCs

Motorcycle clubs were not always exclusively male in the early years. It wasn't until much later that the big clubs removed women from full patch membership. Many of the big clubs of yesteryear, including some 1% clubs actually had full patch female members. Motorcycle manufactures played a role in helping women achieve status and membership where it did occur.

During the early 20th century, while limited, motorcycle manufacturers made a concerted effort to illustrate women riders in their advertisements and encourage women to participate in motorcycle clubs in the following ways:

Print Advertisements

Although print advertisements in magazines, newspapers, and catalogs were primarily targeted towards males—with an emphasis on performance, technical aspects of their motorcycles, and appealing to the speed and adventure-seeking spirit—some ads sought to highlight the emerging trend of female riders, featuring women experiencing the lifestyle and adventure in the same manner as their male counterparts.

Manufacturers published newsletters and sponsored sections in motorcycle club publications to feature stories and news related events relevant in motorcycle communities. These newsletters often highlighted women riders by promoting their accomplishments and involvement in motorcycle clubs. With this positive representation, manufacturers aimed to inspire more women to join clubs.

Women's Auxiliary Groups

Several women's auxiliary groups, such as the Motor Maids of America (1940), began to form with the support of motorcycle manufacturers. These groups provided a platform for women to connect, share their experiences, and participate in club activities. Manufacturers recognized the importance of supporting these women's groups to promote female involvement in motorcycle clubs. It was these women's auxiliary groups that took hold in the early MC culture, especially on the Black biker set.

Women's Riding Competitions

Motorcycle manufacturers sponsored women's competitions, such as endurance races, hill climbs, and motocross events. These sponsorships not only promoted the brand but also showcased women's riding skills and their involvement in the sport. By highlighting women's achievements in competitive settings, manufacturers aimed to inspire more women to engage in motorcycling.

1910s:

The Formation of Formal Clubs and the First MC

The first documented MC in the United States was "Yonkers Motorcycle Club," established in 1903 in New York. By the 1910s, MCs had a more formal structure. These clubs allowed riders to share knowledge and experiences related to riding skills, maintenance, and repair. Members could rely on the expertise and assistance of fellow club members, fostering a sense of community and mutual support. During this time, clubs organized group rides to provide opportunities to explore new areas, participate in social events, and experience the joy of riding together. The connections established in these club events transitioned from friendships into communal bonds with a tight-knit brotherhood.

Military Connection of Vets to MCs

During World War I, motorcycles played a crucial role in military operations. The connection between motorcycles and the military influenced the formation of motorcycle clubs, with many clubs having ties to military veterans. Military veterans who had served as motorcycle dispatch riders during the war often formed clubs upon returning to civilian life. These clubs allowed former servicemen to continue their passion for motorcycles and maintain the camaraderie they experienced in the military. Many who were mentally ill with what was then known as "combat fatigue" later to be known as post-traumatic stress disorder, found that MCs were the only place where they were understood by brothers that had experienced the same horrors in war. In those days the military did not provide the kinds of support it does for war veterans today, so MCs offered not only a military connection and camaraderie but also a mental health connection and loving support that the government was slow to understand it needed to give. Returning vets brought military-like structure to MCs that originally started out as family clubs and gatherings of close-knit friends. These clubs introduced structure that included Sgt-at-Arms, Road Captains, and other command positions in the MC. Bylaws began to make MCs look, operate, and feel like paramilitary organizations.

MC Governing Bodies

With the establishment of organized clubs came the recognition of the need for regulation, political action, and support within the growing motorcycling community. Consequently, this period witnessed the formation of regional and national motorcycle clubs and the establishment of governing bodies to hold them accountable. The first were the Federation of American Motorcyclists (FAM) and the Motorcycle and Allied Trades Association (M&ATA).

FAM

The formation of the FAM can be traced to the New York Motorcycle Club, whose members in early 1903 saw the need for a national motorcyclist organization. The enactment of the New York City law requiring the registration of motorcycles as motor vehicles, further signified the need to create such an organization. This law was seen as a direct act by the government to extract money and taxes from bikers and to create laws targeting them.

Club members and independent riders recognized the need for organizations that centered on biker's rights would be required to adequately lobby and protect bikers against predatory laws, policies, and politics that targeted bikers and portrayed them in a negative light. Bikers have always been a wild and free loving people unconstrained by societal norms and impervious to fear and danger. They have been misunderstood and vilified from the moment they started riding their iron horses – a perception that is still prevalent today.

FAM officially formed during a meeting of 93 biker enthusiasts on 7 September 1908 in Brooklyn, New York. The meeting was chaired by George H. Perry and one notable attendee was George M. Hendee of the Indian Motorcycle Company, who brought 109 membership pledges from the New England area (AmericanMotorcyclist.com, AmericanMotorcyclist.com).

During this meeting, officers were appointed, including R.G. Betts of New York as president, committees were formed, and a constitution was drawn up. Article I, section 2 of the constitution stated:

> Its objects shall be to encourage the use of motorcycles and to promote the general interests of motorcycling; to ascertain, defend and protect the rights of motorcyclists; to facilitate touring; to assist in the good roads movement; and to advise and assist in the regulation of motorcycle racing and other competition in which motorcycles engage .

During its 16-year existence, FAM developed competition rules and rider classifications, dealt with restrictive ordinances in cities like Chicago, Illinois and Tacoma, Washington, and wrestled with funding and membership concerns. In 1915, FAM had 8,247 members; however, with the start of World War I the number of potential members decreased significantly causing the organization to go out of business in 1919 (AmericanMotorcyclist.com, AmericanMotorcyclist.com).

M&ATA

Throughout FAM's existence, one clear indication of the health and vitality of the fledgling American motorcycle industry was the formation of several trade associations. Among the earliest was the

Motorcycle Manufacturers Association, formed in 1908, was created to represent and regulate motorcycle manufacturers, accessory makers, and distributors. In November 1916, the M&ATA. was formed. (AmericanMotorcyclist.com, AmericanMotorcyclist.com).

When FAM eventually folded due to a decrease in membership, the M&ATA was left without a counterpart to represent the riders. Although M&ATA was controlled by the motorcycle industry, the M&ATA "Educational Committee" began registering riders and clubs to support motorcycle activities in 1919, while the "Competition Committee" managed the former FAM's racing responsibilities (AmericanMotorcyclist.com, AmericanMotorcyclist.com).

After five years of growth, the "Educational and Competition Committee" was named the "American Motorcycle Association" (AMA). The M&ATA later united with scooter trade representatives to become the MS&ATA. And in 1969, it merged with the West Coast Motorcycle Safety Council to form the Motorcycle Industry Council, which continues today.

1920s:

Expansion of MCs

In the 1920s, marks a significant growth in the number of motorcycle clubs as motorcycles gained widespread popularity as a mode of transportation and a symbol of freedom and adventure. Some of the reasons clubs enjoyed the increased popularity are as follows:

Increased Motorcycle Ownership:

The 1920s witnessed a surge in motorcycle ownership, as motorcycles became more affordable and accessible to a broader range of people. This increase in ownership contributed to the growth of MCs, as more individuals sought opportunities to connect with fellow riders and enthusiasts. The availability of various motorcycle models and brands also added to the appeal, with riders forming clubs around specific motorcycle brands or types.

Regional and Local Clubs:

As motorcycle ownership increased, regional and local motorcycle clubs proliferated. These clubs catered to riders within specific geographic areas, providing a sense of community and camaraderie. Regional and local clubs organized regular rides, social events, and gatherings, offering riders the opportunity to connect, share experiences, and explore new destinations together. These clubs became important hubs for riders to exchange information, plan trips, and form lasting friendships.

Social and Recreational Activities:

MCs in the 1920s focused not only on riding but also on socializing and recreational activities. Club members organized picnics, parties, dances, and other social events that allowed riders and their families to come together in a fun and festive atmosphere. These activities fostered strengthened the bonds between club members by providing opportunities for riders and their families to socialize, relax, and enjoy the company of like-minded individuals who shared a passion for motorcycles.

Motorcycle Tours and Endurance Runs:

The 1920s saw the rise of motorcycle tours and endurance runs, which became popular activities among MC members. These events involved riding long distances, often crossing state lines, or exploring scenic routes. MCs organized and participated in these tours and endurance runs, which allowed riders to test their skills, experience the thrill of long-distance riding, and explore new areas.

Racing and Competitions:

Club members participated in organized races, both on dirt tracks and road circuits, competing against one another and other clubs. Racing events provided an avenue for riders to showcase their skills, push the limits of their motorcycles, and gain recognition within the motorcycle community. It also allowed clubs to demonstrate their prowess and build relationships through friendly competition.

Supportive Community:

MCs in the 1920s often provided support and assistance to their members. Riders would help one another with mechanical issues, offer advice on maintenance and repairs, and provide a network of support for any challenges or hardships faced by fellow club members. The sense of community within MCs extended beyond riding and social activities. Clubs acted as a support system for riders, creating a sense of belonging and solidarity among members. The expansion of MCs in the 1920s reflected the growing popularity of motorcycles as a mode of transportation and a source of recreation. Further providing riders with community, friendship, and adventure, contributing to the thriving motorcycle culture of the era.

The American Motorcyclist Association

The American Motorcyclist Association (AMA) was the next logical progression in governing bodies that would exist to police, support, and lobby for the biker clubs' communities. It was established in 1924. The AMA played a crucial role in providing support and structure to motorcycle clubs, serving as a national governing body for motorcycle activities and competitions.

"The slogan of the AMA will be: An Organized Minority Can Always Defeat an Unorganized Majority." (*Western Motorcyclist and Bicyclist*, May 20, 1924).

The Motorcycle & Allied Trades Association (M&ATA) began registering riders in 1919, and by early 1924, it claimed about 10,000 members. On May 15 at a meeting in Cleveland, the directors of the M&ATA proposed to create the "American Motorcyclist Association" as a division of the M&ATA. The new AMA would control rider registration and activities, issue sanctions for national events, and serve motorcycle industry members.

The registered M&ATA riders were transferred as AMA charter members, while individual AMA membership dues were set at $1 per year. The motorcycle industry was represented in the AMA in three membership classes: "Class A," which included large motorcycle companies; "Class B," which included supply and accessory companies; and "Class C," which included motorcycle dealers (AmericanMotorcyclist.com, American Motorcyclist Association).

Membership growth was at the top of the early AMA's list of priorities. As Parsons stated in the May 20, 1924, issue of *Western Motorcyclist and Bicyclist*: "Plans are under way to start membership contests and build up the AMA to a live and active fighting organization for the benefit of the motorcycle riders of America. Instead of the 10,000 members now registered with the M&ATA, it is expected that the AMA will have a membership of 50,000." (AmericanMotorcyclist.com, American Motorcyclist Association)

Concerns about restrictive government action against the motorcycling community were among the primary reasons behind the creation of the AMA. In fact, laws and ordinances threatening the freedom of "motor bicyclists" were the impetus for the creation of many early motorcycling clubs and organizations. As an announcement in August 1903, before the creation of the Federation of American Motorcyclists (FAM), stated: "The particular character of the motor bicycle has left its status open to various definitions, and as a result ... laws applying to big motor cars are brought to bear on motorcycles with oppressive force .... To combat such measures, to insist that the highways are free to all alike, and

that the right to use them is irrevocable, is one of the objects to be served by organization. It is an object that should appeal to every motorcyclist with red blood in his veins."
(AmericanMotorcyclist.com, American Motorcyclist Association)

It wasn't until a rash of legislation in the 1960s, though, that motorcycling organizations began to realize how important legislative activity would become to the future of the sport. At that time, the MS&ATA (Motor Scooter & Allied Trades Association) began to concentrate on government relations efforts on behalf of the motorcycle industry, while the AMA saw the need to focus on laws and regulations threatening to riders. This led to the formation of the AMA's Legislative Department, with a mission to "... coordinate national legal activity against unconstitutional and discriminatory laws against motorcyclists, to serve as a sentinel on federal and state legislation affecting motorcyclists, and to be instrumental as a lobbying force for motorcyclists and motorcycling interests." (AmericanMotorcyclist.com, American Motorcyclist Association)

The AMA was a whites-only organization from its inception in 1924 until the 1950s, not allowing African Americans to join for its first 30 years. A 1930 AMA membership application form, on display at the Harley-Davidson Museum, included the statement "membership is limited to white persons only". This segregation occurred at a time in American history when many motorcycle dealerships refused to sell motorcycles to Black riders, forcing an entire population to create their own culture. The museum exhibit has examples of distinctive uniforms worn by motorcycle clubs, both AMA sanctioned, and those from the separate culture of Black or racially desegregated clubs that proliferated as a consequence of the AMA segregation policy, such as the Berkeley Tigers MC from the San Francisco Bay Area.

Prior to the acceptance of Black members, the term outlaw motorcycle club could refer to either a white counterculture biker club that was "uninterested in 'square' events and competitions", or else a club that accepted non-white members and was therefore not allowed to participate in the AMA. In the 1920s and 1930s, Black hill climbing racer William B. Johnson evaded the whites-only restriction and obtained an AMA membership card, which allowed him to compete around the Northeastern United States and become perhaps the first Black AMA member.

After the racist policy was abolished, AMA-sanctioned motorcycle clubs thrived in the era after World War II when motorcycle sales soared, and club membership appealed to "better-adjusted" American veterans who enjoyed group participation and operated under strict bylaws that held club meetings and riding events.

In 1995, AMA President Ed Youngblood said that as a consequence of this racist policy from 1924 to the 1950s, Blacks continued to be underrepresented in AMA events for decades after the segregationist policy was rescinded. That year, Youngblood presented Black AMA member Norman Gaines in their membership advertisement in the campaign "I want to protect my rights as a motorcyclist. That's why I'm an AMA member" in both the AMA member magazine and *Motorcyclist* magazine.

Still little could be done to erase the stigma of the racist policies of the AMA among Black clubs on the Black biker set and therefore there was never a popular registering among them to participate in the AMA. The Black Biker set developed its own governing bodies, rules, regulations, racing events, and lobbying groups. Though the AMA has tried with various outreach programs to enlist Black clubs among their ranks, those efforts have gone largely unnoticed and unappreciated, proving that old wounds heal slowly.

1930s-1940s:

Community Support

Despite the economic challenges of the Great Depression and the disruptions caused by World War II, MCs of the 1930s and 1940s continued to contribute to their communities and provide a sense of unity and support for their members. These clubs played a vital role in maintaining the spirit of motorcycling during a tumultuous period in history.

Motorcycle clubs organized charity rides and fundraising events in an effort to alleviate hardships for those affected by the Great Depression. These rides allowed club members to use their passion for motorcycles to make a positive impact in their communities. Club members would collect donations, ride to specific destinations, and distribute the funds or supplies to charities, orphanages, or individuals in need. These events showcased the generosity and community spirit of motorcycle clubs.

MC were actively engaged in community service activities by volunteering for local initiatives and providing assistance during natural disasters or emergencies. Club members would come together to support their neighborhoods, demonstrating the positive impact that MCs could have beyond their recreational activities.

Support for Military Personnel

In the 1940s, with World War II underway, many club members enlisted in the armed forces, while remaining club members and women's auxiliary groups worked to maintain connections with those serving overseas. Clubs organized care packages, sent letters, and held events to honor and support their fellow club members serving in the military. These efforts helped boost morale and fostered a keen sense of community within the MC.

Post-War Disillusionment:

The aftermath of World War II contributed to the emergence of OMCs. Many veterans, returning from the war, struggled to reintegrate into society, felt disillusioned and disconnected. MCs, particularly OMCs, provided a sense of purpose and belonging by offering an outlet to rebel against societal norms and express their dissatisfaction with the status quo.

Motorcycle Maintenance and Repairs:

MCs of this era continued to provide assistance and expertise in motorcycle maintenance and repairs. The tight-knit community allowed riders to rely on fellow club members for guidance and support in keeping their motorcycles in good working condition. Club members would share tips, techniques, and knowledge about motorcycles, helping each other troubleshoot issues, perform repairs, and enhance their riding experience.

Recreational Riding and Group Tours:

Recreational riding remained an essential aspect of MC activities during the 1930s and 1940s. Club members would organize group rides, exploring scenic routes, countryside areas, and landmarks. These rides provided an escape from the challenges of the times and offered riders an opportunity to enjoy the freedom and adventure that motorcycles provided. Group tours became popular, with riders venturing on longer journeys to new destinations.

Friendship and Brotherhood:

Motorcycle clubs in the 1930s and 1940s were not just about the activities but also about fostering strong bonds of friendship and brotherhood among members. Club meetings, social gatherings, and events created a sense of belonging and support within the motorcycle community. Club members relied on each other for companionship, shared experiences, and mutual support during challenging times. The camaraderie within these clubs helped riders forge lasting friendships that extended beyond their love for motorcycles.

Emergence of Outlaw Motorcycle Clubs

Prior to the 1970s, the term "outlaw motorcycle club" (OMC) referred to either a white counterculture biker club that was "uninterested in 'square' events and competitions" or a club that accepted non-white members and was therefore not allowed to participate in the AMA.

The emergence of outlaw motorcycle clubs (OMCs) during the 1930s and 1940s marked a significant shift in the MC culture. These clubs, often associated with a rebellious and nonconformist image, represented a departure from the traditional MCs of the time. Being an outlaw then could simply mean your club was not acknowledged by the AMA which meant you were outlaw to the AMA, or it could mean you were a part of a counter-culture club which would soon become the entire meaning of outlaw MC in the United States.

Outlaw Reputation:

OMCs gained notoriety for their defiance of societal norms and their association with criminal activities. The term "outlaw" referred to the MC's refusal to adhere to established rules and regulations—both within society and the motorcycle club community defined by the AMA. Outlaw clubs were known for their distinct visual style, often incorporating elements like leather jackets adorned with club patches, skull motifs, and rebellious symbols, further contributing to their counterculture reputation.

The Hollister Riot:

In 1947, the Hollister Riot played a pivotal role in solidifying the image of OMCs. At a motorcycle rally in Hollister, California a large gathering of riders participated in rowdy behavior which led to confrontations with law enforcement. Media coverage of the event sensationalized the actions of a few individuals, depicting the entire motorcycle community as unruly and dangerous. This portrayal further cemented the outlaw image and led to a heightened public interest in these clubs.

Nonconformity and Counterculture:

OMCs embraced a nonconformist ideology, rejecting societal norms and conventions. They sought freedom from social constraints and perceived limitations, emphasizing their own code of conduct and hierarchy within the club structure. These clubs often adopted an "us against the world" mentality, creating a strong bond among members and a sense of exclusivity. They created their own rules, rituals, and modes of operation, distinct from mainstream motorcycle clubs and society at large.

Criminal Involvement:

Some outlaw clubs became involved in illegal enterprises, though not all. Over the decades OMC members have been charged and convicted for drug trafficking, running prostitution rings, gun running, racketeering, murder and more. Recently some OMCs have been convicted of being criminal organizations. In some cases, the Department of Justice (DOJ) has even attempted to use asset forfeiture laws to strip targeted OMCs of their colors.

1950s-1960s:

A New Era in MCs

During the 1950s and 1960s, MCs underwent significant changes in their culture and image. These decades witnessed the rise of various motorcycle subcultures, including both mainstream clubs and more notorious OMCs.

Mainstream Motorcycle Clubs:

Mainstream motorcycle clubs, such as those who were members of the AMA, continued to thrive during this period. These clubs focused on promoting motorcycle riding as a recreational activity, organizing group rides, social events, and local competitions. Mainstream clubs maintained a positive public image and adhered to rules and regulations set forth by governing bodies like the AMA. They often participated in charity rides, parades, and community events, projecting a sense of camaraderie and community involvement.

OMCs 1950s – 1960s:

The 1950s and 1960s saw the emergence and growth of OMCs that gained notoriety for their rebellious nature and alleged involvement in criminal activities. Some well-known outlaw clubs that flourished during this time included the Hells Angels, Outlaws, Mongols, Sons of Silence and Bandidos. These clubs became known as the Big 5. OMCs often adopted distinctive patches, colors, and insignias to identify themselves and assert their independence from mainstream society. These clubs operated outside the boundaries of traditional MC culture creating a sense of fear and fascination in the public eye. Some adopted Nazi styled symbolism such as wearing Swastikas and SS lightning bolts and other characteristics to purposely repulse and repel the general public.

The Rise of Black OMCs 50s – 60s

The rise of Black OMCs can be attributed to various factors, including social and cultural shifts, denial of membership in white MCs with racist admission policies, a desire for autonomy, and a sense of community among African American motorcycle enthusiasts.

Cultural Expression and Identity:

African Americans have a long history of using motorcycles as a means of personal expression and freedom. Motorcycles provided a platform for African Americans to assert their independence and challenge societal norms. The OMC subculture offered an avenue for Black riders to embrace their identity, express their individuality, and form communities based on shared experiences and interests.

Social and Political Climate:

The emerging civil rights movement and the broader social and political climate played a significant role in the rise of Black OMCs. African Americans were fighting for equal rights, autonomy, and self-determination. OMCs offered a sense of empowerment and resistance against oppressive systems. They provided a space where Black riders could assert their freedom, challenge stereotypes, exude MC dominance within their regions, and create their own rules and standards.

The Influence of Existing Clubs:

Existing Black motorcycle clubs and social organizations paved the way for the establishment of Black OMCs. Clubs like the East Bay Dragons Motorcycle Club, founded in 1959 in Oakland, California (ChatGPT Artificial Intelligence), and the Outcast Motorcycle Club, established in the 1967 in Detroit Michigan (Georgia.gov), laid the foundation for the development of Black OMC culture (ChatGPT

Artificial Intelligence). The Chosen Few (CFMC) is one of the oldest, predominantly African American motorcycle clubs in the United States. It was established in Los Angeles, California, in 1959. The club was founded by a group of African American riders who shared a passion for motorcycles and brotherhood. The Chosen Few MC played a significant role in shaping the Black OMC culture particularly on the West coast. It served as a pioneering club that paved the way for the establishment of other Black motorcycle clubs in subsequent years. Over time, the Chosen Few MC has expanded, and additional chapters have been established in various locations (ChatGPT Artificial Intelligence). The Wheels of Soul MC was established in Philadelphia, Pennsylvania, in 1967. It was founded by a group of African American riders who shared a passion for motorcycles and brotherhood. The Wheels of Soul MC has since expanded and gained recognition as one of the prominent African American OMCs in the United States (ChatGPT Artificial Intelligence). The Sin City Deciples MC was founded in Gary, Indiana, in 1966. It was established by a group of individuals who shared a passion for motorcycles and brotherhood. The club has since expanded its presence and has established chapters in various locations across the United States. The Hell's Lovers Motorcycle Club is a multi-ethnic motorcycle club founded in Chicago in 1967. One of the first integrated biker clubs in Chicago, the club was founded by Frank "Claim-Jumper" Rios after he was denied membership in another motorcycle club (Wikipedia). The Thunderguards MC originated in 1965 in Wilmington, Delaware. One of the club's founders, "Buckie", was responsible for giving the club its name. The first members and founders of the Thunderguards were: Buckie, Junkyard, Fishman, Billy C., Charlie, Gordie, and Cuppie (Prezi.com).

Black Pride

These clubs fostered a sense of brotherhood, encouraged motorcycle riding, and represented Black pride and self-determination. They inspired future generations of Black motorcyclists to form their own OMCs.

Following the years of exclusion, Black people continued to be underrepresented in AMA events for decades after the segregationist policy was rescinded.

Little could be done to erase the stigma of the racist policies of the AMA among Black clubs on the Black biker set and therefore there was never a popular registering among them to participate in the AMA. The Black Biker set developed its own governing bodies, rules, regulations, racing events, and lobbying groups. Though the AMA has tried with various outreach programs to enlist Black clubs among their ranks, those efforts have gone largely unnoticed and unappreciated, proving that old wounds heal slowly.

Black MCs fostered a sense of brotherhood, encouraged motorcycle riding, and represented Black pride and self-determination. They inspired future generations of Black motorcyclists to form their own OMCs.

Community and Support Networks

Black OMCs served as a community support network, offering camaraderie, mentorship, and resources to their members. They provided a sense of belonging and solidarity, especially in the face of racial discrimination and marginalization. Black OMCs organized rides, social events, and community outreach initiatives, contributing positively to their local communities and challenging negative stereotypes associated with traditional OMCs.

Cultural Impact and Representation

The rise of Black OMCs had a cultural impact, as they challenged the predominantly white narrative of outlaw motorcycle clubs. Black OMCs showcased their unique style, aesthetics, and contributions to the motorcycle club culture, gaining recognition within the broader motorcycling community. They also insisted in all areas of the country where they arrived that they alone act as the governing bodies of all Black and mixed raced predominately Black MCs within their jurisdictions thereby removing Black MC subservience to white OMCs. After their establishment of chapters in a particular state, MC protocols were enacted that demanded when white OMCs had problems with Black 99%er MCs, they were mandated to settle those problems through Black OMCs and not take direct action on Black and predominately Black MCs.

The emergence of Black OMCs played a significant role in diversifying the motorcycle club landscape and providing a space for Black riders to celebrate their identity, autonomy, and brotherhood.

Greaser Subculture:

The 1950s and 1960s saw the emergence of various motorcycle subcultures, each with its unique identity and style. One such notable subculture was the "greasers" or "rockers," characterized by their love for motorcycles, leather jackets, and rock 'n' roll music. These subcultures had their own clubs and gatherings, often associated with a particular fashion style and rebellious attitude. They represented a countercultural movement, challenging societal norms and embracing a sense of freedom and nonconformity.

Motorcycle Racing:

Motorcycle racing continued to be popular during the 1950s and 1960s. Road racing, motocross, and dirt track racing gained significant attention, with skilled riders competing in national and international competitions. The Isle of Man TT race continues to be a prestigious event attracting talented riders from around the world. Legendary racers such as Mike Hailwood, Giacomo Agostini, and Barry Sheene made their mark during this era, captivating motorcycle enthusiasts and inspiring a new generation of riders.

Motorcycle Culture in Popularity:

The 1950s and 1960s marked a period of increased popularity and fascination with motorcycles and motorcycle culture. The release of iconic films like "The Wild Ones" (1953) starring Marlon Brando and "Easy Rider" (1969) starring Peter Fonda and Dennis Hopper further fueled the interest in motorcycles and the rebellious image associated with them. Motorcycles became symbols of freedom, adventure, and individuality, attracting a wider range of enthusiasts and creating a sense of intrigue around MCs and the biker lifestyle. Overall, the 1950s and 1960s were a transformative period for MCs. Mainstream clubs continued to promote recreational riding and community engagement, while OMCs and MC subcultures challenged societal norms and captured public attention with their rebellious image. These decades laid the foundation for the diverse motorcycle culture we see today.

1970s-1980s:

The 1970s and 1980s were marked by a mix of mainstream MCs, the increasing violence of OMCs, the rise of new motorcycle subcultures and the push for safety and legislation.

OMCs 70s – 80s:

OMCs remained a significant presence during the 1970s and 1980s. Clubs like the Hells Angels, Outlaws, and Bandidos continued to expand their influence and reputation, sometimes involved in criminal activities. Outlaw clubs maintained their distinct patches, colors, and hierarchies, projecting an image of independence and defiance. Their association with rebellion and the biker lifestyle continued to captivate public fascination and draw both admirers and detractors.

The 1970s and 1980s were also marked by a series of conflicts and wars among various outlaw motorcycle clubs (OMCs). These conflicts often stemmed from territorial disputes, control over criminal activities, and clashes between different club ideologies.

The 1% Diamond and the OMC

The "1%" diamond patch is a symbol associated with OMCs and is often worn as a badge of honor by members who consider themselves outside the bounds of mainstream society. The history behind the 1% patch dates back to an infamous incident that occurred in Hollister, California, in 1947. The event, known as the Hollister riot or the Hollister incident, took place during the Fourth of July motorcycle rally organized by the American Motorcyclist Association (AMA). The rally attracted a large number of motorcycle riders, including members of various motorcycle clubs. However, the event turned chaotic, with reports of excessive drinking, reckless riding, and confrontations with law enforcement.

The media coverage of the Hollister incident sensationalized the events, depicting motorcycle club members as unruly and lawless. One particular photograph published in Life magazine showed a man wearing a cut-off denim vest with a "13" patch, which was associated with the Boozefighters Motorcycle Club. The article accompanying the photograph mentioned that "99% of motorcyclists are law-abiding citizens," implying that the remaining 1% were troublemakers. This statement has been historically attributed to having been said by the AMA, however the AMA has stated that they can find no written evidence they ever made this statement. Still, in response to this portrayal, some OMC members embraced the label of the "1%" and began wearing a diamond-shaped patch with "1%" or "1%er" stitched on it. This patch symbolized their rejection of societal norms and their identification as part of the outlaw biker subculture.

The 1% patch became a powerful symbol within the outlaw motorcycle club community, signifying a defiant attitude, a commitment to a lifestyle outside the mainstream, and a rejection of authority. It served as a way for club members to differentiate themselves from mainstream motorcycle riders and to assert their independence and nonconformity.

It is worth noting that while the 1% patch is associated with OMCs, not all members of these clubs engage in criminal activities. The patch is primarily a symbol of defiance, camaraderie, and a shared subculture, rather than an indicator of illegal behavior. However, it has been associated with the outlaw image and is often viewed with suspicion by law enforcement and the general public.

The OMC Wars:

The 1970s and 1980s witnessed several notorious OMC wars, most notably the conflicts between the Hells Angels and the Outlaws Motorcycle Clubs. These conflicts primarily occurred in the United States and Canada but also had ripple effects in other parts of the world. The wars were driven by a combination of factors, including the desire for dominance in the criminal underworld, control over lucrative drug trafficking operations, territorial disputes, and personal vendettas between club members. The conflicts often involved violent confrontations, including shootings, bombings, and ambushes. These acts of violence resulted in casualties among club members and innocent bystanders, leading to heightened public and law enforcement scrutiny of OMCs.

Criminal Activities and Rivalries:

Criminal activities, particularly drug trafficking, played a significant role in fueling the conflicts between OMCs during this period. The control over drug territories and distribution networks led to intense rivalries and violent clashes. The lucrative nature of drug trade and other illicit activities attracted both established and emerging MCs seeking wealth and power. This further intensified the competition and conflicts among various OMCs vying for dominance in the criminal underworld.

Ideological Differences:

Ideological differences also contributed to the conflicts between OMCs. Each club had its own set of values, rules, and code of conduct, and clashes often occurred when these ideologies clashed. Some clubs maintained a strict hierarchy and adhered to a code of conduct within their club. Other clubs had a more decentralized structure and resisted the dominance of larger clubs. These ideological differences, combined with the desire to expand their influence and protect their club's reputation, fueled tensions and led to violent confrontations.

Law Enforcement Crackdown:

The conflicts and criminal activities of OMCs in the 1970s and 1980s drew significant attention from law enforcement agencies. The escalating violence and public perception of OMCs as criminal organizations prompted increased law enforcement efforts to dismantle these clubs. Government agencies implemented stricter measures, including targeted investigations, surveillance, and arrests, aimed at disrupting the criminal activities of OMCs. These actions often resulted in high-profile court cases and convictions of club members involved in criminal enterprises.

Chopper Subculture

The 1970s and 1980s witnessed the emergence of new motorcycle subcultures that became popular and influential. One notable subculture was the "chopper" scene, inspired by the custom-built motorcycles featured in the movie "Easy Rider" (1969) built and engineered by Black men who contributed the chopped look to the American biker world. Chopper enthusiasts modified their motorcycles, often stripping them down and adding custom parts to achieve a unique look. This subculture celebrated individuality, creativity, and a free-spirited attitude towards motorcycle customization.

Racing and Competitions:

Motorcycle racing continued to thrive during the 1970s and 1980s with road racing, motocross, and dirt track racing gained popularity attracting both amateur and professional riders. Iconic racers like Kenny Roberts, Freddie Spencer, and Eddie Lawson achieved remarkable success, contributing to the growth of motorcycle racing as a mainstream sport. The increasing televised coverage of races also helped bring the excitement of motorcycle competitions to a broader audience.

Safety and Legislation:

The 1970s and 1980s saw increased efforts to promote motorcycle safety and introduce legislation to regulate the industry. Safety organizations and government agencies focused on rider education, helmet laws, and improved road infrastructure to reduce accidents and improve rider safety. These initiatives aimed to address the growing number of motorcycle riders and the need for responsible riding practices, ensuring a positive public perception of MCs and riders.

Overall, the 1970s and 1980s were a dynamic period for motorcycle clubs. Mainstream clubs continued to foster a sense of community among riders, outlaw clubs maintained a reputation for independence and new subcultures emerged celebrating customization and individuality. Motorcycle racing flourished and efforts were made to promote safety and legislation to support the growing number of riders.

1990s-Present

From the 1990s to present day, MCs have been marked by both continuity and changes.

OMCs Exponential Growth

From the 1990s to the present, OMCs have continued to have a significant impact on motorcycle culture and have seen fluctuations in their numbers and influence.

The 1990s witnessed a proliferation of OMCs, with the existing major clubs expanding their membership and new clubs emerging and popping up on the scene. This growth was fueled by various factors, including the appeal of the biker lifestyle, a sense of rebellion, and the allure of brotherhood and camaraderie. Some would say that possessing the diamond and a three-piece patch has become an irresistible fashion statement to new folks coming onto the sets. With new laws and RICCO predicates being aimed at traditional OMCs who attempt to regulate the set, many standards have been lowered or even dropped. Many clubs that would have never been allowed to wear a diamond are now no longer challenged. New OMCs are appearing every day trying to exert their will and make names for themselves. This causes an unstable environment for everyone.

OMC Conflicts and Violence

The 1990s and early 2000s were marked by conflicts and violent clashes between rival outlaw motorcycle clubs. These conflicts often arose from territorial disputes, competition over criminal activities, or disagreements between club members. Some of these conflicts gained media attention, further enhancing the public perception of OMCs as criminal organizations.

OMC Law Enforcement Scrutiny

OMCs faced increased scrutiny from law enforcement agencies during this period. Authorities targeted clubs they believed were involved in criminal activities, leading to extensive investigations, arrests, and prosecutions. This scrutiny contributed to ongoing legal battles and attempts to label certain clubs as organized crime groups. In one instance the Mongols MC was targeted for eleven years by federal authorities that took them to court in an attempt to use civil asset forfeiture and trademark laws to confiscate their colors. The club was able to keep their colors, but they were fined and faced other serious sanctions for portions of the case where they did not prevail. Their legal bills were extensive, and a lesser club would have been crushed fighting their legal battles.

OMC Internal Changes and Leadership Shifts

OMCs experienced internal changes, including leadership shifts and power struggles. Some clubs saw the rise of a new generation of leaders, while others faced challenges in maintaining their traditional structures and values. These internal dynamics affected the direction and operations of the clubs.

OMC Global Reach:

OMCs expanded their reach globally during this period, establishing international chapters and forming alliances with other clubs around the world. The globalization of OMCs allowed for increased networking, collaboration, and exchange of ideas and resources.

OMCs Influence on Popular Culture

OMCs continued to capture public attention through their portrayal in popular culture, including movies, television shows, and books. These depictions, although often sensationalized in shows like *"Sons of Anarchy,"* contributed to the perception of OMCs as symbols of rebellion, freedom, and the outlaw lifestyle.

OMCs Decline in Numbers

While the popularity of OMCs remained significant, some clubs experienced a decline in membership during the late 2000s and early 2010s. Factors such as increased law enforcement pressure, changing societal attitudes, and the aging of club members have been cited as possible reasons for this decline.

OMCs Persistence and Resilience

Despite challenges and fluctuations in membership, OMCs have demonstrated resilience and have maintained their presence within the motorcycle subculture. Certain clubs have even expanded their activities beyond traditional criminal pursuits, focusing on charity work, community involvement, and organizing motorcycle events.

MCs Growth and Diversification

MCs continued to grow in numbers and diversity. Not only did OMCs such as the Hells Angels, Outlaws, Bandidos, Outcast, Chosen Few, and Wheels of Soul expand their presence, but new clubs also emerged, catering to different riding styles, interests, and communities.

Popularity of Riding Groups

In addition to traditional OMCs, riding groups and social clubs became more prevalent. These groups often focused on riding together, promoting camaraderie, and organizing charitable events or community initiatives.

Women in Motorcycle Clubs

The 1990s to the present witnessed a notable increase in the participation of women in motorcycle clubs. More women became members of both coed and women-only clubs, challenging the male-dominated image of motorcycle clubs and fostering a more inclusive environment. Throughout their history, women's MCs have served as social networks, fostering camaraderie, and providing a sense of belonging for riders. They continue to be an integral part of the motorcycling culture in the United States, offering opportunities for like-minded women to connect and share their passion for motorcycles. MC set coalitions have even become more receptive to allowing female MCs a seat on their councils whereas in previous times women were often not even allowed to speak in these meetings. Times are changing and women are being recognized!

Riding for a Cause

Many motorcycle clubs and riding groups became actively involved in charity work and community service. They organized fundraising events, toy runs, and rides to support various causes, showcasing the positive impact of the motorcycle community.

Evolving Riding Styles and Subcultures

The 1990s to the present day saw the emergence of various riding styles and subcultures, such as sport bike riders, adventure riders, café racer enthusiasts, and custom bike builders. These subcultures formed their own communities and clubs, contributing to the diverse landscape of motorcycle culture.

Globalization of Traditional MCs, alternative MCs and LEMCs:

Traditional and law enforcement MCs expanded their presence beyond national boundaries as well during this time period. The Blue Knights LEMC, for instance, became one of the largest MCs in the world with over 16,000 members internationally, and hundreds of chapters in countries worldwide. Other MCs like the Ruff Ryders are also international clubs with thousands of members and chapters in countries all over the world. These alliances and chapters of major clubs were established, leading to the formation of global networks and connections between clubs in different countries.

Technology and Social Media Impact

The rise of the internet and social media platforms allowed motorcycle clubs and riders to connect, communicate, and organize events more efficiently. It provided a platform for sharing experiences, promoting club activities, and fostering a sense of community.

The effect of the movie Biker Boyz on the Black biker set

The movie "Biker Boyz," released in 2003, had a heavy impact on the Black club set culture. I was honored to work on the film as a technical advisor and helped bring this iconic movie to the Black biker set.

Biker Boyz Increased Visibility

"Biker Boyz" brought greater visibility to the Black motorcycle set culture and showcased the excitement and camaraderie of MCs in the African American community. This exposure helped shed light on a subculture that had not received significant mainstream attention before.

Biker Boyz Inspiration and Empowerment

The movie inspired individuals to join clubs within the Black motorcycle set culture to pursue their passion for motorcycles more actively. It showcased skilled riders, promoted the spirit of brotherhood, and encouraged Black bikers to chase their dreams and overcome challenges.

Biker Boyz Fashion and Style Influence

"Biker Boyz" contributed to shaping the fashion and style preferences within the Black MC set culture. The movie featured a variety of motorcycle gear, custom bikes, and distinctive aesthetics that influenced the choices and preferences of riders in terms of clothing, accessories, and bike customization of the day.

Biker Boyz Debate and Discussion

The movie sparked debate and discussion within the Black club set culture regarding its portrayal of MCs and the authenticity of the experiences depicted. It encouraged conversations about representation and the dynamics of club life, creating a space for riders to share their perspectives and opinions.

The history of motorcycle clubs is diverse and complex, with individual clubs having unique experiences and dynamics. The historical developments mentioned above provide a general overview of the trends and changes that have occurred within the motorcycle club culture from the 1990s to the present day. It is by no means an exhaustive list.

CHAPTER 7
How Do MCs Operate

Now that you know the history of motorcycles, MCs and how they came about it wouldn't be a bad idea to understand how they operate so that you can matriculate easily around them. This chapter is dedicated to giving you a crash course in MC operations. This information is not exhaustive. For more detailed information about MC protocol and biker set operations, I recommend referencing many other books I've written on these topics. Still, this information will give you a working knowledge upon which you can expand.

Note: As I've said before, these lessons and observations are from my lengthy experience as a full patched member, retired Chapter President, and retired National President of the Mighty Black Sabbath Motorcycle Club Nation. There are a lot of others who have a great deal of experience on the MC set who have a different take on things and would explain them a different way. That's okay! If your Prez thinks things are slightly different or entirely different than what I am telling you in this book, listen to them as well. Then study and draw your own conclusions.

The Makeup of the MC

The greater extended MC family is made up of several components. Not all MCs will have these components, and some will have more or less but basically –depending upon the scope, size, and age of the MC— you can expect to see something like this respectively by order of seniority:

- National Officers (if a national club)
- Regional Officers (if a national or regional club)
- Nomads (if a national or regional club)
- Local Officers (local chapter)

- Full patch brothers
- Prospects
- Women's Auxiliary or 'Properties Of'
- Honorary members
- Hang-arounds
- Brother clubs
- Support clubs
- Social Clubs (to which this book is created)
- 'Friends of the Club'
- Supporters

National Officers

A national MC will be led by national officers often referred to as the National Executive Board or Committee. You can typically expect to see:

- National President (National)
- National Vice President (National VP)
- National Sergeant at Arms (SAA) or Enforcer
- National Secretary
- National Business Manager
- National Treasurer
- National Road Captain

These are the supreme leaders of the MC. You may hear them called affectionately "The Nationals" or anyone of them referred to as "National" but that is generally reserved for the National "P" (Prez) himself. So, it is often acceptable to refer to the National "P" as "National" or anyone you may see wearing a patch indicating "National" on it.

Note: International MCs may have a leadership board one level above nationals and will have the same positions only with the title "International" before the positions.

Note: There aren't as many International MCs on the Black biker set at the time of the writing of this book but you will see it more often on the White set and amongst 1%er and outlaw clubs.

Responsibilities of the Nationals

The responsibilities of national officers can vary depending on the specific club and its organizational structure. However, there are some common responsibilities you should expect to see:

Leadership:

Nationals are responsible for providing leadership and guidance to the club at the national level. They set the overall direction and vision of the club and work to ensure that the club's values, goals, and objectives are upheld.

Governance and Administration:

They are involved in the governance and administration of the club. They oversee the club's bylaws, rules, and regulations, ensuring compliance and proper functioning of the organization. They also handle club finances, membership management, and other administration.

Communication and Representation:

The national president is the main point of contact and representation for the club at the national level. He communicates with regional officers facilitating the flow of information and ensuring effective communication within the club. He also represents the club in external interactions with other motorcycle clubs, organizations, or the public.

Event Coordination and Planning:

National officers coordinate and plan national-level events, such as rallies, rides, or conventions. They work with local chapters to organize these events, ensuring they align with the club's values and provide meaningful experiences for members.

Conflict Resolution:

National officers resolve conflicts or disputes within the club and between chapters or charters. They act as mediators and work to find amicable solutions, promoting harmony and unity among members.

Promoting Club Culture and Values:

National officers are responsible for upholding and promoting the club's culture, traditions, and values. They foster a sense of camaraderie, brotherhood/sisterhood, and mutual respect among members. They also develop and implement programs or initiatives that align with the club's mission and values.

Growth and Expansion:

National officers expand the club's reach by establishing new chapters or affiliations, both domestically and internationally. They evaluate potential new chapters, oversee their formation, and provide guidance to ensure consistency and adherence to the club's standards.

What Is a National MC

An MC is generally expected to have five chapters or charters in five states and have been in existence for five years before it is recognized as a national MC on the Black biker club set. Other sets may operate similarly. And yes, you may know a few clubs that have national presidents and national officers that don't meet that standard. Often those clubs run into major problems with 1%er clubs when they are attempting to expand. But for every so-called rule of MC protocol, there are exceptions so don't be surprised when you see them. It is what it is.

"Chapter" versus "Charter"

The terms "chapter" and "charter" are often used interchangeably in the context of MCs, but they can have slightly different meanings depending on the club and its organizational structure. Some MCs will recognize the differences between a chapter and a charter as follows:

Chapter:

> In an MC, a chapter refers to a local branch or subdivision of the club that operates within a specific geographical area. A chapter is typically established in a particular city, region, or state. It serves as a local representation of the larger club and operates under the umbrella of the national or international organization. The chapter is usually led by a chapter officer or a chapter president, along with other officers responsible for managing the affairs of the chapter. Chapters often have their own set of bylaws and rules that are in line with the overall club's guidelines.

Charter:

A charter, like a chapter can refer to a local branch or subdivision of a national or regional MC that operates within a specific geographical area, but it most often refers to a branch that largely operates on its own without governance from the central body, national/international president or executive governing board. This protects a club from laws that would make all members guilty of the actions of one or more charters or members in a charter. Laws like the Racketeer Influenced and Corrupt Organizations (RICO) Act is a United States federal law that was enacted in 1970. It provides for extended criminal penalties and civil liability for individuals involved in organized crime. RICO is designed to combat racketeering activities, including illegal activities conducted by organized crime groups. Other laws like civil asset forfeiture laws are also designed to target centrally governed MCs. The charter system seeks to avoid those complications by allowing clubs to operate independently without authorization from nationals.

What is a Regional MC

A regional MC is a club that may have many chapters/charters in one state or in one region but hasn't grown to the level of a national MC having five chapters/charters in five states.

What is a Local MC

A local MC has one chapter in one location. It has a local

- President (Prez)
- VP (VP or Vice Prez)
- SAA or Enforcer
- Secretary
- Treasurer
- Business Manager

- Road Captain
- Public Relations Officer (PRO)
- Full patch brothers (and full patch sisters in a coed MC)
- Prospects
- Women's auxiliary or 'Properties Of'
- Honorary members
- Hang-arounds
- Brother clubs
- Support clubs
- Social Clubs (SCs that's you!!)
- 'Friends of the Club'
- Supporters

Note: Not all MCs have road captains, business managers, or PROs. In fact, PROs are almost uniquely on the Black MC set exclusively. On other MC sets you'll see the Secretary performing that job.

Traditionally an MC needs five members to get blessed. These members make up the top five officers:

- Prez
- VP
- SAA/Enforcer
- Secretary
- Treasurer

Chapter President

The Prez of a local chapter is responsible for leading the MC in its direction, traditions, club culture, discipline, public relations, relationships with MCs external to the club and dominant outlaw or 1%er MCs on the set.

In a traditional MC a president doesn't vote unless it is to break a tie. This is because more than anything it is his job to reflect in leadership the will and direction of the MC. He is the ultimate servant of the officers and members of the extended family. His job is to deliver to the MC its will as determined by vote. He may provide guidance, leadership, and direction but in the greater scheme of things he is merely a conduit to provide the pathway to ensure the desires of the voting body of the MC are carried out. The voting body of a traditional MC are the full patch brothers in good standing. You may run into an MC with a dictator or strongman as the leader who thinks he is God and is to be obeyed like some kind of king, ruler, or potentate—but that situation is counter to MC protocol and how MCs are properly run.

Note: Refer to my Amazon number one best-selling book "President's Bible Chronicle I Principles of Motorcycle Club Leadership" for more in-depth information about this position.

Chapter VP

The VP plays a crucial role in supporting the president in the overall management and functioning of the MC and in carrying out his duties. He collaborates closely with him to make decisions, develop strategies, and implement club initiatives. In the absence of the president, the VP will assume his responsibilities and act as the interim leader. The VP assists in overseeing the day-to-day operations of the club. He coordinates club meetings, events, and activities, ensuring that they align with the club's goals and objectives. He is often the "bad" guy being the "heavy" by executing the Prez's orders and initiating discipline so the Prez can remain the "good" guy of the club. The VP ensures the Prez operates in accordance with the club's vote and bylaws. Though he is second in charge of the MC if he does his job correctly, often the club won't notice he even exists. Being a good VP is an art. He is seldom seen or noticed but must be up-to-speed at all times in case he must step in and take the reins if the "P" becomes incapacitated or unable to fulfill his job duties.

Chapter SAA/Enforcer

The sergeant-at-arms is an important position within the MC. While the specific responsibilities can vary between clubs, there are some common duties associated with the role of a SAA you can expect:

Club Security:

The SAA is responsible for ensuring the security and safety of the club and its members. This includes maintaining vigilance during club meetings, events, and rides to identify and address any potential threats or security issues.

Enforcing Club Rules:

The SAA helps enforce the club's bylaws, rules, and codes of conduct. He ensures all members adhere to the established protocols and standards of behavior within the club. This includes addressing any violations or misconduct and taking appropriate disciplinary actions when necessary.

Preserving Club Traditions and Protocols:

The SAA upholds the traditions, rituals, and protocols of the club. He ensures that club ceremonies, rituals, and traditions are conducted with respect and in accordance with the club's customs.

Managing Club Property:

The SAA oversees the club's property and assets. This can include maintaining and safeguarding club-owned items such as clubhouses, meeting spaces, club equipment, merchandise, and inventories.

External Relations and Security:

The SAA represents the club in interactions with other MCs, law enforcement agencies, or the public when it comes to security-related matters. He may coordinate security arrangements for club events and rides and serves as a point of contact for external security concerns.

Conflict Resolution:

The SAA assists in resolving conflicts or disputes within the club. He is a mediator, helping to facilitate open communication and finding resolutions that maintain harmony within the club. He also intervenes in situations where conflicts arise during club activities.

Ride Formation and Safety:

As I have previously stated, not all clubs have road captains. In those cases, the SAA often plays a role in organizing and leading club rides. He ensures proper ride formation, communicates ride instructions to members, and promotes safe riding practices within the club. He may also coordinate with road captains and assistant road captains or other ride leaders like tail gunners, road guards or others to maintain a cohesive and safe riding experience for the MCs that utilize those positions.

Specific responsibilities and authority of an SAA can vary between MCs. Their exact powers are located in the club's bylaws. The role may also involve additional duties or specific requirements based on the club's culture, size, and internal dynamics. The SAA typically works closely with other club officers and the club's leadership to maintain a strong and unified club environment. In some clubs they are picked specifically by the President as the SAA will normally be expected to be wherever the President is whenever he moves. In other clubs they are voted in. But next to the President the SAA is perhaps the second most important and powerful officer in the MC.

Note: Refer to my Amazon number one best-selling book "Sergeant-at-Arms Bible Soldier/Sergeant of the Brotherhood" for more in-depth information about this position.

Chapter Secretary

The secretary holds a crucial administrative role and is responsible for various tasks related to documentation, communication, and record-keeping. The specific responsibilities may vary between different clubs, but here are some common duties associated with the role of a secretary you may expect to see:

Meeting Coordination:

The secretary schedules church, sends out meeting notices to club members, and prepares the meeting agenda.

Meeting Minutes:

During church, the secretary takes detailed minutes of the discussions, decisions, and actions taken. These minutes serve as an official record of the meeting and are circulated among club members upon request. The secretary ensures that accurate records are maintained and kept up to date.

Club Correspondence:

The secretary handles incoming and outgoing club correspondence and other forms of communication on behalf of the club. He also maintains contact lists of club members and other relevant contacts.

Club Records and Documentation:

The secretary is responsible for maintaining important club records and documentation. This can include membership records, bylaws, financial records, event attendance lists, and any other relevant paperwork. He ensures that these records are organized, secure, and easily accessible.

Membership Administration:

The secretary manages the MC's membership administration. He oversees membership applications, member emergency contract information and other documentation as needed. He may also manage prospect administration, provide membership requirements documents, and facilitate the onboarding process for newly patched brothers.

Financial Record-Keeping:

In some clubs, the secretary may assist in financial record-keeping. He works closely with the treasurer and business manager to maintain accurate records of club finances, including income, expenses, and dues. The secretary may also help prepare financial reports and assist with budget planning.

Reporting and Documentation:

The secretary may be responsible for preparing various reports and documentation on behalf of the club. This can include monthly or annual reports, event summaries, membership statistics, or any other documentation required by the club's leadership, governing bodies, or external entities.

General Administration:

The secretary may assist in general administrative tasks as needed, such as organizing club files, managing club calendars, and coordinating club-related logistics. He may provide support to other officers and club members with administrative needs or inquiries.

The role of a secretary in an MC requires good organizational skills, attention to detail, and effective communication abilities. He plays a vital role in maintaining club records, facilitating communication, and ensuring smooth administrative operations within the club.

Chapter Treasurer

The treasurer holds a critical role in managing the club's financial affairs and ensuring the proper handling of funds. Here are some common duties associated with the role of a treasurer:

Financial Record-Keeping:

The treasurer is responsible for maintaining accurate and up-to-date financial records for the club. This includes tracking income, expenses, and any other financial transactions. He must ensure that all financial activities are properly documented and recorded.

Budget Planning:

The treasurer often plays a key role in budget planning for the club. He collaborates with other club officers to develop a budget that outlines projected income and anticipated expenses. He helps monitor the club's financial performance against the budget and provides financial insights to guide decision-making.

Membership Dues and Finances:

The treasurer manages the collection of membership dues and fees from club members. He maintains records of member payments, tracks outstanding dues, and provides regular reports on the club's financial status. He may also work closely with the club secretary and business manager to ensure accurate membership records.

Financial Reporting:

The treasurer prepares financial reports and statements for the club's leadership and members. This includes regular reports on income, expenses, account balances, and financial trends. The treasurer presents these reports during club meetings or as requested by the club's governing bodies.

Banking and Financial Transactions:

The treasurer handles banking activities on behalf of the club. This involves opening and maintaining a bank account in the club's name, depositing funds, writing checks, or authorizing electronic payments, and reconciling bank statements. The treasurer ensures that financial transactions are conducted securely and in accordance with the club's policies.

Fundraising and Sponsorships:

In some cases, the treasurer may be involved in coordinating fundraising efforts or seeking sponsorships for club activities and events. He may collaborate with other club members to identify fundraising opportunities, maintain donor records, and manage funds raised. He may also work within his responsibilities to manage the club's charitable fundraising and giving efforts.

Financial Compliance:

The treasurer ensures that the club's financial activities comply with relevant laws and regulations. He may be responsible for filing any necessary tax forms or reports, as well as maintaining proper documentation for auditing or financial review purposes or managing the club's 501.3c.

Financial Planning and Advice:

The treasurer provides financial advice and recommendations to the club's leadership. He analyzes financial data, identifies trends, and offers insights to support informed decision-making. The treasurer may also assist in financial planning for future club initiatives, such as purchasing new equipment or organizing larger events.

The role of a treasurer requires financial acumen, attention to detail, and a strong sense of responsibility. He plays a crucial role in maintaining the financial health of the club, ensuring transparency, and supporting the club's overall objectives.

Chapter Business Manager

The business manager position is very common on the Black MC set but not as popular among outlaw, 1% or white MC sets. The office can be seen as a variation of the treasurer's job and in many MCs his duties will be divided between the treasurer and the secretary. But in clubs that do have the business manager position he typically handles various administrative and operational tasks to ensure the smooth functioning of the club with an emphasis and specialized knowledge of business management as opposed to a secretary who will be more administrative in his specialty, or a treasurer that will be more slanted toward accounting and fiscal responsibility. Here are some common responsibilities associated with the role of a business manager:

Financial Management:

The business manager is responsible for overseeing the club's financial affairs. He may manage the club's budget, track income and expenses, manage club investments, handle financial transactions, and ensure that proper financial records are maintained. The business manager may work closely with the treasurer to ensure accurate and transparent financial management.

Club Business Operations:

The business manager is involved in managing the day-to-day business operations of the club. This can include coordinating meetings, events around club events and business opportunities. He handles logistics, such as securing venues, arranging equipment, and coordinating with external vendors or suppliers as needed.

Club Business Communication:

The business manager will be responsible for club communication and correspondence regarding business matters. He handles internal and external business communications on behalf of the club, including emails, newsletters, announcements, and other forms of communication. He ensures that club members are informed of important updates regarding all business matters.

Documentation and Record-Keeping:

The business manager maintains club business records and documentation. The business manager ensures that these records are organized, accessible, and up to date.

Business Contracts and Relations:

The business manager handles external business relations on behalf of the club. This can include establishing and maintaining rental agreements, managing club properties, evaluating contracts the club may enter, and managing financial dealings with attorneys, realtors, or other professional services the MC may require. The business manager may look after the club's intellectual properties, handle lawsuits, hire attorneys, accountants, or other services the MC may need. The business manager represents the club in external meetings, events, or collaborations to ensure the best financial interests of the MC as it conducts business.

Club Administration:

The business manager may assist in general club administration, providing support to other club officers and members as needed. This can include assisting with event planning, managing club resources or assets, coordinating club merchandise or branding, and addressing administrative needs or inquiries.

The role requires sharp business acumen, organizational skills, attention to detail, and the ability to handle multiple tasks and responsibilities simultaneously.

Chapter Road Captain

The road captain plays a vital role although he is the junior officer in the MC. The road captain is responsible for how the MC looks and rides on the road! In many MCs' bylaws this junior officer assumes the authority of president while the MC is on the road. In this capacity he is responsible for various duties related to planning, coordinating, and executing rides. Here are some common responsibilities associated with the role of a road captain you will see in many MCs that have them:

Ride Planning:

The road captain is involved in planning club rides, including selecting the route, determining the duration and stops along the way, and considering any special requirements or preferences of the club members. He takes into account factors such as road conditions, traffic, weather, and the skill levels of the riders to create an enjoyable and safe riding experience.

Pre-Ride Briefing:

Before each ride, the road captain conducts a pre-ride briefing for all participating club members, guests, cars, trucks, chase vehicles, support clubs and all others who will be in the pack. This includes reviewing the planned route, highlighting any potential hazards or points of interest, discussing riding formations and signals, and addressing any specific instructions or guidelines for the ride. The road captain ensures that all riders are well-informed and prepared for the journey.

Leading the Ride:

During the ride, the road captain takes the lead position in the group formation (in some MCs). He sets the pace, maintains proper spacing between bikes, and follows safe riding practices. The road captain acts as a role model for other riders, demonstrating responsible and defensive riding techniques.

Group Management:

The road captain is responsible for managing the group dynamics during the ride. He ensures that riders stay together as a cohesive unit, maintain proper spacing, and follow the established riding formations. The road captain may also assist in resolving any issues or conflicts that arise within the group during the ride. In many club bylaws he is able to levy fines, discipline, and suspensions while on the road. Woe be to anyone who may cross him on a trip or be foolish enough to "act-a-fool" or "cut-up" in the pack!

Safety and Traffic Management:

The road captain prioritizes the safety of the riders during the ride. He keeps a vigilant eye on the road conditions, traffic, and potential hazards. He may make decisions regarding route adjustments or stops to ensure the safety and well-being of the pack. He communicates important information, such as road hazards or upcoming turns, using established hand signals or communication systems.

Communication and Coordination:

The road captain maintains effective communication with the riders throughout the ride. He may use hand signals, radios, or other communication devices to relay information to the group. He coordinates with other club officers or road crew members to ensure a smooth and organized ride experience.

Ensuring Rider Compliance:

The road captain enforces club riding rules and guidelines during the ride. He monitors the behavior and adherence of the riders to ensure that everyone follows safe riding practices and respects the rules of the road. He may provide guidance or reminders to individual riders when necessary.

Ride Evaluation:

After each ride, the road captain may conduct a post-ride evaluation or debriefing. This allows for feedback and discussion about the ride experience, identifying any areas for improvement or adjustments for future rides. He may gather input from the riders and incorporate it into future ride planning.

The position of a road captain requires strong leadership skills, knowledge of safe riding practices, and effective communication abilities. He plays a critical role in ensuring the smooth operation of club rides, promoting rider safety, and fostering a positive riding experience for all club members. He ensures that "MC" means "move-the-crowd" on two wheels, looking good, safe, smooth, and professional. He must be an exemplary rider, one of the best in the MC. When people exclaim how sharp the MC looks while pounding the ground on two, it is to the road captain that the club owes its gratitude.

Chapter Public Relations Officer (PRO)

The PRO is a fairly new position found almost exclusively on the Black MC set. Many clubs have a distorted view of what a PRO truly is focusing this position on setting up parties and networking between clubs. This is a poor usage for the position. For clubs that use them the public relations officer (PRO) is responsible for managing the club's public image and handling external communications. Their role involves promoting positive relationships with the public, media, external MCs, and other organizations. Here are some common responsibilities associated with the role of a public relations officer:

Media Relations:

The PRO serves as the primary point of contact for media inquiries and facilitates interactions between the club and the media. He coordinates press releases, interviews, and media coverage related to club events, activities, or community involvement. The PRO ensures that accurate and positive information is communicated to the media.

Public Image Management:

The PRO works to maintain and enhance the club's public image. He develops strategies to promote the club's positive reputation, values, and contributions to the community. The PRO may coordinate public relations campaigns, social media presence, and other promotional activities to shape public perception of the club.

Community Engagement:

The PRO plays a key role in fostering positive relationships with the local community. He seeks opportunities for the club to engage in community service, charity events, or other initiatives that contribute to the well-being of the community. The PRO may coordinate with local organizations, government entities, or charitable causes to establish partnerships or collaborative efforts.

Club Representation:

The PRO represents the club in external events, meetings, or public forums. He may attend community meetings, motorcycle rallies, charity events, or other gatherings to represent the club and promote its values and activities. The PRO ensures that club members present themselves professionally and positively during these engagements.

Online Presence and Social Media Management:

In today's digital age, the PRO often manages the club's online presence and social media accounts. He creates and shares content that highlights the club's activities, events, and positive contributions. The PRO may engage with online followers, respond to inquiries or comments, and ensure that the club's online presence aligns with its image and values.

Crisis Management:

In the event of a crisis or negative publicity, the PRO plays a crucial role in managing the club's response. He works to minimize damage to the club's reputation, address concerns or misconceptions, and handles media inquiries or statements. The PRO may collaborate with club leadership and legal advisors to develop appropriate crisis communication strategies.

Internal Communication:

The PRO also facilitates internal communication within the club. He may coordinate newsletters, club updates, or announcements to keep members informed about upcoming events, news, or other relevant information. He ensures that internal communication channels are effective and efficient.

Branding and Merchandising:

The PRO may be involved in branding initiatives and merchandise management. He helps develop and maintain the club's visual identity, logo usage, and branding guidelines. The PRO, working closely with the business manager, may oversee the production and distribution of club merchandise, ensuring quality control and adherence to licensing requirements, if applicable.

The role of a public relations officer requires excellent communication skills, a positive and professional demeanor, and the ability to effectively represent the club to the public and media. He plays a crucial role in managing the club's reputation, building relationships, and promoting a positive image both within the motorcycle community and the wider public.

Nomad

In the context of an MC, a nomad is generally a very senior member of a national or regional MC who does not have a fixed chapter or geographical area to call home. They are banished from the MC into nomadism either by choice or sometimes by club necessity or as a result of disciplinary action. They have the freedom to travel and represent the club in different regions or territories but must have the experience, strength of character, MC protocol knowledge, maturity, mental acuity, and toughness to represent entirely on their own for extended periods, often in enemy territory, without support or resupply from the MC. You will typically only see nomads in 1% MCs. The role of a nomad within a motorcycle club can vary, but here are some general aspects of their responsibilities:

Representing the Club:

Nomads serve as ambassadors of the MC, representing its values, traditions, and brotherhood wherever they travel. They may attend events, visit other chapters, or establish connections with other clubs or individuals on behalf of the MC.

Building Relationships:

Nomads focus on establishing and maintaining relationships with other chapters, clubs, and individuals in the motorcycle club community. This involves fostering positive interactions, promoting unity, and facilitating cooperation between different entities.

Support and Assistance:

Nomads are often called upon to provide support and assistance to other club members, chapters, or allied clubs. They often travel great distances, wherever required to accomplish these tasks.

Reporting and Communication:

Nomads play a crucial role in keeping the club informed about the activities, dynamics, and developments in the regions they visit. They provide valuable information and insights into competing clubs' leadership and members, facilitating informed decision-making in the MC.

Maintaining Club Standards:

Nomads uphold the club's standards, policies, and code of conduct, ensuring that the club's reputation and integrity are maintained wherever they go. They serve as examples of loyalty, respect, and commitment to the MC's values. They may be assigned to discipline rogue elements within the MC or presidents who are challenging national authority.

Flexibility and Adaptability:

Nomads embrace a lifestyle of flexibility and adaptability. They are comfortable being on the road and away from a fixed chapter, adjusting to different environments, and integrating themselves into various MC communities.

The specific responsibilities and expectations of nomads may vary between MCs.

What is a Full Patch Brother

A full patch brother is a member who has earned his place in the MC at the most basic level. He has been voted in by the full membership of the MC (in a traditional MC) and is commonly referred to as "the most powerful member of the MC." Full patch brothers are also referred to as "regular fucking members" (RFO) and for many it is the only position to which they aspire.

The responsibilities of full patch brothers can vary depending on the specific club's rules, traditions, and organizational structure. However, here are some common responsibilities associated with full patch brothers:

Club Loyalty:

Full patch brothers are expected to demonstrate unwavering loyalty to the MC. They are committed to upholding the club's values, traditions, and code of conduct. They support the club's objectives and work towards its collective goals.

Club Unity and Brotherhood:

Full patch brothers foster a sense of unity and brotherhood within the club. They build strong bonds with their fellow club members and prioritize the well-being and camaraderie of the brotherhood. They actively contribute to creating a positive club culture and maintaining a sense of unity among the members.

Club Support and Participation:

Full patch brothers actively participate in club activities, events, and meetings. They show support for the club's initiatives and contribute to its success. They may take on various roles or responsibilities within the club, such as organizing events, volunteering for club projects, or representing the club in external engagements. They support and uphold their officers in their duties by setting them up for success!

Club Security and Protection:

Full patch brothers play a role in ensuring the security and protection of the club, its members, and its extended family. They are vigilant in safeguarding the club's interests, assets, and reputation. They may contribute to maintaining the club's confidentiality, enforcing club rules, and addressing any threats or conflicts that may arise.

Club Tradition, Etiquette and Protocol:

Full patch brothers adhere to the club's traditions, etiquette, protocol, and hierarchy. They respect the club's chain of command and follow established rules and traditions. They serve as role models for other club members, embodying the values and standards set by the club.

Club Representation:

Full patch brothers represent the club in a responsible and respectful manner. They understand that their actions and behavior reflect on the entire club and its reputation. They maintain a positive image both within the MC community and the public.

Club Development and Growth:

Full patch brothers contribute to the growth and development of the club. They may provide mentorship and guidance to newer members, helping them understand and embrace the club's culture. They actively participate in club meetings, discussions, and decision-making processes to contribute their insights and ideas.

Club Unity in Conflict Resolution:

Full patch brothers play a role in conflict resolution within the club. They strive to maintain unity and resolve internal disputes or disagreements in a constructive manner. They mediate conflicts, promote open communication, and work towards finding resolutions that align with the best interests of the club.

Good Standing

Full patch brothers are expected to maintain their status "In Good Standing." This means that they must follow the bylaws to adhere to at least the minimum standards in club membership as required. In some clubs that means to be current on dues, meet minimum ride and club participation rules, maintain an operating motorcycle, ride a yearly minimum number of miles and other requirements. Not being in good standing can result in a full patch brother being fined, suspended, physically disciplined, or put "OUT BAD" of the MC brotherhood.

What is an MC Prospect/Probate/Probationary

A prospect in a motorcycle club is an individual who is seeking membership and is in the process of proving their worthiness and commitment to the club. Prospects are essentially probationary members who are working towards earning their full patch and becoming full-fledged members of the club. The job of a prospect typically includes the following responsibilities:

Club Familiarization:

Prospects are expected to learn about the history, values, traditions, and rules of the motorcycle club they aspire to join. They study the club's bylaws, code of conduct, and any other club-specific information provided to them.

Club Support:

Prospects assist full patch members and officers in various club activities and events. They may help with setting up and taking down equipment, organizing rides, providing support during club functions, or any other tasks assigned to them by the club's leadership.

Club Education:

Prospects engage in a process of learning and skill development within the club. They may receive training on motorcycle safety, riding techniques, club protocols, and other aspects of club life. They demonstrate a willingness to learn and improve themselves to align with the club's standards.

Club Integration:

Prospects actively engage with the club's members, fostering relationships and establishing a sense of camaraderie. They participate in club meetings and social events, interacting with full patch members and getting to know them on a personal level. They seek guidance from experienced members and show respect for the club's hierarchy.

Club Loyalty:

Prospects demonstrate their loyalty to the club and its members. They prioritize the interests of the club and show support for its objectives and activities. They prove their dedication by consistently attending club events, following club rules, and supporting the club's reputation.

Club Contributions:

Prospects contribute to the overall well-being of the club. They may take on specific tasks or responsibilities assigned to them by the club's leadership, such as assisting with fundraising efforts, community service projects, or maintaining club facilities. They demonstrate their commitment and willingness to contribute to the club's success.

Personal Development:

Prospects work on personal growth and character development during their prospect period. They strive to embody the values and ideals of the club, both on and off their motorcycles. They may be expected to maintain a certain level of personal conduct and integrity as representatives of the club.

Prospect Evaluation:

Prospects are continuously evaluated by full patch brothers and club officers to determine their suitability for membership. The evaluation considers factors such as dedication, commitment, loyalty, adherence to club rules, and compatibility with the club's culture. The length of the prospect period can vary among different motorcycle clubs.

Each club has its own unique set of rules, requirements, and traditions for prospecting. The prospect period serves as a trial period to assess the prospect's fit within the club and their ability to uphold its values and standards. It is also important that SC members not trifle with prospects while they are working. They are trying to gain admittance into the MC and if you are flirting with them, distracting them, or hindering them from excellent job performance, you risk costing them longer prospecting times, punishment (possibly physical abuse), suspensions, and fines. Remember they are always under the watchful eye of their full patch brothers. They never get to take a break while operating on the MC set because they are earning their way into the MC. Stay clear of them and let them do their work. That is the biggest favor you can do them.

Note: It is not considered appropriate to ask most prospects their names in many clubs. Some may only be able to refer to themselves as "P1," "P2," "Probie," or the like. Let them tell you what to call them then respect that.

Note: It is never appropriate to call a 1% prospect by the name "Prospect." 1% MCs require that their brothers (even their prospective brothers) are always referred to with respect. They also consider their prospects senior to the most senior officer of any club that is not a 1%MC. So, they will absolutely NOT tolerate an SC member talking "down" to one of their prospects. Don't ever make that mistake as the correction could be very public and highly embarrassing. If you haven't been introduced to them and don't know what to call them then call them by the name of their club until you are told to do otherwise. For instance, it is far better to say, "Hello Screaming Eagles MC how are you" than it is to say, "Hey prospect come over here!"

Note: Prospects only prospect for their own MCs. Even if you have been in your SC forever you will never be appropriate in attempting to give an order to the prospect of any MC. A women's organization on the biker set will never have that privilege. It is important to always know your place on the set if you want to navigate efficiently and without drama.

Women's Auxiliary of an MC

The most protected women on the MC set are women who are associated with a biker club. Those two groups are Properties and Auxiliaries. Unfortunately, women's SCs will never hold the same level of respect and protection as the women who wear the same colors of an MC. If an MC cannot protect its women, then it is useless in a male dominated culture. To that end we will discuss women's auxiliaries first.

A women's auxiliary of an MC is a separate organization or group associated with a motorcycle club that consists of female members who support and contribute to the club's activities and objectives. They wear some version of that MC's patch. The women's auxiliary is typically composed of female partners, spouses, family members, or close friends of the full patch brothers. While the specific roles and responsibilities can vary between different motorcycle clubs, the women's auxiliary often performs the following functions:

Support Club Activities:

The women's auxiliary provides support to the MC by assisting in organizing and participating in club events, rides, and fundraisers. They may help with event planning, coordination, logistics, and promoting club activities.

Community Involvement:

The women's auxiliary may engage in community service and outreach initiatives on behalf of the club. They may organize or participate in charitable events, fundraisers, and volunteer activities to support local causes and make a positive impact in their communities.

Social and Networking Activities:

The women's auxiliary creates opportunities for social interaction and networking among its members. They organize gatherings, social events, and meetings to foster a sense of camaraderie and friendship within the auxiliary group.

Support for the Full Patch Brothers:

The women's auxiliary provides emotional support and encouragement to the full patch brothers. They are there to offer a listening ear, provide assistance, and create a sense of unity and support within the larger motorcycle club community. They can also be a source of wisdom to prospects and hang-arounds.

Promoting the Club's Values:

The women's auxiliary serves as ambassadors for the MC, promoting its values, mission, and positive image. They may engage in public relations efforts, representing the club at community events.

Fundraising and Financial Assistance:

The women's auxiliary may contribute to the club's financial stability by organizing fundraisers, participating in revenue-generating activities, paying dues, and providing financial assistance when needed. This support helps the club fulfill its objectives and maintain its operations.

Communication and Coordination:

The women's auxiliary serves as a communication channel between the club members and the broader community. They may facilitate communication and coordination among club members' families, relay important information, and provide updates on club activities.

It's important to note that the structure and activities of a women's auxiliary can vary between different motorcycle clubs. Some clubs may have formalized auxiliary organizations with established leadership positions and specific bylaws, while others may have more informal arrangements. The primary purpose of a women's auxiliary is to support the MC and contribute to its overall success while fostering a sense of community and camaraderie among its female members. Although SCs can become very close to the MC and receive protection and love from the full patch brothers, the women wearing the patches of the MC will always be exclusive family.

Properties Of an MC

The property of is a relationship that is not often understood by others who are not in the lifestyle. Why a woman would want to be called a property is not something that everyone can understand. Suffice it to say that the most important thing I would want to convey to you is that it doesn't mean chattel property as in slavery or ownership of someone's soul, body, or spirit. This doesn't mean that women haven't been abused. But even wives have been abused so don't let a word (property) throw you off, it is the symbolism of protection, overwatch, support, love, and loyalty they are given that makes them desire to be property of the MC nation to which they engage completely. As I have said before they are among the most protected groups on the biker clubs' set. Properties are on both the Black and the white set and they should not be trifled with as the entire club will turn up to protect them if necessary. A showdown between properties and an SC will always be a losing interaction for the SC.

Properties can be found in both 99%er traditional MCs, outlaw MCs, and 1% MCs. I have even known some riding clubs (RCs) that have had properties of believe it or not. But most often you will see them in outlaw and 1% MCs.

In the context of an MC, the term "property" can also refer to a member's significant other or spouse. In that case you may see her patch reflect the term "Property of Shady One." It would mean she was the property of a particular member named "Shady One." It is important to note that a property does not have to be romantically involved with a full patch brother to wear his "Property Of Shady One" tag. A property's immediate supervisor is known as her sponsor. In most things he will speak for her especially in matters pertaining to the club. A property of can also have a patch the designates her "Property of the Eagle Cliffs MC." She will still have a club sponsor who speaks for her even though she doesn't bear his name tag. Sponsors can also have multiple properties. They are not limited to just one.

Property's roles can vary depending on the specific club's culture and traditions. Here are some common roles and responsibilities associated with being a property:

Support and Loyalty:

The primary role of a property is to support her sponsor who is a member of the motorcycle club. This includes being loyal to the club, respecting its rules and values, and standing by her sponsor through the club's activities and endeavors.

Club Participation:

Properties participate in club events and functions alongside their sponsors. They attend rides, parties, fundraisers, and other activities organized by the club.

Socializing and Networking:

Properties engage in socializing and networking within the MC community. They build relationships with other MCs' properties adding allies to the family.

Community Engagement:

Properties participate in community engagement activities organized by the MC. This can include charity donations, and volunteer work to support local causes and give back to the community.

Supporting Club Functions:

Properties assist with various tasks related to club functions, like setting up camps, cooking at field meets, organizing rally events, watching over the children, and providing entertainment around campfires.

Emotional and Physical Support:

Being a property involves offering emotional support to her sponsor, especially during the challenges and demands of club life. Properties provide understanding, and encouragement to their sponsor to aid in navigating the responsibilities and commitments associated with being a club member. They have also been known to provide physical support including aiding in war and battle. A property will always have her sponsor's back.

Respecting Club Hierarchy:

Properties are expected to respect the club's hierarchy and chain of command. They should understand and abide by the club's rules and protocols, recognizing the authority of the club's officers and leadership.

Some clubs may have more defined expectations and guidelines for properties, while others may have a more relaxed approach. Communication and understanding between the sponsor and his property are crucial to ensure a healthy and supportive relationship within the MC community.

Honorary Members of the MC

An honorary member is an individual who is recognized and granted a special status by the club. Unlike full patch members or prospects who go through the usual initiation and prospecting process, honorary members are typically invited to join the club based on their exceptional contributions, achievements, or significance to the club or the motorcycle community. Here are some key aspects of being an honorary member:

Recognition:

Honorary membership is a way for the club to recognize an individual's notable accomplishments, support, or contributions to the MC or the broader motorcycle community. It is a mark of respect and appreciation for their involvement and dedication.

Symbolic Inclusion:

By bestowing honorary membership, the club is essentially extending an honorary patch or symbol to the individual. This patch or symbol may differ from the traditional club patches worn by full patch members and prospects but represents a special affiliation with the club.

Association with the Club:

Honorary members are associated with the MC and often enjoy certain privileges and benefits. They may be invited to attend club functions, participate in rides, or be involved in club activities. They are recognized as part of the club's extended family or support network.

Support and Representation:

Honorary members are expected to support and represent the club positively. They may be called upon to act as ambassadors for the club, promoting its values, and contributing to its reputation. This can include attending events, speaking on behalf of the club, or lending their expertise or influence on club initiatives.

Relationship with Full Patch Members:

Honorary members develop close relationships with full patch members of the club. Often, they may have a mentor-like role, providing guidance and support to club members, especially in areas where they possess specialized knowledge or experience.

Non-voting Status:

In most cases, honorary members do not have voting rights within the club's decision-making processes. Their membership is honorary and does not grant them the same level of privileges in club affairs as full patch members. However, their opinions and perspectives may be respected and considered by the club's leadership.

Each club has its own criteria for granting honorary membership and may define the expectations and privileges associated with this status. Honorary membership is typically an honorary title and does not necessarily entail the same level of commitment or obligations as full membership. You will not see them often on the MC set, but if you do see an honorary member, you can rest assured he did something very special to get an honorary patch others had to prospect to achieve.

Hang-arounds

A "hang around" is a term used in MC culture to describe an individual who is interested in joining a motorcycle club and is in the process of getting to know the club and its members. A hang around is essentially an informal status that precedes becoming a prospect or a full patch member. Here are some key aspects of being a hang around:

Observation and Familiarization:

As a hang around, the individual spends time around the club, attending club events, and getting to know the club members. They observe the club's activities, traditions, and dynamics to gain a better understanding of the club's culture and values.

Building Relationships:

Hang arounds use this period to build relationships and establish rapport with club members. They interact with club members, participate in conversations, and engage in social activities to develop connections within the club community.

Club Etiquette and Respect:

Hang arounds are expected to adhere to the club's rules, protocols, and customs. They demonstrate respect for the club, its members, and the club's property. Following club etiquette and showing proper behavior is essential during this stage of affiliation.

Support and Assistance:

Hang-arounds may assist the club in various ways, such as helping with event setup, cleanup, or other tasks as requested. They demonstrate their commitment to the club and their willingness to contribute and be of assistance.

Getting Vetted:

The hang around period allows club members to evaluate the individual's compatibility with the club and assess whether they would be a good fit. Club members observe the hang around's character, commitment, and dedication to determine if they should proceed to the next stage of becoming a prospect.

The specific process and duration of the hang around period can vary between MCs. Some clubs may have a structured and formalized hang around period, while others may have a more informal approach. The purpose of this stage is for both the hang around and the club to assess mutual compatibility and determine if the hang around will progress to the next stage of club membership. Most hang-arounds do not wear club colors, but they may wear support t-shirts.

Brother Clubs of an MC

A brother club can also be known as a support club or affiliated club but for the purposes of this book it is a separate motorcycle club that has a close relationship and affiliation with another MC that recognizes that club as an equal and respects it enough to call it "brother." Brother clubs often share common values, interests, and camaraderie with their brother MC, and they work together to support each other and promote the MC lifestyle. Here are some key aspects of brother clubs:

Mutual Relationship:

A brother club maintains a formal or informal relationship with the brother MC. They have a mutual respect and bond based on shared interests and values within the motorcycle club culture.

Support and Association:

Brother clubs provide support to their brother MC in various ways. This can include attending and assisting with their events, participating in joint rides or runs, and showing solidarity in club matters. They contribute to the overall unity and strength of the MC community.

Shared Values and Protocol:

Brother clubs align themselves with the values, protocols, and expectations of their brother MC. They adhere to similar club customs, rules, and codes of conduct, reinforcing a sense of brotherhood and common identity within the MC culture.

Patch or Colors:

Brother clubs may have their own distinctive patches or colors, separate from those of their brother MC. These patches typically display their club's name, logo, and other identifiers. However, brother clubs often wear a "brotherhood" patch or a specific patch indicating their affiliation with their brother MC.

Relationship Dynamics:

Brother clubs maintain a respectful and cooperative relationship with their brother MC. They understand and respect each other and work in harmony with them. The level of involvement and collaboration can vary depending on the specific arrangement and dynamics established between the clubs.

Autonomy and Independence:

While brother clubs have an affiliation with their brother MC, they maintain their own autonomy and independence. They have their own leadership structure, club activities, and decision-making processes. However, major decisions or actions may be discussed or coordinated with the brother MC to ensure alignment and support.

It's important to note that the specifics of brother club relationships can vary between different motorcycle clubs. Each club has its own policies and agreements regarding brother club affiliations. These relationships are based on mutual respect, support, and shared values, enhancing the sense of brotherhood and community within the MC culture.

Support Clubs of an MC

A support club, also called a satellite club or puppet club by law enforcement, is a separate motorcycle club that has a formal affiliation with a dominant MC. Unlike a brother club, which maintains autonomy, a support club exists primarily to provide direct support and assistance to the dominant MC. Here are some key aspects of support clubs:

Relationship with the Dominant MC:

A support club has a close and formalized relationship with the dominant MC. They are established as a subordinate club to the dominant MC and operate under their authority and direction.

Support and Assistance:

The primary role of a support club is to provide various forms of support to the dominant MC. This can include assisting with club events, security, fundraising efforts, and other tasks as required. Support clubs are dedicated to serving the interests and needs of the dominant MC.

Patch or Colors:

Support clubs typically wear patches or colors that clearly indicate their affiliation with the dominant MC. These patches often include the dominant MC's name or logo, along with the support club's own identifiers. The patches and colors signify the support club's allegiance and dedication to the dominant MC.

Hierarchy and Structure:

Support clubs operate within a hierarchical structure, with the dominant MC holding the highest authority. They follow the rules, protocols, and customs established by the dominant MC and are subject to their directives. The support club's leadership may have direct communication and coordination with the leadership of the dominant MC.

Relationship Dynamics:

Support clubs maintain a subservient role to the dominant MC. They work closely with the dominant MC's members and support their initiatives and activities. The relationship is characterized by loyalty, respect, and a sense of shared purpose within the MC community.

Limited Autonomy:

Unlike brother clubs or independent MCs, support clubs have limited autonomy and independence. They operate under the guidance and supervision of the dominant MC, and major decisions or actions are often made in consultation with the dominant MC's leadership.

The dynamics and arrangements between support clubs and dominant MCs can vary between different MCs. The specific roles, responsibilities, and expectations of support clubs are determined by the dominant MC, and support club members are expected to prioritize the interests and goals of the dominant MC above their own.

Social Clubs (SCs) on the biker set

SCs are unique to the African American biker club experience. SCs are groups of women (mostly African American) who operate their clubs on the Black biker clubs' set, in support of Black MCs while simultaneously doing charitable work for their communities at large. As such, they have etched themselves into a place of existence among Black biker clubs not customary for women on any MC set no matter the race. That is because women are not often included in today's male dominated world of biker clubs and their voices are consequently muted. Black women's SCs; however, have flourished on the MC set because they have learned to understand the MCs around them and found their role as support clubs therein enriching the MC set with their beautiful presence. Many of these SCs are set up administratively much like the MCs they support. Some even have the same officer positions, ranking structure, operational standards, and traditions as MCs—including prospecting their sisters before allowing them to become members.

SCs are heavily regulated on the set by both dominant and 99%er MCs and serve the set largely in a support capacity. In many regions they are restricted to wearing certain colors of vests and are required to have a sponsoring male MC to be included within coalitions on the set.

An SC is a separate organization that has a formal affiliation with its sponsoring MC and does maintain a level of autonomy over its own affairs. In many instances an SC will become almost as close to its sponsoring or brother club as an auxiliary club especially if that club doesn't have auxiliaries or properties. An SC consists of female members who support and contribute to the sponsoring club's activities and objectives. They may wear a support patch or other affiliation patch of their sponsoring club. The members aren't necessarily composed of female partners, spouses, family members, or close friends of their sponsoring MC. While the specific roles and responsibilities can vary between different motorcycle clubs, SCs often performs the following functions:

Support Sponsoring Club Activities:

SCs provides support to their sponsoring MC by assisting in organizing and participating in club events, rides, and fundraisers. They may help with event planning, coordination, logistics, and promoting club activities.

Community Involvement:

SCs absolutely engage in community service and outreach initiatives on behalf of themselves and sometimes their sponsoring club. They organize or participate in charitable events, fundraisers, and volunteer activities to support local causes and make a positive impact in their communities.

Social and Networking Activities:

SCs create opportunities for social interaction and networking among their sisters. They organize gatherings, social events, and meetings to foster a sense of camaraderie and friendship within their extended family.

Support for the Full Patch Brothers of Their Sponsoring MC:

SCs provide emotional support and encouragement to the full patch brothers of their sponsoring MC.

Fundraising and Financial Assistance:

SCs organize fundraisers, revenue-generating activities, and provide financial assistance to the communities they support.

The structure and activities of SCs can vary between different organizations. Some may have formalized organizations with established leadership positions and specific bylaws, while others may operate more informally.

Friend of the Club

The term "friend of the club" typically refers to an individual who is not a member of an MC but is considered a trusted and respected associate or supporter of the club. This person may have a close relationship with one or more members of the club or have demonstrated consistent support and camaraderie towards the club and its members. Here are some key aspects of being a friend of the club:

Trusted and Respected Associate:

A friend of the club is someone who is trusted and respected by the members of the MC. They have earned the club's confidence and have established a positive rapport with the club's members.

Support and Camaraderie:

A friend of the club actively supports the club and its members. This can involve attending club events, participating in rides or runs, providing assistance when needed, and showing solidarity with the club's activities and causes.

Loyalty and Discretion:

A friend of the club understands the importance of loyalty and discretion. They respect the club's privacy, maintain confidentiality regarding club matters, and do not engage in activities that may bring harm or negative attention to the club.

Mutual Respect and Trust:

The friendship between a friend of the club and the club's members is built on mutual respect and trust. The friend of the club values the club's culture, traditions, and values and conducts themselves in a manner that aligns with the club's principles.

Limited Privileges:

While a friend of the club may enjoy some privileges or benefits associated with their association, such as attending club events or socializing with club members, they do not have the same level of involvement or decision-making authority as full members of the MC.

Recognized Affiliation:

The club may formally recognize the friend of the club's association by granting them a specific designation or insignia that indicates their status. This can include a "friend of the club" patch, pin, or other identifiers.

The exact meaning and significance of "friend of the club" can vary between different MCs. The club's bylaws and internal policies define the criteria for recognizing and maintaining such friendships, and the extent of involvement and privileges may differ from club to club.

Club Supporters

A supporter of a motorcycle club (MC) is an individual who is not a member of the club but shows their support and loyalty to the club and its members. Supporters are often friends, family members, or acquaintances of club members who align themselves with the club's values, ideals, and activities. Here are some key aspects of being a supporter of an MC:

Loyalty and Support:

Supporters demonstrate their loyalty and support to the MC by actively participating in club events, rides, and activities. They may attend club functions, rallies, or gatherings to show solidarity with the club and its members.

Respect for the MC:

Supporters have a deep respect for the MC, its history, and its members. They adhere to the club's code of conduct, traditions, and values. They understand and respect the hierarchy and authority within the MC and follow the guidance of club members.

Representation:

Supporters may wear clothing or accessories that identify them as supporters of the MC. This can include wearing club merchandise, such as T-shirts or patches, or displaying stickers or decals on their vehicles.

Relationship with Club Members:

Supporters often have personal relationships with club members, whether as friends, family members, or acquaintances. They maintain close bonds and enjoy the camaraderie of being associated with the MC.

Mutual Respect and Trust:

The relationship between supporters and club members is built on mutual respect and trust. Supporters understand the importance of discretion and confidentiality when it comes to club matters and respect the privacy of club members.

Limited Involvement:

Supporters do not have the same level of involvement or responsibilities as full members of the MC. They are not part of the club's decision-making processes, governance, or leadership structure. However, they may be invited to participate in certain club activities or events based on the club's discretion.

The exact role and expectations of supporters can vary between different MCs. Some clubs may have formalized supporter programs or designated roles, while others may have more informal arrangements. The level of involvement and privileges granted to supporters are determined by the MC and may differ from club to club.

Summary of Motorcycle Club Operations

Motorcycle clubs operate on an international, national, regional, and local level. Traditional MCs generally have officers on each level. The terms I have used to describe these officers can be different based on the club, its location, or bylaws. For instance, some clubs have state bosses instead of regional presidents or enforcers instead of Sgt at Arms while some clubs have all of those positions. Other clubs call their leaders "commanders" instead of presidents. In fact, my club, the Mighty Black Sabbath MC Nation once called our presidents "First Rider" back during our humble beginnings. My point here is that for any rule I may have spoken there is another MC somewhere doing it differently, naming it differently, or calling things different names based on their rules and bylaws. Learn the functions of how MCs operate in your area, and you'll be okay no matter where you travel and experience MCing.

The Social Clubs Bible

CHAPTER EIGHT

The Social Club, Biker Club's, Sets, Relationships, Protocol, & Moving Around

Your depth of understanding of the way things work inside and outside of your SC will determine your level of success and perhaps your club's level of success while operating on the MC set. Your knowledge of Motorcycle club protocol (MC protocol) will dictate your every move, how you are respected, how you are treated and how your club sisters move, are respected, and treated. Yes, one woman can spoil it for everyone acting scandalous, naive, whorish, or stupid so you don't want to be "That Girl!" Be smart enough to know your shit out there on the set. It is a grownup environment for grown women who are wearing their grown woman panties, prayed up, laced up with eyes wide open. Immature or naïve girls will be eaten alive on the set. "Trust me what I tell you!"

A Deeper Explanation and Look at the "Set"

The term "biker club set" refers to the subculture or community of MCs and their associated activities, values, and lifestyle. It encompasses the network of clubs, riders, and enthusiasts who participate in MC culture and engage in activities such as group rides, social gatherings, and club events.

The biker club set is characterized by a strong sense of camaraderie, brotherhood/sisterhood, and shared interests among its members. It revolves around the passion for motorcycles, riding, and the unique culture that has developed within the motorcycle club community.

Within the biker club set, there are different clubs with their own distinct identities, structures, and affiliations. These clubs range from traditional MCs, which adhere to a strict set of protocols and hierarchies, to riding clubs, social clubs, or support clubs that cater to specific interests or demographics.

Members of the biker club set often wear club colors or patches that signify their affiliation and loyalty to a particular club. They participate in club activities, adhere to club rules and traditions, and contribute to the overall sense of brotherhood/sisterhood within the set.

The biker club set has its own customs, rituals, and code of conduct to which members adhere. This can include displaying respect for other clubs and riders, adhering to riding etiquette and safety practices, and upholding the values of loyalty, honor, and integrity that are central to the biker club set.

Overall, the biker club set is a vibrant and diverse community that fosters a strong sense of identity and camaraderie among its members. It provides a space for motorcycle enthusiasts to connect, share experiences, and engage in the unique lifestyle and culture associated with motorcycle clubs.

Everywhere you are that clubs operate, visit, ride, hang out in, party at, or pass by regularly is part of the biker club set.

MC Protocol

All MC sets are governed by a set of rules known as motorcycle club protocol (MC protocol). MC protocol exists within the club for conduct between members, and outside of the club for conduct between MCs and organizations that support them. If you are going to operate safely and freely on the MC set you will have to learn MC protocol and have a strong understanding of how it works in the area you are in, in areas you visit, and areas to which you may relocate. MC protocol is like politics and all politics are local. That is to say that what you can do in one place may or may not work in another.

Inner-club MC Protocol

Inner-club MC protocol refers to the set of rules, customs, and traditions that govern the behavior and interactions within an MC. These protocols exist in all MCs and are in addition to bylaws that will establish particular rights, policies, traditions, and rules of the MC. MC protocol is more universal and transcends differences between MCs. It is so universal that if you understand MC protocol you can operate within almost any MC. That is because these protocols are established to maintain order, respect, and unity within the club and to uphold the values and identity of the club members. While specific protocols will vary between different MCs, there are some common elements that are often seen in all MCs:

Club Colors and Patches

MCs have their unique colors and patches that represent their club identity. These colors and patches are considered sacred and should be treated with utmost respect. Unauthorized individuals should not wear or display MC colors or patches.

Respect for Club Hierarchy

MCs typically have a hierarchical structure with designated officers and positions. Members are expected to show respect and deference to higher-ranking members, including officers and club leaders.

Club Meetings and Communication:

Regular club meetings are held to discuss club matters, make decisions, and maintain communication among members. It is important for members to attend and actively participate in these meetings.

Riding Formation and Etiquette

MCs often have specific riding formations and protocols to ensure safety and unity during group rides. Members are expected to follow the designated formations and adhere to riding etiquette, including proper hand signals, maintaining formation, and promoting safe riding practices.

Club Events and Activities

MCs organize various events and activities, such as charity rides, parties, or club runs. Members are expected to participate and contribute to these events to support the club and its initiatives.

Loyalty and Brotherhood/Sisterhood

MCs emphasize loyalty to the club and its members. Members are expected to prioritize the interests and well-being of the club and its members, fostering a strong sense of brotherhood/sisterhood and camaraderie.

External Club Interactions

MCs often have protocols for interacting with other motorcycle clubs or individuals in the riding community. These protocols may include showing respect to other clubs, maintaining proper conduct during encounters, and adhering to established rules and agreements.

Internal MC Protocol Summary

Learn how MC protocol works within MCs and you can move your MC respectfully and safely through almost any interaction with a traditional MC. You can almost always find certain practices nearly the same in every MC so once you know how it works you can hang out with any MC on any set without even knowing anything personal about that club.

Intraclub MC Protocol

MC protocol between motorcycle clubs refers to the set of rules, customs, and protocols that govern the interactions and relationships between different motorcycle clubs. These protocols are established to promote mutual respect, maintain order, and minimize conflicts between clubs. Here are some common elements of MC protocol between motorcycle clubs:

Respect for Club Colors and Patches

MCs place a high value on their club colors and patches as symbols of their identity and allegiance. It is important for members of one club to show respect and not wear the colors or patches of another club without permission.

Permission and Courtesy

When visiting another MC's territory or attending their events, it is customary for members of one club to seek permission or notify the host club in advance. This demonstrates respect and helps maintain good relations between clubs.

Greeting and Acknowledgment

When members of different clubs encounter each other, it is customary to exchange greetings and acknowledge each other's presence. This can involve hand gestures, such as extending a closed fist or nodding, to show recognition and respect. On the Black set we hug. Hugs are plentiful and they are everywhere. Men hug women who are not their own and women hug men they do not know. Men hug men and different club brothers hug each other.

People outside of the Black set are often blown away when they are received with love and hugs from everyone they meet. For example, it is not customary on the white set for one club to hug the women or properties of another club. On the Black set it is done without thinking. If you have a significant other that you are bringing on the set, ensure that you educate him/her that hugs are in abundance. Be prepared to give and receive them.

Communication and Diplomacy

If issues or conflicts arise between clubs, it is important to address them through open and respectful communication. This can involve designated club representatives or leaders engaging in discussions to find amicable resolutions.

Non-Interference

Motorcycle clubs generally respect each other's internal affairs and decisions. Clubs should refrain from interfering with the internal matters, disputes, or conflicts of other clubs unless invited or necessary to maintain peace and order.

Protocol at Events

When multiple clubs gather at events or rallies, there may be specific protocols to ensure smooth interactions and minimize potential conflicts. This can include designated areas for each club, protocols for introductions, and guidelines for behavior and conduct.

Avoidance of Territory Disputes

MCs often have established territories or areas where they have a presence. It is generally expected that clubs respect each other's territories and avoid encroachment or territorial disputes to maintain harmony.

Protocol for Riding Together

When multiple clubs ride together, there may be protocols for riding formation, order, and communication to ensure safety and coordination during group rides.

Intraclub MC Protocol Summary

It's important to note that MC protocol between motorcycle clubs can vary based on the specific clubs involved, regional customs, and the relationships between clubs. Communication, respect, and a willingness to adhere to established protocols are key to maintaining positive relations and minimizing conflicts between motorcycle clubs. As an SC member the more you know about MC protocol and how it works the better off you will be when practicing MC protocol on the set.

Hierarchy of Clubs on the Set

There is a pecking order of biker clubs on the set. It is vitally important that each participant understands exactly what their station is in that pecking order. This is known as the hierarchy of the biker clubs set. There can be some argument between the biker club scholars at to exactly what the hierarchy is so below I will provide you with my opinion as to what that organizational chart looks like:

- 1%er MC Nations
- 1%er Support MC Nations (brother clubs)
- Supporter MCs
- Outlaw MCs (Diamond Clubs)
- Law Enforcement MCs (LEMCs)
- Traditional MCs (male)
- Veteran's MCs
- Non-Traditional MCs

- - Christian MCs
  - Masonic MCs
  - First Responder MCs
  - Sober MCs
  - Coed MCs
  - BACA and Anti Child Abuse
- Female MCs
- Motorsports Clubs
- Riding Clubs
- Patriot Guard and Specialty Biker Groups
- Motorcycle Organizations
- Motorcycle Safety Organizations
- Motorcycle Rights Organizations
- Social Clubs

Understand that the pecking order of clubs has been well established in US history. There are many people that will argue that it shouldn't be that way, or they will argue, "Who died and made any one organization more important than another," and all of those arguments are true and make a lot of sense. But the bottom line is that as an SC you are most likely not going to be involved in any or all of those arguments on the MC set. You need to know how things are first, before worrying about how they should be. Reality is real so make sure to always keep it real. There has been plenty of bloodshed establishing these parameters and there are those willing to go to great extremes of violence to preserve these customs. So, take the time to learn and understand the customs, traditions, values, and hierarchies that you will be held accountable to know as your SC operates on the set.

In the biker club set, particularly within the traditional MC culture, the hierarchical structure defines the relationships and roles among different clubs. Here is a general outline of the hierarchy commonly seen in the biker club set:

1% Outlaw Motorcycle Clubs (OMCs)

1% OMCs are considered the top tier of the hierarchy. These clubs, also known as "1%er" clubs, have a well-defined structure, established bylaws, and a reputation for being independent and nonconformist. They often have multiple chapters and follow a strict code of conduct. OMCs have their own set of rules and protocols and are known for their distinct patches and colors. They run the MC set sometimes by violence if it comes to that. There is much you will learn about dealing with OMCs. Learn MC protocol and follow it and you will not have much to fear from OMCs.

1% MC Support Clubs

Support clubs, also called "puppet clubs" by law enforcement or "feeder clubs," or "brother clubs" are affiliated with an 1% OMC. They have a close relationship with the dominant 1% OMC and support its activities and values. Support clubs often wear patches or colors that show their affiliation and may assist the 1% OMC with tasks such as security, fundraising, or other club-related activities.

Note: Two 1% OMCs can be brother clubs on equal levels, and one is not a support club of another. In that case the two clubs have established a brotherhood of equality, respect one another, perhaps fight together, and backup one another.

Supporter MCs

Supporter MCs are a newer phenomenon on the MC set, especially on the Black set. These are support clubs but not on as high a level as a brother club or a higher-level support club. They normally wear a support patch of the 1% OMC and enjoy their protection but are not expected to operate on as high a level of commitment. A lot of these kinds of clubs were not allowed to operate on the set unless they put on a support patch. They still enjoy a high status on the set because they are protected and carry out the interests of the 1% OMC.

Outlaw or Diamond MCs

There is another class of OMC out there that is not considered a 1% OMC. They are called outlaw clubs. They are not necessarily found in all areas of the country. Some will wear a diamond, but their diamond won't have the 1% in it. You may see a 13 in that patch, the letter M, a fist, there is even a 99% diamond club or two out there. Though not 1% OMC nations, they move independently and are given the respect of an outlaw club. They are able to move without hassle or intimidation.

Note: Some 1% OMC support or brother clubs are given diamonds without 1% marking in them too.

Riding Clubs

Riding clubs are organizations of motorcycle enthusiasts who come together for the primary purpose of riding motorcycles. While they may share a similar passion for riding, they typically do not have the same structured hierarchy as MCs. Riding clubs may have their own set of officers or leaders, but they usually do not have the same level of formality or strict protocols as OMCs or support clubs.

Law Enforcement MC (LEMCs)

A law enforcement motorcycle club (LEMC) is a motorcycle club whose members are primarily current or retired law enforcement officers, including jailers, police officers, sheriff's deputies, state troopers, and federal agents. These clubs are formed by individuals who share a passion for motorcycles and have a background or affiliation with law enforcement.

Purpose of LEMCs

The primary purpose of LEMCs is to provide camaraderie, support, and a sense of community among members who share a common bond through their law enforcement careers. LEMCs often engage in various activities, including group rides, charity events, fundraisers, and community outreach programs.

LEMC Patches

Their patches almost always incorporate law enforcement symbols, such as badges, emblems, guns, and handcuffs to reflect their background and affiliation with law enforcement.

LEMCs versus Law Enforcement Agencies

LEMCs should not be confused with official law enforcement agencies or departments. LEMCs are independent social and recreational organizations composed of law enforcement officers who come together voluntarily to pursue their shared interests in motorcycles and promote fellowship among fellow law enforcement professionals.

LEMC Operations

LEMCs typically operate in accordance with local laws and regulations, and their activities are focused on promoting positive relationships within the law enforcement community and the broader community they serve.

LEMCs Hated by the Set

It is important to know that LEMCs are almost universally hated by Traditional MCs, and especially OMCs, and 1%er OMCs, their support clubs and almost all others. Often LEMCs are accused of trying to be cops in the daytime and act out their passions as tough guys at night, but then arresting MCs in the day, while acting like thugs at night. They often operate entirely on their own and aren't included in biker coalitions, COCs, or other kinds of biker organizations on the set. If your SC gets too close to an LEMC it will most likely be ostracized off the biker set.

Why are LEMCs Hated by MCs

Most MCs hate them because they do not have to follow any protocols to exist, ride, or operate on the MC set. No one is going to mess with a group of off duty cops that is in their right mind, so dominant MCs leave them the hell alone. That is why they are so hated. It is felt that they hide behind their badges when they are confronted, and that sentiment may or may not be true.

Traditional MCs

A traditional MC refers to a club that follows the established customs, values, and protocols commonly associated with the motorcycle club culture. These clubs will be male only MCs and may have women's auxiliaries or properties of as part of their extended families. But it is important to note that in a traditional MC, women do not have a voice in the operations of the male brotherhood. They can be extremely misogynistic and sexist in nature. These clubs often have a rich history and adhere to a set of traditions that have been passed down through generations of members. Traditional MCs are known for their strong sense of brotherhood, loyalty, and commitment to the biker lifestyle. Here are some key characteristics of a traditional motorcycle club:

Club Structure and Hierarchy

Traditional MCs typically have a hierarchical structure with specific officer positions such as President, Vice President, Secretary,

Treasurer, and Sergeant at Arms. These positions hold specific responsibilities and authority within the club.

Club Colors and Patches

Traditional MCs have distinct club colors and patches that represent their club identity and affiliation. These patches often include the club's logo, name, and location. The club's colors and patches are considered sacred and should be treated with respect.

Clubhouse

Many traditional MCs have a dedicated clubhouse where members gather, hold meetings, and socialize. The clubhouse is often seen as the club's home and serves as a central hub for club activities.

Riding and Brotherhood

Traditional MCs place a strong emphasis on motorcycle riding and brotherhood. Group rides, road trips, and attending rallies or events together are common activities that help foster a sense of camaraderie among members.

Club Events and Activities

Traditional MCs often organize club events, parties, charity rides, and fundraisers. These events not only provide opportunities for members to bond but also allow the club to contribute positively to the community.

Club Protocol and Etiquette

Traditional MCs have specific protocols and etiquette that members are expected to follow. This includes showing respect to fellow members, obeying club rules, adhering to riding formations, and demonstrating proper conduct both within the club and in public.

Club Affiliations and Alliances

Traditional MCs may form alliances or have relationships with other motorcycle clubs, such as being part of a larger federation or maintaining friendly associations with specific clubs. These affiliations are often based on mutual respect and shared values.

Traditional MC Summary

Each club may have its own unique history, rules, and culture that contribute to its identity. Respect for club traditions and adherence to established protocols are highly valued within traditional MCs.

Veteran's MC

A Veterans Motorcycle Club (VMC) is an MC composed primarily of military veterans or active-duty service members. These clubs are formed by individuals who have served in the armed forces and share a bond through their military experience and love for motorcycles. The primary purpose of a Veterans MC is to provide a supportive and brotherhood-oriented community for veterans. These clubs often engage in various activities that promote camaraderie, support for veterans, and community involvement. Some of the common activities include group rides, veteran recognition events, charity fundraisers, and participating in military-related ceremonies or parades.

Their patches may include military symbols, insignias, or flags to honor their military service and showcase their veteran status.

It's important to note that Veterans MCs are not officially recognized or affiliated with any government or military organization. They are independent social and recreational organizations formed by veterans to create a sense of brotherhood, support, and connection with fellow veterans who share a passion for motorcycles.

Veterans MCs often uphold values such as honor, loyalty, respect, and service, which are rooted in military traditions. They may also have specific requirements for membership, such as honorable military service, or may be open to veterans from all branches of the military.

Veteran's MCs Summary

Veterans MCs play a significant role in providing a supportive network for veterans, promoting awareness of veterans' issues, and engaging in activities that honor and remember those who have served in the armed forces.

Non-Traditional MCs

A non-traditional MC refers to a club that deviates from the conventional norms and practices commonly associated with traditional MCs. These clubs may have alternative structures, values, or activities that differentiate them from the traditional MC culture. They may be coed and allow women to be officers even rising to the level of president. Here are a few examples of non-traditional motorcycle clubs:

Christian MCs (CMCs)

A Christian motorcycle club (CMC) is an MC whose members are primarily individuals who identify as Christians and have a shared passion for motorcycles. These clubs combine their love for motorcycles with their Christian faith, creating a community of riders who seek to live out their faith while enjoying the biker lifestyle. The primary focus of a Christian motorcycle club is to promote fellowship, brotherhood/sisterhood, and outreach within the context of their Christian beliefs. They typically incorporate elements of worship, prayer, and Bible study into their club activities. Some Christian motorcycle clubs also engage in charitable work, community service projects, and missions to spread their Christian values and help those in need. Here are a few key aspects of a Christian motorcycle club:

Faith-based Focus

Christian motorcycle clubs place a strong emphasis on their Christian faith. They may gather for regular fellowship meetings, Bible studies, and prayer sessions. Their club activities often incorporate elements of worship and spiritual growth.

Evangelism and Outreach

Many Christian motorcycle clubs engage in evangelistic efforts to share their faith and the message of Christianity with others. This can involve participating in rallies, events, and rides where they have the opportunity to interact with non-Christians and share their personal testimonies.

Brotherhood/Sisterhood

Christian MCs foster a sense of brotherhood/sisterhood among their members. They create a supportive and inclusive community where riders can connect, build friendships, and encourage one another in their Christian walk. Some Christian MCs do not allow women and operate more traditionally. Others do allow women.

Community Service and Charity

CMCs often participate in community service projects and charitable initiatives. They may organize fundraisers, support local charities, or engage in outreach activities to help those in need within their communities.

Code of Conduct

CMCs typically have a code of conduct that aligns with Christian values and ethics. This may include guidelines on behavior, language, respect for others, and adherence to traffic laws.

CMCs Summary

It's important to note that Christian motorcycle clubs may have different denominational affiliations or theological perspectives. While they share a common belief in Christianity, the specific expressions of their faith and club activities can vary. The primary goal is to create a community where Christian bikers can come together, support one another, and live out their faith in the context of their shared love for motorcycles. CMCs typically must do everything traditional MCs have to do to get their blessings to operate on the set. Even though they may be religious they are still human. Many are recovering from alcohol and other life vices. Don't be surprised to see them acting out on the set like other biker clubs or drinking too much, or even fighting. This is a criticism that has been aimed at them throughout the years. Remember they are people too and also remember they are bikers not choir boys – even though they may actually sing in the choir.

Masonic MCs

A Masonic MC is a motorcycle club that consists of members who are Freemasons. Freemasonry is a fraternal organization that dates back centuries and is focused on moral and spiritual development, personal growth, and philanthropy. Masonic motorcycle clubs bring together Freemasons who share a love for motorcycles. These clubs provide a platform for Freemasons to connect, ride together, and promote the values and principles of Freemasonry within the motorcycle community. The specific activities and focus of Masonic motorcycle clubs may vary, but they typically incorporate elements of brotherhood, charity, and community involvement. Some common features of Masonic motorcycle clubs include:

Freemasonry and Motorcycle Brotherhood

Masonic motorcycle clubs aim to unite Freemasons who also enjoy riding motorcycles. They provide a platform for like-minded individuals to bond over their shared interests, strengthen their brotherhood, and create lasting friendships.

Charitable Endeavors

Masonic motorcycle clubs often engage in charitable activities and fundraising events. They may raise funds for Masonic charities, local community organizations, or support various causes aligned with the principles of Freemasonry.

Masonic Symbols and Rituals

Masonic motorcycle clubs may incorporate Masonic symbols, such as the square and compass, into their club patches, apparel, or other branding. They may also incorporate Masonic rituals or ceremonies into their club activities to maintain a connection to the traditions and values of Freemasonry.

Fellowship and Brotherhood

Masonic motorcycle clubs prioritize fostering a sense of fellowship and brotherhood among their members. They provide opportunities for socializing, networking, and building strong relationships based on mutual respect and shared values.

Masonic Values and Ethics

Masonic motorcycle clubs uphold the values and ethics of Freemasonry. This includes principles such as integrity, truthfulness, compassion, and respect for others. Members are expected to conduct themselves in a manner that reflects these values both on and off their motorcycles.

Masonic MCs Summary

Masonic MCs are not officially recognized or endorsed by Freemasonry as a whole. They are independent social and recreational organizations formed by Freemasons who share a passion for motorcycles and desire to connect with other Freemasons in the motorcycle community.

First Responder MCs

First Responder MCs are motorcycle clubs composed of active or retired first responders, such as police officers, firefighters, paramedics, and other emergency service personnel. These clubs bring together individuals who share a common bond of serving in these demanding and often high-stress professions. The primary purpose of First Responder MCs is to create a supportive community for first responders who have a passion for motorcycles. These clubs provide a platform for members to connect, ride together, and support one another both on and off the road. They offer a sense of camaraderie and understanding among those who have experienced the unique challenges and rewards of serving as first responders. Some key aspects of First Responder MCs include:

Brotherhood/Sisterhood

First Responder MCs prioritize fostering a strong sense of brotherhood/sisterhood among members. They create a supportive and understanding environment where individuals can bond over their shared experiences as first responders and motorcycle enthusiasts.

Motorcycle Riding

First Responder MCs organize rides and events for members to enjoy their shared passion for motorcycles. These rides may range from casual outings to longer road trips or participation in motorcycle rallies and events.

Charitable Activities

Many First Responder MCs engage in charitable initiatives to give back to their communities. They may organize fundraising events, participate in charity rides, or support causes related to first responder support, public safety, or community well-being.

Advocacy and Awareness

Some First Responder MCs also advocate for issues affecting first responders and promote awareness of the challenges they face. They may participate in public events, fundraisers, or campaigns to raise awareness about the importance of supporting first responders.

Respect and Service

First Responder MCs emphasize the values of respect, service, and commitment to their profession and communities. Members are expected to uphold high standards of integrity, professionalism, and ethics both in their first responder roles and as representatives of the club.

First Responders MCs Summary

It's important to note that each First Responder MC may have its own specific structure, rules, and activities, as they are independent organizations. However, the common thread among these clubs is the shared bond of first responders coming together to enjoy their love for motorcycles and support one another in their challenging professions.

Sober MCs

Sober MCs are motorcycle clubs that are specifically focused on maintaining a sober and drug-free lifestyle. These clubs bring together individuals who have chosen to abstain from alcohol and drug use and provide a supportive community for those seeking a sober way of life. The primary purpose of Sober MCs is to create a safe and supportive environment for members who want to enjoy the camaraderie and brotherhood/sisterhood of motorcycle clubs without the presence of alcohol or drugs. These clubs often organize activities and events that promote sober living and provide opportunities for members to connect, ride together, and support one another on their sober journey. Here are some key aspects of Sober MCs:

Sobriety

Sobriety is the central focus of Sober MCs. Members commit to living a drug-free and alcohol-free lifestyle. This commitment is essential for membership and participation in club activities.

Support

Sober MCs provide a supportive community for individuals in recovery or those who have chosen to live a sober lifestyle. Members can share their experiences, offer support to one another, and serve as positive role models for those seeking a sober way of life.

Fellowship

Sober MCs promote fellowship and camaraderie among members. They organize rides, events, and social activities that allow members to bond, share their love for motorcycles, and enjoy the company of like-minded individuals who value sobriety.

Outreach and Service

Many Sober MCs engage in outreach and service activities to support the recovery community and raise awareness about the benefits of a sober lifestyle. They may participate in community events, charity rides, or support organizations that provide resources and assistance to those in recovery.

Positive Lifestyle

Sober MCs promote a positive and healthy lifestyle. Members strive to uphold values such as integrity, accountability, and personal growth. The focus is on fostering a supportive and inclusive community that encourages individuals to thrive in their sobriety.

Sober MCs Summary

It's important to note that each Sober MC may have its own specific structure, rules, and activities, as they are independent organizations. However, the common goal among these clubs is to provide a space for individuals to connect, ride, and support each other in their commitment to living a sober life.

Coed MCs

A coed MC, also known as a mixed-gender or coeducational motorcycle club, is a club that welcomes both male and female members. Unlike traditional motorcycle clubs that may have separate chapters or clubs for men and women, coed motorcycle clubs embrace inclusivity and offer equal membership opportunities to riders of all genders. The primary purpose of a coed motorcycle club is to bring together individuals who share a common passion for motorcycles and riding. These clubs provide a supportive and inclusive environment for riders to connect, socialize, and participate in motorcycle-related activities. Members of coed motorcycle clubs often enjoy group rides, attend motorcycle events and rallies, and engage in various social and community service activities. Here are some key characteristics of coed motorcycle clubs:

Gender Equality

Coed motorcycle clubs promote gender equality and do not restrict membership based on gender. They provide equal opportunities for men and women to join, participate, and hold leadership positions within the club.

Inclusivity and Diversity

Coed motorcycle clubs embrace diversity and welcome riders from different backgrounds, regardless of their gender, race, ethnicity, or age. They foster an inclusive community where members can connect and share their love for motorcycles.

Group Rides and Events

Coed motorcycle clubs organize group rides, where members come together to explore scenic routes, enjoy the freedom of riding, and bond with fellow riders. They also participate in motorcycle events, rallies, and charity rides as a group.

Social Interaction

Coed motorcycle clubs prioritize social interaction among members. They may organize regular meetings, social gatherings, and events that provide opportunities for riders to connect, share experiences, and build friendships within the club.

Safety and Education

Coed motorcycle clubs often promote safety and offer educational resources to their members. They may conduct riding clinics, share tips on motorcycle maintenance and safety gear, and encourage ongoing learning to enhance riders' skills and knowledge.

Community Involvement

Many coed motorcycle clubs engage in community service and charitable activities. They may organize fundraisers, participate in charity rides, or support causes that are important to their members and the local community.

Coed MC Summary

It's important to note that the specific activities and culture of coed motorcycle clubs can vary. Some clubs may have a specific focus, such as adventure riding, sport biking, or cruiser riding, while others may be more diverse in terms of riding styles and interests. Ultimately, coed motorcycle clubs aim to create an inclusive and supportive community for riders of all genders to enjoy the camaraderie and thrill of motorcycle riding.

Biker Social Clubs

Biker social clubs are motorcycle-oriented groups that emphasize socializing and networking among members. These clubs may focus on creating a welcoming and inclusive environment for individuals who share a passion for motorcycles. They may organize social events, gatherings, and rides to foster camaraderie among members.

Charity MCs

Charity clubs are motorcycle clubs that primarily focus on philanthropic activities and community service. These clubs use their passion for motorcycles to raise funds for charitable causes, participate in charity rides, and organize events to support their chosen charities. The emphasis is on giving back to the community rather than strictly adhering to the traditional MC culture.

Vintage Motorcycle Clubs:

Vintage motorcycle clubs are centered around a shared love for vintage or classic motorcycles. These clubs focus on preserving and celebrating vintage motorcycles, organizing rides and events that showcase these historic bikes, and providing a platform for enthusiasts to connect and share their passion.

BACA and Anti Child Abuse MCs

BACA stands for Bikers Against Child Abuse. BACA is a non-profit organization and a motorcycle club dedicated to supporting and empowering children who have experienced abuse. The organization's primary mission is to create a safe environment for abused children, to empower them, and to help them overcome the fear associated with their abuse. The members of BACA are motorcycle enthusiasts who use their love for motorcycles and the biker lifestyle to make a positive impact in the lives of abused children. They work closely with local and state authorities, as well as child advocacy agencies, to aid and support children in need. The key principles and activities of BACA include:

Empowerment

BACA members aim to empower abused children by showing them they are not alone and that they have a support system. They provide emotional support, encouragement, and a sense of security to these children.

Safety

BACA members work to create a safe environment for abused children. They often establish a physical presence by attending court hearings, visitations, and other situations where the child may feel unsafe. They also assist children in feeling secure in their homes and communities.

Advocacy

BACA acts as an advocate for abused children within the legal and social systems. Members attend court proceedings and meetings, help the child understand the legal process, and support them in navigating through the system.

Awareness

BACA raises awareness about child abuse and works to prevent its occurrence. The organization promotes education and community outreach to spread awareness about the issue and provide resources for prevention and support.

Support

BACA members offer ongoing support to children and their families. They maintain regular contact, participate in activities with the child, and provide a sense of stability and protection.

BACA and Specialty MC Summary

There are hundreds of specialty MC organizations that operate like BACA. They have many different names and missions that range from helping abused children, to helping abused women and animals to protect migrants, all the way to stopping human trafficking. These kinds of MCs operate independently from law enforcement agencies and are not affiliated with any specific religious or political group. Their organizations are solely focused on aiding and support to abused children and needed causes don't engage in illegal activities. BACA chapters and clubs like them are present in various locations around the world, and the organizations continue to grow as more individuals join the cause to fight for world causes and a brighter future for the downtrodden.

Non-Traditional MC Summary

It's important to note that non-traditional MCs may still have their own set of rules, protocols, and expectations for members. While they may deviate from the traditional MC culture, they still cultivate a sense of community, camaraderie, and shared interests among their members.

Female MCs

Women's MCs are motorcycle clubs specifically formed and catered to women riders. These clubs provide a supportive and inclusive community for women who share a passion for motorcycles and riding. Female MCs empower women riders, promote camaraderie, and create a space where women can connect, socialize, and participate in motorcycle-related activities. The primary focus of female MCs is to celebrate women in motorcycling and provide a supportive environment for their members. Here are some key aspects of female MCs:

Empowerment

Female MCs empower women riders by fostering a sense of independence, confidence, and empowerment through motorcycling. They encourage women to pursue their passion for riding and provide a platform for women to support and uplift each other.

Camaraderie and Sisterhood

Female MCs foster a sense of camaraderie and sisterhood among their members. They provide opportunities for women to connect, build friendships, and share experiences related to riding, motorcycles, and the biker lifestyle.

Riding and Events

Female MCs organize group rides and participate in various motorcycle events and rallies. These rides and events allow women to come together, enjoy the thrill of riding, explore new routes, and create lasting memories.

Skill Development and Education

Female MCs offer riding clinics, workshops, and educational resources to help women enhance their riding skills, knowledge of motorcycle mechanics, and safety practices.

Advocacy and Support

Some female MCs are involved in advocacy work related to women's issues in motorcycling. They may advocate for increased visibility and representation of women riders in the industry, promote safety initiatives, and support causes that are important to their members.

Community Engagement

Female MCs often engage in community service and charitable activities. They may organize fundraisers, participate in charity rides, and support local organizations that focus on women's empowerment, safety, or other related causes.

Female MCs Summary

Temale MCs may have different names, structures, and focuses depending on the specific club and its mission. Some clubs may be independent, while others may be affiliated with larger motorcycle organizations. The main goal is to provide a supportive and empowering community for women riders, allowing them to connect, grow, and thrive in the world of motorcycling. They are received with respect on the biker set today especially among the Black biker set. This was not always the case. They have won their reputation through superior riding skills, honor, and respect.

Motorsports Clubs (MSCs)

An MSC is an organization or group of individuals who share a common interest and passion for various types of motorsports activities. These clubs bring together enthusiasts who enjoy participating in or supporting motorsports events, such as car racing, motorcycle racing, off-roading, karting, drag racing, autocross, and more. They are not considered MCs but often hang very closely on the MC set because they do ride motorcycles. In many cases you can't tell them apart from MCs in their operation and get down. Also, many MSCs are coed with both men and women riders. One of the most famous motorsports clubs is called Ruff Ryders. They happen to be bigger than most biker clubs on the Black biker set with international chapters worldwide. They started as a street promotion team and spread out worldwide as a fun loving, highly stylized biker organization doing crazy stunt riding, racing, and promotions.

Riding Clubs:

Riding clubs are often less formal than traditional MCs and focus primarily on the enjoyment of motorcycle riding. They may have less hierarchical structures and fewer strict protocols. Riding clubs may have a more relaxed atmosphere and may not adhere to some of the strict traditions and customs of traditional MCs. Still, many of them have colors usually in the form of a one-piece patch though there are some with three-piece patches, some have bylaws, and some hangout with motorcycle clubs exclusively.

Riding clubs are generally thought of as requiring less commitment from their members than traditional MCs. In many cases all you have to do is purchase their patches and you are a member. But this is not true of all riding clubs. In fact, many look so much like MCs, that dominant MCs are now requiring them to do the exact same things traditional MCs have to do to get a blessing to ride on the set. Still as such RCs are at the lower spectrum of the clubs set in order of hierarchy.

Patriot Guard and Specialty Biker Groups

The Patriot Guard Riders (PGR) is a volunteer organization in the United States that was formed in 2005. The PGR's primary mission is to honor and show respect for fallen military service members, veterans, and first responders during funerals, memorials, and other commemorative events. They attend these events to provide a physical presence, demonstrate support, and shield grieving families from any disruptions or unwanted attention. Here are some key aspects of the Patriot Guard Riders:

Flag Line and Escort

The PGR members often form a flag line, holding American flags, to create a solemn and respectful corridor for the funeral procession or memorial service. They may also provide motorcycle escorts to ensure the safe and dignified transportation of the fallen service member or veteran.

Patriot Guard Missions

The PGR responds to requests from families, funeral homes, military organizations, or community groups to stand in honor of fallen heroes. These missions may include military funerals, memorial services, burials, and other related events. The PGR coordinates with the family and event organizers to ensure their presence is appropriate and welcomed.

Non-Confrontational Presence

The PGR conducts its activities in a non-confrontational manner and operates within the bounds of the law. Their focus is on providing support, respect, and honor to the fallen heroes and their families. They do not engage in counter-protests or confrontations with any opposing groups.

Veterans and First Responders Support

The PGR also extends their support to living veterans, active-duty military personnel, and first responders. They may participate in welcoming home ceremonies, send-offs for deployed troops, homecomings, and other events that recognize and appreciate the service and sacrifice of these individuals.

Motorcycle Community

While the PGR is open to all individuals who support their mission, it has a strong presence within the motorcycle community. Many PGR members are motorcycle riders who use their bikes to honor the fallen and show solidarity. However, participation is not limited to motorcycle riders, and individuals can support the PGR's mission in various capacities.

PGR and Specialty MCs Summary

The Patriot Guard Riders are just one example of so many specialty groups of MCs that have carved out a space in service to community and mankind. The services provided are varied and plentiful and though they are on a lower level on the MC scale of hierarchy, they are well recognized and respected for their contributions. In the case of the PGR, they have gained recognition and respect for their unwavering commitment to honoring those who have served their country. Their volunteer efforts have made a significant impact in providing comfort and support to grieving families while paying tribute to the fallen heroes and their service to the nation.

Motorcycle Organizations

Motorcycle organizations are groups or associations that bring together individuals with a shared interest in motorcycles and motorcycling. These organizations serve various purposes, ranging from promoting motorcycle safety and advocacy to fostering camaraderie among riders. Here are some common types of motorcycle organizations:

Motorcycle Safety Organizations

Motorcycle safety organizations focus on promoting safe riding practices, rider education, and raising awareness about motorcycle safety issues. They may offer training courses, organize safety campaigns, and collaborate with government agencies and other stakeholders to improve motorcycle safety on the roads.

Motorcycle Enthusiast Groups

These groups are formed by individuals who share a passion for motorcycles and motorcycling but may not have the formal structure or requirements of MCs or riding clubs. Enthusiast groups often gather around specific motorcycle brands, models, or riding styles and provide a platform for enthusiasts to connect, share knowledge, and participate in events or rides together.

Motorcycle Organizations Summary

It's important to note that the specific nature, purpose, and structure of motorcycle organizations can vary widely. Some organizations may have national or international reach, while others may be more localized or regional. Additionally, the level of formality, membership requirements, and activities can differ from one organization to another.

Motorcycle Rights Organizations (MROs)

MROs are groups that advocate for the rights and interests of motorcyclists. They work to protect the rights of riders, promote motorcycle safety, and influence legislation and policies that affect motorcycling. Here are some key characteristics and activities of motorcycle rights organizations:

Legislative Advocacy

MROs actively engage in legislative advocacy at the local, state, and national levels. They monitor proposed laws and regulations that could impact motorcyclists' rights and safety. MROs work to ensure that motorcyclists' voices are heard by lawmakers, providing input, lobbying for favorable legislation, and opposing measures that could be detrimental to riders.

Rider Education and Safety

MROs often promote rider education and safety initiatives. They may organize training courses, workshops, and awareness campaigns to educate riders about safe riding practices, proper gear usage, and defensive riding techniques. MROs may collaborate with government agencies, motorcycle safety organizations, and training providers to improve rider safety.

Legal Support and Representation

MROs may provide legal support and representation for motorcyclists. They may offer advice, resources, and referrals to riders facing legal issues related to motorcycle accidents, insurance claims, unfair treatment, or discriminatory practices. MROs may also establish legal defense funds to help riders with legal costs and advocate for fair treatment within the legal system.

Awareness and Outreach

MROs work to raise awareness about motorcycling issues and promote a positive image of motorcyclists. They may organize events, rides, and rallies to showcase the benefits of motorcycling, engage with the public, and foster a sense of community among riders. MROs may also participate in community service activities and charitable initiatives to give back to society.

Networking and Support

MROs provide a platform for riders to connect, share information, and support one another. They offer opportunities for riders to network, exchange ideas, and discuss common challenges and experiences. MROs often have local chapters or state organizations that facilitate communication and collaboration among members.

Membership and Grassroots Involvement

MROs rely on the support and involvement of individual riders. They encourage motorcyclists to become members and actively participate in their initiatives. MROs often organize meetings, forums, and membership events where riders can voice their concerns, share input, and contribute to the organization's efforts.

MROs Summary

Examples of well-known motorcycle rights organizations include the Motorcycle Riders Foundation (MRF), American Bikers Toward Education or A Brotherhood Against Totalitarian Enactments (ABATE), National Coalition of Motorcyclist (NCOM), American Motorcyclist Association also known as American Motorcycle Association (AMA) and many others. These organizations, along with numerous regional and local MROs, play a vital role in protecting the rights and interests of motorcyclists and promoting a safe and favorable environment for riders.

Social Clubs

Female SCs on the Black biker set sit near the bottom of the hierarchy ladder of biker club organizations on the biker set. It is important to know one's place in all things in which you endeavor. This is where clubs see you regardless of where you see yourself. Understanding these facts empowers you to know how to maneuver, manipulate, navigate, and negotiate your SC into the best position possible.

MC Hierarchy Summary

The hierarchy and structure of the biker club set can vary between different regions and subcultures. Not all motorcycle clubs fit neatly into these categories, and there can be variations and exceptions based on the specific dynamics and traditions of different clubs.

CHAPTER NINE
Overcoming Challenges Facing Black Women in SCs On the Biker Set

Black women hanging out on the biker club set have come a long way in how they are treated and respected but there is still a long way to go. Let's start by discussing the general dynamics of being a Black woman in an SC on the Black biker set.

Overcoming the Basic Bullshit and Succeeding

Generally, Black women who associate with the Black MC set face a variety of challenges:

Gender Dynamics and Patriarchy

On many MC sets, particularly those rooted in traditional biker culture, there is a strong male-dominated hierarchy. Women often find themselves navigating this predominantly male environment where their perspectives, opinions, and contributions are undervalued or dismissed. This creates barriers to leadership positions or decision-making roles as a leader of an SC on the set. This masculine dominated environment offers limited opportunities for Black women to shape their own club activities, culture, or policies. However, because MC protocol is localized, SCs in one area may have more autonomy than SCs in others.

On today's set SCs are often paired with so-called "brother" clubs—which, if allowed can simply be a group of men overlooking and second guessing the decisions of an autonomous SC. This can be a real pain in the ass for all the obvious reasons. Therefore, it is important to enter such forced relationships with the determination to run your SC as a separate and independent entity. As these "brother" clubs, who are, in theory, there to educate the SC, often need direction and education themselves. Their ideas of MC protocol philosophies are made up as they go. They get into echo-chambers among the brothers and convince themselves that what they are talking about is actually MC protocol deciding that the agreements established among themselves should be mandates for your SC. Balderdash! One of my favorite sayings is, "I don't mind following MC protocol what I do mind, however, is being asked to follow MC per-your-call. That I ain't never fixin' to do!" Never allow your SC to be caught up in a blind-leading-the-blind situation.

Your SC's bylaws, customs, rules, traditions, discipline, and day-to-day operations should never be up for discussion or compromise with an outside MC. You set your culture, no one else! Remember they are a brother club, in many cases forced on you, not your daddy! Your internal club business is not up for discussion with outsiders. Only dues payers in good standing get a vote on your SC's policies, traditions, culture, and operations. This can be tricky when circumstances get messy, and your members want to gossip outside of the SC and run to the brother club to bring some sort of consequence or sanction against the SC because they can't get their way. Discussing club business with outsiders is an absolute no, no in biker culture. Punish that behavior sternly, swiftly, and without question. Be ruthless in keeping your SC's autonomy because this is paramount to maintaining control of your sisterhood.

Exclusion and marginalization

Black women often face exclusion and marginalization within the MC culture especially after male authority is put in check when dealing with female officers on their same level. This happens when men are incapable of dealing with the intersecting identities that women have reached in achieving the same rank and titles they have attained in their clubs. For instance, they refuse to see a female president of an SC as a capable leader with as much clout, authority and competence to lead as they feel they have. As a result, they will attempt to fall back on old tropes, stereotypes, bias, and discrimination to mute their voices causing them to be overlooked, laughed at, or their experiences and perspectives to be diminished or invalidated at every opportunity they can. They also foster this disrespect among their members causing them to frequently overlook the rank, leadership and contributions of SC leadership, effectively dismissing them—especially in combined meetings or functions attended by the MC and the SC simultaneously. By reducing and overstepping officers and presidents in front of their own SCs they seek to cause a sense of invisibility where a president and her officers could feel like outsiders within their own SCs. A wise SC president will never allow herself or her officers to be diminished in any capacity by an outside entity especially in front of her SC. She won't allow a brother club to attempt this, a coalition to try it, or a dominant. Always remember that no one respects a president who cannot demand it and command it! No one gives orders to your MC above the president and her officers.

Know your value and your worth! Recall the historic and legendary accomplishments of the SCs of yesteryear. These woman's clubs are the origin story from whence your legacy and strength is derived. Those women faced obstacles and challenges so perplexing that is hard to comprehend how any of them survived and yet they rose— lifting others as they climbed! They refused to be left to spoil because of the ill will and bad intentions of others. Self-respect, dignity, and confidence are not markers of arrogance, they are indicators of the power of knowing one's worth. Allow no MC to exclude or marginalize your SC in any situation. The SC's life matters. The SC's wants matter. The SC's desires matter. If what concerns the SC is important to the SC, it must be addressed otherwise the SC should never mind finding another direction upon which to head. The compass of righteousness, fair play, equal and respectful treatment shall always determine the course of the day and the actions to be followed in all matters. This goes for the Black woman as well as the woman's SC.

Objectification and Hyper-sexualization

Women entering the set almost instantly face a barrage of objectification and hyper-sexualization by hormone-crazed Black bikers—obsessed with the pursuit of "catching and releasing" anyone willing to fall for their bullshit narratives, false promises, and immaturity long enough to give them a quick piece of tail and a good time. A sad but not new fact among this group. Historically, Black women in biker culture have been portrayed as sexual objects or accessories, reinforcing harmful stereotypes like the ones your ancestors faced by their overseers and plantations masters when they landed upon these shores! It is an insane proposition to expect women to accept the burden that their contributions are only as valuable or desirable as their willingness to "put-out" sexual gratification to any "Bozo the Clown" wearing a set of club colors on his back and riding a Harley Davidson motorcycle down the street. This objectification and over sexualization allows bikers to reduce the value of our beautiful Black goddesses to their physical appearance, undermining their agency and individuality. The pursuit of these harmful tropes spurned by hypersexuality permits bikers to treat our women as though they are "devoid of morality, sexually wanton and underserving of true romance, commitment, chivalry, dignity and respect." The result is these women are treated like groupies in pursuit of rock stars of a band where the bikers are portrayed as the band members and the SC members their prey. The sad part is to what extent do the SC sisters play an intended or unintended role in igniting and fanning the exotic flames of these toxic and unhealthy pursuits? The solution is found in putting down these sex-starved dogs and make them always treat you with respect and dignity in every situation.

Start Out Like You Can Hold Out

It starts with how you mentally approach your membership in the SC and your participation on the set and the reasons for which you attached from day one. If your reasons for entry are merely for the parties, free sex, unencumbered relationships, and messiness you will find more partakers than you can count on your fingers and toes. However, if your reason for entry is to participate in a sisterhood and reap the benefits of belonging to an extended family, perform community service, enrich the African American social construct and better the lives of others while exploring the vibrant, exciting, and unusual subculture of MC society, then there are some things you should consider before embarking on this lifestyle. And I would say perhaps you should consider this proposition; "Start out like you can hold out!" When speaking with Bull Baby ("BB") Angela Peterson, co-founder of Black Diamond Duchezz SC in Atlanta, GA, I asked her what she thought might be good topics for a book such as this. Surprisingly, she said, "Whatever you do, own it! If you're gonna be a ho on the set, then be a good ho. Own it! But always remember that once that bell has been rung, it will be next to impossible to un-ring it. So, make sure that you start out like you can hold out. If you don't want to be thought of as a ho, never act like one."

The Surprising Effect of the MC Set

Women are often surprised by the freedom, strength, and masculinity that exudes from the roughneck biker brothers the first time they experience the set. These Black males are the rock stars of their own environment created by them, for them, to exalt, satisfy, and challenge them. They are the kings of their biker world even if they have no more importance than being a janitor in the outside world. That is because in an MC a mere janitor could rise to be a national president of a mighty MC giving him more power, access, and influence than any other janitor on the planet. You don't have to be a superstar CEO or rocket scientist to lead an MC, you only have to be a virtuous leader of men or extremely conniving, or manipulative, or a dishonest dictator fool. So, do not be fooled when entering the set as it is like any other place on Earth in that people are not always what they seem. And it takes time to get to know them before allowing them into your personal space.

And yet, women are often utterly thrilled and inspired at the absolute virility of these soulful brothers who ride dangerously on iron constantly pushing one another and competing endlessly over every little thing. On the set, alpha males dominate alpha males and differences can be settled with words, fists, bullets or bombs but no matter what differences will be settled in the ways that men settle scores. The biker set is a hardcore environment run by the toughest of the bad boys. And good girls are often attracted to bad boys! Be that as it may, a girl must watch herself and closely guard her conduct because the set is always watching, and the set sees everything.

Bikers On the MC Set Gossip More Than Women

I can remember one of my particularly sexually uninhibited female acquaintances who started hanging around the MC set many years ago. She was an airline stewardess and was quite freaky about things and didn't mind open relationships, orgies, sex partner swapping, and that sort of thing. So, when she emerged onto the biker set, with all the freaks, she felt right at home. One day she called me up to ask if it would be acceptable for her to bed one biker if she had previously bedded his club brother. I said, "Sure, if you want the reputation of being an easy to lay ho!" She asked me why that would be if everyone were adults? To which I informed her, "If you want to be treated with dignity you must carry yourself always in a dignified fashion and sometimes that requires sacrifice. You must spurn your base instincts and carnal desires to hold out for the bigger payout in the end because alpha males in biker clubs don't often share well with their club brothers—especially women and conquests. Oh, it's okay for them to be loose with the women but when women return the favor in kind, they discover the major flaw in biker set culture. That is that bikers have frail egos, are immature as Hell and as a result they gossip worse than women!" I recommended she explore a more discrete crowd with which to share those kinds of exploits. On the biker set she should stay reserved and keep her legs closed for as long as possible so as not to become the story of the day shared among brothers like a wildfire spreading on the dry grasses of the great Oklahoma plains.

All New Women are New Meat on the Set

One thing to remember is that if you are a newcomer to the set, you are considered "new meat" to every clubber you encounter. It doesn't matter who you are, you will attract a lot of attention because men on the biker set rove in packs like wild dogs looking for whom they may devour. A lot of women who view themselves to be less attractive, morbidly obese, or afflicted with whatever defect that has caused them to be alone and unpursued in life, will be overwhelmed at the attention they receive the moment they hit the club set. Do not be fooled! Though the offers may be plentiful and widely varied, you are still classified as "new meat" and a task list checkoff for 99% of the males who will pursue you. Take the time to establish a sensible relationship on a sensible time scale so as not to end up broken hearted. Love and romance are virtually non-existent on the MC set.

My Club Brother Train and the Big, Sexy Girls

I once had a club brother, I'll call "Train." He had an affinity for the large and sexy women on the set. At one point he had more than 20 relationships going on simultaneously. Each and every woman thought they were somehow special and exclusive to Train, and each was heartbroken to discover they had been lied to, tricked, and taken for a fool. Remember, the set is a place brothers use to get off like rock stars and SCs are the killing fields filled with the groupies upon which they prey. Properties, auxiliaries, and women's organizations that belong to the club are somewhat protected. SCs are not.

Limited Support Networks

As a male dominated environment, the set has been specifically designed to invalidate women and be uncaring towards their opinions and experiences and therefore offers limited support networks that cater to the needs of women. This can lead to feelings of isolation and difficulty in finding camaraderie and understanding about women's issues among MCs and the greater set. This is where the understanding and loving sisterhood of the SC becomes invaluably important.

Catty Petty Women

Women gathered in female-dominated environments, tend to become competitive, catty, and petty. Even on the MC set, where many odds are stacked against the SC success, some women would rather fight against each other and divide than stand together to fight the true enemies of the SC.

You must remember that inside the SC is your refuge. You never turn on the SC or the sisters in it. Never repeat gossip, never spread gossip, never discuss club business outside of the SC. Never talk about it on your pillow, don't discuss it with your parents, your priest, your family, or your best friend. Never tell your sponsor club your internal club's business. I've witnessed a lot of SCs do this over the years. There is no outside organization that can come in and make things right within your SC. You cannot let anger, ego, pettiness, or jealousy make you run to another MC or dominate club and tell them your SC's internal business. To do so would be the utmost level of betrayal to your SC and the sisterhood. If you have a problem work it out at the table, like a woman, face-to-face with your sisters. If a sister calls you up to talk shit about another sister, pause the conversation immediately and say, "Before we go another step let's get this sister on the phone so she can defend herself against these accusations." Don't be so ready to believe the vilest, unkind, horrid things about another sister just because someone claims it to be so. Don't hate a sister because she had a bad experience with someone else. Always treat a sister how she treats you, not how she supposedly treated someone else who told you their story from their perspective. After all, there are limited support networks for women on the biker set. You don't want damage the one you have by sabotaging the one organization that should be your largest support network—the sisterhood of your mighty SC nation. Never turn on that!

Safety concerns

MCs, especially those affiliated with outlaw or the 1% subcultures, can be associated with risky behaviors or illegal activities. You may face additional concerns for your safety when participating with these clubs, both in terms of your personal safety within the club and potential encounters with law enforcement or rival groups. Once again, the most valuable tool at your disposal is your sisters within your SC. If you are new to the set—listen and learn! And if you know what's going on—teach!

You must be alert and remain aware of your surroundings at all times. Always use the buddy system when going out on the set. Rule number one: If you come with your girls, leave with your damned girls! This is rule number one of the buddy system. The set can be a cool place to hang out, but it can also be extremely dangerous. You should think of going out on the set like going to a college frat party—not everyone there is worthy of trust or consideration. Sure, some guys will be chivalrous and walk you to your car, but there are plenty of guys willing to walk you to your car because they slipped something into your drink and are biding time while they wait for you to pass out. The best advice I can give is to NEVER trust anyone in any situation that would give them power over your life or safety. Never be so quick to get laid by a perfect stranger just because he has a nice motorcycle, a cowboy hat, seems exotic, and smells of masculinity. Until you know him, he is no better than Jeffery Dahmer. Women do come up dead and missing on the set so, don't be that girl!

Don't Just Be Jumping on Just Anyone's Motorcycles

I can't tell you how many horror stories I've observed throughout my nearly 35 years on the biker set involving women who climbed on the back of some guy's Hawg never to be seen alive again. Not because they were kidnapped, raped, and taken away (although that has happened), but because they were killed in a traffic accident by a drunk or unskilled rider showing off with a woman on his bike he didn't know and didn't have sense enough to protect by riding like he had some goddamned sense. Clubbers don't always think, especially when they've been drinking, so be wise enough to take a raincheck on that midnight ride with a stranger you've met by chance while both of you were drinking. Liquor and motorcycles never mix well. Especially with immature rock stars exploiting new meat and taking unnecessary chances as they offer rides in the middle of the night.

The average Harley weighs around 1,000 pounds. Combine that with a rider and his passenger and you're approaching 1,300 pounds, if not more. An inexperienced passenger, unfamiliar with how to lean with the bike, can cause it to be very unstable. A simple counter lean when the rider is trying to lean into a curve can throw the entire motorcycle off course and into oncoming traffic. Add this to an inexperienced rider who hasn't really had too many passengers on the back of his bike. And believe me, when he asks you to go for a ride, he will never be truthful about his inexperience. Now, if you add alcohol and a penchant for showing off, like speeding, driving aggressively, or riding faster than weather, road conditions, or visibility may allow, and you have the perfect recipe for disaster.

In short, "Stay the fuck off of folks' bikes you don't know." Not everyone who rides a motorcycle knows how to ride it well enough to give you a ride. Bikes are fast, cool, and fun to be a passenger on. Let your club sisters guide you in finding a responsible someone from your sponsor club to give you rides and teach you how to passenger safely.

Hard Head Not Hard Enough to Withstand the Fall

I'll never forget this beautiful woman I met one night at a club and invited out for a ride. The only problem was I only had one helmet in a helmet law state. So, I made the decision to give her my helmet and I rode without one. She wrapped her arms and legs around me and squeezed me so tight I felt like a turtle with a shell on my back. Man, what a sexy and romantic night it was riding under the stars.

That same night, from the same party, another guy convinced an SC member to take a ride on his bike only he decided he would wear the helmet and didn't tell her that it was against the law for her not to be wearing a helmet. The cops saw them and attempted to pull him over for the helmet violation, only he failed to mention that he had warrants out for his arrest. (Now, you'd think a guy who had warrants out for his arrest wouldn't take the chance of riding a motorcycle illegally with a passenger who wasn't wearing a helmet. Like, who does that? He did.) He made the command decision to run from the cops with an innocent passenger on his bike wearing no helmet, while at speeds in excess of 100 mph. So, when he crashed, she died from head injuries while his protective gear kept him from getting one scratch. Learn the lesson from this cautionary tale and don't let it happen to you!

Brittany Morrow: The Queen of Road Rash

If you take a moment to look up the search terms "road rash queen" you will find the story of a Brittany Morrow from the United Kingdom (UK). In an instant, Brittany Morrow's life changed with the decision to ride pillion (back seat) on a friend's bike, which nearly led to her death on September 25, 2005. The crash skinned her alive, removing skin from all over her body. The only protective gear she was wearing at the time was, in her words, "an ugly red helmet." As a result, she spent two months in the hospital and received skin grafts on over 50 percent of her body. Since the accident, pictures of her injuries and articles about her experience have been posted across the internet. In 2006, as a cautionary tale for other riders, Brittany wrote a full account of the accident and her experiences in recovery. It was published online and embraced throughout the community, but soon began appearing in forums and websites around the world, with Brittany affectionately becoming known as the "Queen of Road Rash". As her popularity swelled, Brittany was invited to attend safety conferences to tell her story in person as a way to show riders exactly what can happen and offer information on how to prevent it – even bringing that ugly red helmet as a tangible testimony. So, what exactly happened on that fateful day? Well, that's best explained by Brittany herself...

"Long story short, I got on the back of a stranger's bike wearing a borrowed helmet and no other gear. Then, things went wrong at 120mph – as they tend to do at those speeds – and I tumbled 522ft (160 meters) down the road, skinning myself alive. After nearly a dozen surgeries and almost a year in and out of the hospital and physical rehabilitation, I chose to face my fears and embrace my love of motorcycles by purchasing my own bike. I wanted to set an example for other riders to follow of the best way to both learn to ride and how to dress, whether they are seasoned veterans or brand new to the sport (Bikerider Magazine).

All of the Gear All of the Time

The lessons in the stories I've told you above are simple. Motorcycle riding is an incredibly dangerous sport. If you don't wear gloves you could lose your knuckles on a long slide down an asphalt highway. If you don't have a good riding jacket you could lose your elbows; if you don't have boots, you could lose your feet or toes and if you aren't wearing a helmet you can scrape off your pretty face, lips, eyebrows, and lose your teeth. Most women in SCs wind up on the back of someone's bike at some point during their careers. Take the precautions necessary to be safe.

True Support Means Knowing It All, or as Much as You Can

An SC is a support club so supporters should always be prepared to support. So, as you spend more time on the set, I believe you should know as much as you possibly can. I recommend all SC members get their motorcycle license—even if you don't ever really plan to be a rider. As an SC is a supporter of the set and of their sponsor ("brother") club, and as such you should be able to back them up in every viable way. By earning your motorcycle license, you could ride bike for a brother who consumed too much alcohol at a party, providing major support for the club in getting that brother and his bike back home safely.

You should learn the hand signals the pack uses on rides so that you can watch while riding on the back seat (pillion). This way if he misses a hand signal, you haven't and you can quickly alert him to keep him in lock step with the pack. By becoming a contributor, you've increased your worth to the pack. In fact, my daughter used to give the same hand signals as the pack when she rode on the back of my bike, which she learned as a "Property Of" for an outlaw biker club. I thought it was very cool. Later I knew other women that would also execute the hand signals with the pack while riding passenger. Also, if so inclined and you have AAA or other towing services, consider adding the motorcycle towing package to your subscription. This provides another way you can help brothers get bikes home safely in the event of an emergency, especially if you happen to be passenger on one when the brother breaks down and he doesn't have that subscription himself. Imagine the relief of knowing his sister had his back! Just some things to think about. Remember an SC is a support club so supporters should always be prepared to support.

Learn the Signs of Trouble on the Set

There are many scenarios that can cause things to go awry on the set. These things turn a great social evening into a nightmare. MCs, especially outlaw MCs have wars, strife, turmoil, and physical violence that occurs daily. Generally, SCs and innocent bystanders are left unharmed, but bullets have no qualms about who they strike, and they will strike the innocent as well as the intended. You are going to have to become astute at "reading the tea leaves," to discern when trouble is brewing on the set. Until you know what to expect, always listen to those who know more than you and have been around longer. If you are establishing a new SC, everyone will be inexperienced. Get with a senior SC on the set and formally request to receive some training from them. Do NOT rely solely on your sponsor (brother) club for training as men are not experienced in the operations of the SC life. They live the MC life. You need experienced sisters to help you get along on and understand the SC side of hanging out on the MC set.

The Social Clubs Bible
CHAPTER TEN
DEALING WITH THE 1%, DOMINANTS, DIAMONDS, OUTLAWS, OMGS, AND THE LIKE

Perhaps many of you have skipped ahead to this chapter, so let me put a few disclaimers and caveats out before we go further:

1. These are my own personal opinions, observations, and experiences. As such, they are not carved in stone. Many may disagree with these insights as there are several opinions out there. Mine is not the only one. That being said … I am the mofo authoring this book, so if someone disagrees over zealously ask them to see their book on the subject.
2. Politics are local. Different areas do things differently. Adjust what you have learned in this book to your area. That's okay!
3. Allow for circumstances to change and experiences to vary. This book will age, and conditions will change, cease to exist, or perhaps they never existed in your area.
4. I cannot speak to anything happening outside the United States. I've never participated in MCs outside the United States. Although details outlined within this book may be similar – this is entirely incidental and not intentional.
5. Do your OWN RESEARCH! My thoughts and views are my own. "Beware of false prophets," as warned in the Christian bible, should be heeded in all things. You cannot be misled if you do your own research.
6. I do not speak for anyone's club, not even my own. I speak for myself! Wait, I think I already said that… moving on…

A Quick Overview to Bring You Up-to-Speed

This chapter is designed to familiarize you with the 1% subculture. This is by no means exhaustive. I could write multiple books on this subject and still have a million words left to write. For comprehensive Knowledge, you will need more information and experiences than this book can provide.

What are they called

1% MC

The Black MC set is overseen by the Black 1% MCs in the states or regions in which they reside. 1% is the proper term for these clubs even though they are colloquially called 1%ers.

Dominant MCs

Since 1% MCs are considered the top of the MC hierarchy you often hear them referred to as "dominant" clubs or "dominant" MCs. Colloquially they are referred to as "my dominant" or "the dominant".

Outlaw Motorcycle Gangs (OMGs) Outlaw Motorcycle Clubs (OMCs)

1% MCs and outlaw clubs will all refer to themselves as OMCs. But this is how they perceive themselves. Police organizations and the media often refer to 1% MCs, OMCs, and some 99%er clubs that get in trouble with the law as "OMGs" simply because law enforcement has classified them on the level of criminal street gangs and as such use this designation when referring to them in the news or media outlets.

The Department of Justice describes OMGs as:

OMGs are organizations whose members use their motorcycle clubs as conduits for criminal enterprises. OMGs are highly structured criminal organizations whose members engage in criminal activities such as violent crime, weapons trafficking, and drug trafficking. There are more than 300 active OMGs within the United States, ranging in size from single chapters with five or six members to hundreds of chapters with thousands of members worldwide. The Hells Angels, Mongols, Bandidos, Outlaws, and Sons of Silence pose a serious national domestic threat and conduct the majority of criminal activity linked to OMGs, especially activity relating to drug-trafficking and, more specifically, to cross-border drug smuggling. Because of their transnational scope, these OMGs are able to coordinate drug smuggling operations in partnership with major international drug-trafficking organizations (DTOs) (Department of Justice).

Federal definition. The federal definition of gang as used by the Department of Justice and the Department of Homeland Security's Immigration and Customs Enforcement (ICE), is:

1. An association of three or more individuals;

2. Whose members collectively identify themselves by adopting a group identity, which they use to create an atmosphere of fear or intimidation, frequently by employing one or more of the following: a common name, slogan, identifying sign, symbol, tattoo or other physical marking, style or color of clothing, hairstyle, hand sign or graffiti;

3. Whose purpose in part is to engage in criminal activity and which uses violence or intimidation to further its criminal objectives.

4. Whose members engage in criminal activity or acts of juvenile delinquency that if committed by an adult would be crimes with the intent to enhance or preserve the association's power, reputation or economic resources.

5. The association may also possess some of the following characteristics:

    1. The members may employ rules for joining and operating within the association.
    2. The members may meet on a recurring basis.
    3. The association may provide physical protection of its members from others.
    4. The association may seek to exercise control over a particular geographic location or region, or it may simply defend its perceived interests against rivals.
    5. The association may have an identifiable structure.

(https://nij.ojp.gov/topics/articles/what-gang-definitions Nov 2023)

When referred to in news and media or press conferences, the terms OMGs or biker gangs are normally used to identify them.

This is NOT a designation given to MCs by MCs! MCs should not be referred to as "gangs", because they will go crazy if they hear you call them that. So, it is never cool to ask an MC brother something misinformed like, "To which of these biker gang do you belong?"

There is a reason for the hatred of this term by clubs. If an MC is designated an OMCG (i.e., "gang") then certain gang enhancements will be attached to the group should they ever be charged with crime. These enhancements can add years to prison sentences or additional fines to their final adjudication. In addition, public perception of a gang is horrible, and the legal consequences are grave.

Your own family may question your judgement when they find out you are hanging out with what they might call those "biker gangs" or are in some kind of "women's biker gang," so always correct them, "They are not gangs and we are not gangs' family."

Motorcycle Gang (MG)

At the time of this writing, I do know of two clubs that named themselves the "such-&-such Motorcycle Gang." Yes, they named themselves an MG, like "Puritan MG" believe it or not. Of course, "Puritan MG" is not a real name to my knowledge, but the "MG" part is. So, you might see an OMC self-named MG out there but that is not usual. And even though they are named MG I bet if you asked them, "To which biker gang do you belong," they would get mad at you and scream that they are a club not a gang even though they call themselves an MG.

Diamond Clubs

Most 1% MCs wear a diamond patch containing the words "1%" or "1%er," which is why 1%er MCs are often referred to as "diamond" clubs. However, not all diamond clubs are 1% MCs or 1% MC nations. Some diamond clubs are not quite on the level of hierarchy as a 1% diamond clubs, but they are still high on the MC hierarchy table. These clubs are often referred to as outlaw clubs (OCs) and are not found in every area. Generally, "OMG" is reserved for 1%ers.

NOTE: There are some 99% clubs that are considered OCs just by the way they carry themselves. They don't generally wear diamonds although there is one that wears a 99%NFG diamond. They are highly respected and not generally meddled with because they are known to handle business just as seriously as the 1% clubs, instead they are granted wide authority to run their own affairs. These kinds of clubs are generally 35 years old or older.

Diamond 13 Clubs

As mentioned before, some OMCs that wear diamonds are brother clubs or support clubs to 1% clubs. These clubs often wear diamond 13 patches, especially in Texas and other midwestern or southwestern states. These diamond 13 clubs are not found in all areas of the country.

Diamond 13 Racing MCs (RMC)

There are original racing MCs that also wear a diamond 13 patch. These clubs represent the 13 original racing motorcycle clubs that were outlawed by the AMA because they broke away from them decades ago. They were in fact, among the first clubs to be referred to as "outlaws" though not outlawed by law enforcement; OMCs as you may think of them. There are few of these clubs left, and I'm not sure if any Black RMCs exist, since Black RMCs weren't allowed in the AMA at the time those clubs flourished.

One-Piece, Two-Piece, Three-Piece, and 5 Piece Patches

In OMC culture, the regalia of a 1% MC is typically a Three-Piece patch. A "Three-Piece" patch refers to the number of back patches worn by full patch brothers. A "Three-Piece" patch consists of a top rocker, a center emblem (commonly known as the "club colors" or "club logo"), and a bottom rocker. Each of these elements carries significant meaning within the OMC culture:

Top Rocker

The top rocker usually bears the name of the club and is placed above the club emblem. It signifies the club's name and helps identify its affiliation.

Club Emblem

The center emblem is the main part of the patch and represents the specific club. It often features the club's logo, symbols, and other identifying elements. This emblem is unique to each club and holds great significance within the club's identity.

Bottom Rocker (State Rocker)

The bottom rocker typically displays the geographic location or territory of the MC. It usually contains the name of the city, state, or region where the club is based or claims as its territory.

Once-Piece and Two-Piece Patches

Not all 1% MCs wear a Three-Piece patch. This is seen as more of a standard on the white MC set than it is on the Black MC set, in my opinion. For the longest time, many Black west coast dominant MCs wore One-Piece back patches with no state rockers, and diamond patches without the "1%" or "1%er" nomenclature. As the biker set decreased in size because 1% MCs started spreading out nationally like they hadn't before, around 2015, we started to see these standards change—especially as many Black 1% clubs started to spread across the country to become national powers instead of state and regional powers. We saw sets adopt and envelope cultures. At that time, we saw two-Piece patches begin to emerge with a center patch and a state rocker. At this time, we also started seeing Black dominant clubs adopt the "1%" and "1%er" diamonds for the first time.

Note: There are several white 1% clubs that don't have three-piece patches either. So, it is important to know that the number of pieces in a patch does not necessarily make a club an OMC. Look for the diamond as a general indicator. If you see a 1% or 1%er insignia, then you will know for sure.

The MC Cube and Side Rockers

The "MC Cube" is a small (often diamond shaped) patch placed near (above, below, left, or right) the center patch that contains the initials "MC" to signify that the club is a motorcycle club. This "MC Cube" is also known as the "MC diamond." It holds different meanings depending upon its arrangement. And I have heard it called different called different things like a "Four-Piece" patch. Sometimes you will see the M and the C separated on either side of the logo patch. This is often referred to as a "Five-Piece" patch.

MC Cube Within the Back Patch

When the MC cube is incorporated as part of the center patch or emblem of the back patch, it is typically positioned within the design and not separated from the main patch. This arrangement signifies that the club is recognized as a traditional MC, adhering to the protocols and traditions of the MC culture.

Separated MC Cube

When the MC cube is separate patch either above or below the center patch on the back patch. It is physically distinct from the main patch and can be seen as a standalone element. This arrangement is typically associated with RCs or social riding clubs that do not fully align with traditional MC culture. While these clubs may share a passion for motorcycles, brotherhood, or specific interests, they may not necessarily adhere to the same strict protocols and traditions as traditional MCs.

Side Rockers

Side rockers are additional patches that can be placed on either side of the vest which carry additional club information or slogans, such as the club's motto, founding year, or other relevant details.

Patches Summary

Generally, the Three-Piece patch is considered a significant symbol of membership within the OMC and greater MC community. It signifies the commitment, loyalty, and brotherhood among club members. Wearing a Three-Piece patch without the proper authorization from a recognized OMC is seen as disrespectful and may lead to conflicts or misunderstandings within the MC community. SCs associated with an MC that does not understand these protocols may suffer along with the MC. Although the Three-Piece patch is not restricted to OMCs, it is often perceived this way in many areas as RCs, MMs, SCs, Women's MCs, family MCs and non-traditional organizations generally wear a One-Piece patch. There are meanings to the placement of all patches, with subtle differences in each category that the untrained eye might not recognize.

Hierarchy Among the 1%

There are major players in the 1% game of which you should become familiar if you are to operate on the biker set. Each 1%er MC plays a significant role in their area of influence with some 1% MCs being more "dominant" than others. When you join an established SC, your founder and president should have already figured which 1% MCs are dominant in your area. If you are attempting to establish a new SC, you MUST determine who's set you are operating in and the dominant MC in the area to which your SC will report.

Keep in mind that there are White, Black, Hispanic, and other dominant MCs in existence across the United States, many of which you may never have heard of. You MUST learn about ALL of the dominants are in your area and know them by sight when you see them. The following lists the perhaps most well-known Black or mixed-race dominant clubs in the country:

- Soul Brothers MC
- Chosen Few MC
- Outcast MC
- Sin City Deciples MC
- Hells Lovers MC
- Thunderguards MC
- Wheels of Soul MC
- Street Soldiers MC
- Phantoms MC
- Hawks MC
- THUG Riders MC
- Ching-a-Lings MC

The following lists perhaps the most well-known White or mixed-race dominant clubs in the country:

- Hells Angels MC
- Pagans MC
- Mongols MC
- Bandidos MC
- Outlaws MC
- Warlocks MC
- Sons of Silence MC
- Vagos MC

There are so many more 1% MC than the ones I have named on both the Black and White sets. At least know the ones in your area.

How Do 1% Control the MC Set

1% MCs exert control and influence over the MC set by mutual respect, intimidation, fear, compromise, or violence. MCs and SCs that operate on the set must comply with the regulations and protocols set forth by the dominant MC(s) in the area. In some cases, the dominant will authorize a council run by respected "99%er" MCs, to govern the region and run most of their own affairs, with Black councils controlling the Black MC set and white councils controlling the white MC set. These councils have different names based upon the region in which they govern, including the "Georgia Council" in Georgia, the "Chain" in Texas and on the white MC set, this council is often referred to as the "Confederation of Clubs" or "COC."

There may be hundreds of these kinds of coalitions across the country with some states having coalitions for different areas within the state. Typically, the dominant MC(s) will administer the council or even run their own councils.

It is important to remember that even though these dominant clubs don't always get along and even fight and kill one another, they STILL TALK and COMMUNICATE with one another! They will check in with one another to ensure the MCs and SCs operating in the area have been blessed and are operated under someone's control. Generally, if you have been blessed by one of the dominants or their associated council, you will be recognized by all Black OMCs in your area.

NOTE: White OMCs will not interact with an SC off the Black set as you are not an MC. Since white MCs do not have SCs many wouldn't recognize you for what you are. However, as the set gets smaller, with more Black and white sets mixing and hanging out, white MCs are definitely becoming more aware of the existence of SCs. And, of course, when the Black set visits the white set, they take their SCs with them.

Note: I know I said there aren't really any SCs on the white MC set but here goes an exception to the rule. I do know of one recent case here in Georgia (circa 2023). I was made aware that a white dominant in the area blessed its first Black SC. Now that's crazy but it did happen. Whether or not the Black OMCs will let that blessing stand will be one for us to sit back and observe to see. I mention it to let you know that you shouldn't be surprised by anything you see. All rules are meant to be compromised at some point or another.

What is a Blessing

All non-dominant MCs, MMs, RCs, MSOs, SCs and others that operate on the set will go through an authorization called a "blessing" to get approved to fly their colors without hassle. MCs that refuse to follow this format will likely experience physical altercations in order to maintain their status and existence on the MC set. SCs will be forced into compliance, if need be, as well. It must be understood because it is what it is. If you understand it, you will know how to deal with it. If you are hard-headed it will deal with you.

What steps must an SC go through to get a blessing? It will vary based on the state, city, area, or region; however, here are some of the common requirements you may observe:

Members

- Your SC may need between 5 and 10 members to be recognized on the set.

- You may have to turn in a roster with your member's names and officer positions annually or go through some other procedure to prove you've maintained your numbers.
- You may have to provide contact information for all your club's officers.
- You may have to perform some kinds of social services for the community prior to receiving your blessing.

Sponsoring MC (Brother Club)

In some areas SCs are required to be invited into the coalition by a sponsor MC and you may not receive a blessing without it. The sponsor MC is supposed to guide, educate, and teach the SC. In some cases, there may be a requirement for the sponsor MC to be in existence for an established number of years. A new MC trying to sponsor a new SC may not work.

The sponsor MC must remain compliant with the council. If the sponsor MC becomes non-compliant, this may negatively affect the SC. Prior to partnering with an MC for sponsorship, it is wise to validate the history of the MC to ensure that have maintained their compliance and never been sanctioned by the coalition.

If things go wrong with a sponsor MC there may be procedures to transition to a different sponsor; however, it may not be easy, which is why you need to examine the relationship closely before entering into it. You must also be aware that club hopping will not be allowed. Take your time and make sure that your SC gets along well with your chosen sponsor MC long before you agree to the partnership. My MC has partnered with SCs with dire results for both my MC and the SC. The sponsor MC is senior and will nearly always win its case before the committee or council. Remember it is all male dominated so be careful as most decisions will be decided on behalf of the male MC. So, when you are approaching an MC to see if they want to be your sponsoring club spend some time with them, hang out with them, and make sure that their club culture is something that you want to support and be a part Make sure they're not a bunch of weirdos that expect sexual favors from you and all that kind of dumb shit before things even get started off bad.

Some coalitions may allow you to find a new sponsor MC should you need to depart from your previous sponsor. At which point it is essential that you do not make the same mistake twice. Take your time and choose wisely. Sometimes an MC will get very upset if you no longer want to deal with it and become vindictive. You might be surprised to find folks that were once your brothers, or so-called brothers, can be very mean if they feel like you no longer want to hang out with them. Like I said many of these clubs are full of very immature males. Especially the clubs that have all these millennial babies in them, these guys are run by emotions and feelings like little girls. Make sure to look out for pitfalls. However, if you can't find a new sponsor MC within a certain amount of time you may be removed from the blessed list, so if your SC finds it needs to get away from a sponsor MC make sure you have some place to go before you leave.

Colors

Most coalitions won't allow you to wear "hard colors" for a period of time before your blessing. Hard colors are your vest with your insignia on the back. Also referred to as a "cut." Traditionally, "cut" is reserved for colors on a blue jean cut off vest, but colloquially "hard colors" is often interchanged with the term "cut," which could be spelled "CUTTE" or "KUTTE." Soft colors are considered any kind of a t-shirt with some version of your colors on it. In many coalitions you can wear soft colors during the blessing process. In most cases once you are blessed you are legal to fly. "Legal to fly" means you have been blessed to wear your hard colors.

Annuals, Parties, and Fundraisers

A lot of the rules enforced upon SCs have emerged because they have been far more successful than MCs on the MC set in recent years. This popularity has brought about some jealousy towards them from the MCs as they were being beaten in their own backyard. Nobody is angry at you until you become successful. And I must tell you if given a choice between hanging out with a bunch of hard-leg dudes in an MC or fine-ass social club ladies in an SC, I would choose the SC party each and every time. As SCs began throwing bigger parties with the most people and making more money, they certainly didn't need a bunch of dudes telling them how to throw a party. Yes, SC grew too successful for their own good in the minds of the MCs on the set. In response, coalitions came up with a few rules in an effort to debilitate and retard the growth and success of SCs, with most of the rules focused on the SC parties, annuals and fundraisers that made money.

First and foremost, was the requirement of a sponsor MC – to which we discussed previously. Secondly, they established requirements for how long you must operate on the set before you can throw any kind of a party. With most MC anniversaries held on Saturdays, SCs are forbidden to hold any kind of party, annual, or fundraiser on Saturdays, thus preventing any competition with the MCs on the set. Most recently, SCs are now required to coordinate all events with the sponsor MC. If the sponsor MC's annual is in November and the SC's annual is in April, the SC must switch its annual to November to align with the sponsor MC to allow the sponsor MC to take full advantage of the hard work, contacts, and supporters coming to the SC's function. As a result of these sanctions, you may find the SC throwing parties on Friday which coincides with the meet and greet for the sponsor MC with the sponsor MC having its annual on Saturday. You can see how this arrangement is incredibly beneficial for the sponsoring MC.

Note: In many coalitions, if for any reason you miss your annual anniversary date to throw a party you may also lose the date the following year.

Some coalitions do not allow SCs to throw money-making events the first year on the set. Violations of this requirement will assuredly incur sanctions against the SC for years to come including forbidding all MCs on the set from attending future functions hosted by the SC. You are well advised not to violate the rules set forth by the coalition. Similarly, some coalitions may limit new SCs to one revenue generating event during the first year of operation. These restrictions may require the SC to function on the set without making any money from the set or two to three years. This definitely limits the survivability to only the fittest and most financially viable SCs. As I have said before there are many challenges to overcome being a Black woman on the set.

Should I Sleep with a 1% President to Get my Club Blessed

There are definite difficulties to getting your SC blessed, especially in an area that is closed to new SCs. This may lead you to consider engaging in the world's oldest bartering system in an effort to place your SC in a favorable light to move the "blessing" forward. Don't laugh too loud because I have seen it happen numerous times. Sometimes a president will come straight out and tell you that the only way you are going to get your SC blessed it to make it happen by laying on your back Prez, and no matter if it comes faintly, jokingly, or jarringly the proposition is placed on the table and choice must be made. Once an SC founder asked of me, "Should I sleep with the 1% president because he promised me that if I do, he will make sure that my SC gets blessed with no problems? Do you think he'll keep his promise?"

Let me start by saying ... one thing is certain, no one remains president forever. MC leadership changes frequently without warning or reason. The president may be president for 10 or 15 years, then in a flash he's voted out! So, I would encourage any SC founder to put your stock in doing things the right way because what are you going to do if you get in through a "privileged" way when the privilege is gone? You put your SC at risk when you put your stock in a president who could be voted out and no longer has the influence or the power he once had. If you do things the right way no one can take away all that you have attained. You deserve your spot on the set because you followed the rules to get it, even if it takes a year or two longer than the other way. Believe me, it's okay. I've had some chapters take me three or four years to open, so it's not unheard of that it could take some time to get a blessing in a closed city. Naturally, there are plenty of people who take shortcuts—I can't deny that there aren't—and sure some of them have even been successful, but I would not risk putting your SC in such a precarious predicament. Doing so is like building a house on sand with a poor foundation. It may survive the first storm, but will it survive them all? Whatever you do in the dark will come to the light and people will know if what you did was inappropriate. Because on the set, if you don't know, let me tell you—people talk (gossip)!

The 1% Clubhouse

Many folks are absolutely terrified of the 1% and for good reason, because they have a bad reputation. Be that as it may you will still find times that you will have to deal with them. Keep in mind that they are people just like everyone else. They have feelings, emotions, fears, prejudices, they laugh and cry too. For the most part if you deal with them straight up, they will deal with you the same way. They are not the boogeyman, but they do have a lifestyle not everyone understands, nor can everyone live.

I'll tell you like I tell my own club brothers before we go to a 1% clubhouse. Most of the time if you don't start any shit there won't be any shit. If you don't know how to handle yourself, your temper, or your liquor then don't go! Keep your ass at home! If you are looking for a quick hookup know that many of the good-looking men are already spoken for by properties. Every property there is spoken for by a male sponsor so if every woman belongs to someone it is safe to assume that so does every man. So, don't be on your hunt for a Mandingo Warrior. Always wait instead to be approached. If someone shows interest, it's not crazy to ask if his property is around somewhere that's going to be starting some shit with you because that's not why you are there. Not all experiences will be the same in every 1% clubhouse as each has its own rules.

There are two reasons you may find yourself at a 1% clubhouse:

1. To take care of business
    a. Good relations
    b. Bad relations
2. To party

Good Relations Business

If you are at the clubhouse for business and you are on good terms with the 1% MC, then you can expect a matter-of-fact conversation to handle the business you came to handle.

- Arrive before the agreed upon time. A 1% MC does not see your SC as an equal and will not be impressed if you are late. In the Navy we always said being on time is being late. So always arrive early. In other words, early is on time, on time is late, lates is unacceptable.
- Have your notes prepared and organized. It wasn't very long ago that a woman could not speak in a 1% clubhouse. Times may be changing but attitudes can still be chauvinistic.

- Don't adhere to any kinds of stereotypes like being unorganized, or disheveled, or overly emotional—especially if your problem is with your sponsoring MC, because they will always want to make you appear hysterical. Leave your emotions at the door and come to the table prepared for the business at hand. Remain calm and effective and never elevate your voice with anger or emotion, no matter what they say.
- Make sure to have your appropriate officers with you. For instance, if you are the president make sure that your sergeant at arms is accompanying you. Watch and learn how MC's move. Then make sure your SC moves the same way. The 1% respects power, confidence, and authority. If they see weakness they pounce. If you are the spokesperson, president, or sergeant at arms, then move with authority. Don't try to be something you're not but be confident in who and what you are.
- Remain respectful. All the eye-rolling and neck movements that our sisters can do, displaying the bad attitude and snappy replies will NOT be tolerated in a 1% MC clubhouse. This is a vastly different atmosphere than bossing your little brother, boyfriend or husband around the house. These alpha males will not tolerate loose talk from women—especially in front of their brothers. They may tolerate it, because it is cute, for the first few minutes, but second you blurt out an intellectual low blow, attempting to gain vantage, you will likely receive a response you were not expecting; "Bitch shut the fuck up now I'm talking!" Don't be the one to get caught sitting there with your mouth wide open and tears in your eyes. Keep it professional and about business and it will stay that way.
- Wait until the 1% brother is finished talking before you talk.

- Don't cut brothers off in mid-sentence. This is considered very disrespectful especially coming from a woman.
- Don't act like a know-it-all. Nobody likes a know-it-all. Avoid saying, "I know but..." "I know but..." "I know but...", if you really knew, you probably wouldn't be there for a sit down in the first place.

I know this may all sound a bit cliché, but you must understand it is what it is. You are closer to the barbarian age than you are to the age of enlightenment inside a 1% clubhouse. If you get mouthy you are likely to have the meeting turn on you in a way that you may not have ever imagined possible. And in case you were wondering... yes, they have plenty of properties over there willing to touch your ass up if need be and no man will have lifted a single finger to harm you. Suffice it to say no one gets out of hand at the OMC clubhouse—not men, not women and especially not a visitor.

Bad Relations Business

Well, if you are at the 1% clubhouse to receive a reprimand, you are already off on the wrong foot. One good thing about the MC set is there are usually plenty of warnings before bad shit happens. Most of the time your initial conversations will be warnings and dress downs before any drastic actions or sanctions are taken. Keep in mind that that compliance will be had whatever the cost.

At a bad relations meeting the goal of the 1% club is to bring you in and communicate to you the direction you will be required to traverse to get back in good graces. There won't be many options if any and your acceptance and compliance at that moment will dictate whether, or not, your day gets worse or better.

This meeting usually happens after many warnings or other attempts at communication have occurred so don't be surprised if the dominant president or SAA is short-tempered, rude, or brutally honest.

During this meeting there may be a time you're allowed to voice your opinion about the SC's position, to have a say about your wishes, expectations, or to provide an explanation of what actually occurred from your point of view. And then there will be a time that the dominant will speak. That will not be your time to speak or interrupt! That will be your time to listen and be silent—to acknowledge that you have heard the request (or demand) and to indicate that you will comply. Just think of it like being in court. When the judge (in this case the dominant) is rendering his verdict, he has already heard what you have to say, listened to the evidence (or not), and has made up his mind. The only thing that remains is for you to hear the verdict and abide by the terms.

Warning to Liars—If you are a habitual liar, you better be a damned good and convincing liar because these 1% MCs have eyes and ears everywhere on the set willing to snitch to them like they are the FBI, CIA, and DEA simultaneously! They are good at catching little liars and like most smart prosecutors only ask you questions to which they already know the answers. On the MC set liars are hated as much if not more than anywhere else in the world. Don't get the reputation of being known as a liar on the set. It won't be good for you, and you'll be ostracized everywhere you go. Be honest and stand up for your shit and stand on your shit. If you did it, own it. You might not be liked for your honesty, but you'll absolutely be respected. On the set reputation, respect, and your word are all that you have. Live by that!

When the bad meeting is over, take your lumps, make your corrections, and move on. Don't be too embarrassed and don't worry. If you keep a low profile, I guarantee you someone else will fuck up in a week or so and your incident will be forgotten as their SC takes center stage.

1% Party at the Clubhouse

For the uninitiated, one's first party at the 1% clubhouse can be utterly shocking to one's senses. Be prepared to see adult fun and uninhibited behavior. This is the 1%'s playground. This is their kingdom and their castle where they get to live out their greatest fantasies. If you are a prude, don't go! You may see properties twerking on stripper poles. You may see women in Jell-O® fights or all kinds of other eyebrow raising goings on. Mostly you will see people having an excellent time being themselves. There is no one telling them how to behave, who to be, or what expectations must be met. There's nothing like being the king of one's own domain.

Greetings and Hugs

Upon entering a 1% clubhouse it is customary to greet and hug as many of the brothers and sisters as possible. Attempt to show love to everyone who is willing to receive it. A brief hug and smooch are appropriate and even expected. So, don't act like a cold fish because you can become despised very quickly if folks think you are acting better than everyone else.

On the White biker set it is not so common for such things to happen. In fact, when White MCs come to visit a Black clubhouse, they are often blown away, and made to feel a bit uncomfortable by the love and hugs that they receive.

Boyfriend or Civilian Male

I would say that it's never appropriate to take a boyfriend, husband, or other civilian male like a cousin, brother, or friend to a 1% clubhouse especially if they are not familiar with the MC set. It is also not the place for a male to exhibit jealous or 'protective' behavior. Since he has no colors, he is completely alone and a target for exploitation. If you have a jealous boyfriend or husband a good place for them to wind up knocked-out cold and unconscious on the floor, with multiple fractures is at a 1% clubhouse where they have shown their ass and insulted the brothers in their own clubhouse. Many jealous civilian males cannot understand other men coming up and hugging on their woman—and will take it as a sign of ultimate disrespect and feel compelled to take an action that will get their teeth kicked in! So don't set him up for that kind of failure! If he must accompany you ensure he is schooled up that you will be hugged and maybe kissed on the cheek, sometimes bear hugged, sometimes hugged for a second or two too long (brothers will do that kind of silly shit just to piss your man off)—so if he can't handle it tell him to... "Keep his ass at home!"

Properties Of

As I've said before the properties are at home. You never want to mix it up with a property in her clubhouse. Properties know very well how the 1% mindset works—how they chase women, what goes on in the clubhouse, and who is visiting (including your SC)... Most of the time, they ain't even trippin' so, never trip with a property. Never argue with a property, never get into a pissing contest with a property, in fact, leave them the hell alone. I can promise you this, if you tangle with them, at their clubhouse you will not win. Unless you got some hardcore sisters that are ready to go back-to-back losing all of their hair, makeup, and breaking their heels to get down on a basic level like that backing you like when you were running the streets, then be on your best behavior and never mix it up with the properties.

Never Run Your Mouth Negative

There will be no negative talk about any other club while you are in a 1% MC clubhouse, function, sitting at the bar, or any of that. Believe me when I tell you the walls have ears. That nice old man sitting there at the bar nursing his beer with no colors on could be the retired national president. You and your sisters sitting in there talking negative about his club can cost your SC a whole lot of heartache. Or maybe you're talking about his niece who belongs to another social club. As you can see, problems arise from loose talk. In the United States Navy, we used to say, "loose lips sink ships." That was because back in World War II running your mouth in a bar about where a ship was going could be overheard by a Japanese spy. That spy would relay that information back to high command and now the Japanese Navy would know where that ship was going to be so that they could go and sink it. And your loose lips would have sunken that ship." So never run your mouth loosely on the set. Never engage in loose talk. Especially when you are out on the set at a 1% motorcycle clubhouse. If the wrong person hears what you have to say and doesn't like it, you and your sisters could have hell to pay. Also shut a sister up that's disorderly and running her mouth in a foul way, drunk, incapacitated, or having any other kind of mental inadequacies going on. Get her out of there quickly. Remember you are your sister's keeper and other clubs, including the dominant, will be watching.

Staying Sober

One of the quickest ways to get yourself into trouble is to not be able to handle your substances and alcoholic beverages. Being drunk and out of sorts in a 1% clubhouse is a foolish game you shouldn't play. If you are one of those females who shouldn't be drinking on the set, then don't. Generally, you don't have to worry about being hurt or attacked in a 1% clubhouse or party. But you do have to act like you've got some sense.

1% Support SCs

There is a new trend on the set that involves OMCs inducting SCs as 1% SC support clubs. In fact, in some areas you may even be told that you cannot start an SC without it becoming a "SC support club" for a 1% MC nation. Therefore, there are many SCs that are having this status enforced upon them against their will. This is not just happening to SCs, this is happening to RCs and even car clubs (CCs) as well, so SCs are not alone in facing this challenge.

I don't feel like any SC should become a diamond support SC because it limits everything it can do and as well as the club's freedom the moment it puts that support patch on. The SC immediately takes on the baggage of the OMC including its enemies, problems with law enforcement and potential damage to careers and reputation. Suffice it to say that law enforcement, the greater community, media and employers will never see alignment with an OMC as a positive thing, no matter how many charities you help throughout the year. And consequently, the gang label will ensue and attach itself to your SC like it does OMCs. If the sisters of the SC vote that it is in their best interests to become an SC support club, then that's ok because it is a decision they made. But if it is something that is being forced, I say resist it with all your might! There are ways to remain independent and resist bullying and intimidation from any organization. There is no MC protocol that requires your SC to be a support SC for a diamond club. Ultimately your SC has the right to decline such an offer or demand and instead pursue goals the sister feel are in the best interests of the SC.

CHAPTER ELEVEN
The Prospect's List of 45 Do's and Don'ts to Gain Entry into the SC

One of the most important and incredible journeys you will experience during your SC career is the process of prospecting for your chosen SC. The prospecting journey will set the foundation for everything in your SC career. What you learn during this phase should equip you to build your base to face whatever challenges, losses, or victories you may encounter during your SC life. It is essential you have a successful journey through your prospectship.

In my book the *"Prospect's Bible,"* I outline every step of the prospecting journey. Even though the *"Prospect's Bible"* was written specifically for MCs, SCs will gain a lot of information from its contents, since SCs are intrinsically similar to MCs in their administration and operation. There are a few things I would like to impart to prospects and hang-arounds interested in joining an SC. These 45 basic prospect Dos and Don'ts were shared with me by "T. Solo" founder/President of the "Simply Divas and Dames SC." I would be remiss if I did not also mention T Solo's VP "Sunshine," Business Manager/Treasurer "Foxy," and Founder of the Mother Chapter (Houston) "Essence". When T. Solo first outlined these guidelines to me, I insisted she allow me to share these with you, to which T. Solo graciously agreed. Thank you, T. Solo for your willingness to share these amazing insights with others.

Please note, I have taken the liberty to expound upon this list. Remember no two SCs operate the same way. These are guidelines that will help you prospect for an SC with greater ease and a better understanding of the set:

1 Prospecting is Getting into The Habit of Prospecting

To prospect correctly you must develop the habit of prospecting. Prospecting is not an easy task for anyone. The purpose of prospecting is for the prospect to get to know the SC and the SC to get to know the prospect. Through that process you will prove your worthiness to become a member of the SC, and, in turn, the SC will prove its worthiness to deserve your membership. Prospecting is a complicated relationship that requires fairness and equity on both sides. The SC must realize you are not just cannon-fodder to be used, misused, or abused. By the same token you must understand and learn the SC's customs, traditions, operations, and bylaws while simultaneously learning how to fit in and become part of the club's social construct. When the club fails to fulfill its obligations or the prospective member fails to prove herself, both sides lose. When prospecting works, the process delivers an invaluable sister to the sisterhood and the former prospect gains an SC family for life.

When learning the habit of prospecting, here are a few things you must know:

Everyone Goes Through It

It may seem like everything is set up against you, that everything is intentionally against you, but that's not the case. If you are prospecting for an SC that follows MC protocol rest assured, everyone has traveled a similar path. This is a necessary process you must complete to call yourself a sister and wear the full patch. It's time to put on your big girl panties, grin, and endure.

Your Pride May Take a Few Hits

The act of prospecting is a humbling experience. You may find yourself taking orders from a sister you deem to be beneath your level, but as a full patch sister of the SC, she is actually above your level in the SC. Proverbs 16:18 KJV the Bible states, *"Pride goeth before destruction, and a haughty spirit before a fall."* so stash your pride away so that it doesn't cause you to trip and fall. Prospecting is designed to be humbling and at times can be quite distasteful. The silly little tasks demanded of you have the effect of letting others determine your true personality. It gives the sisters the ability to judge whether you have the true grit to be one of them – are you willing to sacrifice for the sisterhood, are you a liar, do you share, can you be depended on when a sister needs you? Prepare yourself to endure a few mildly humiliating episodes. Afterall it's all in good fun and for most ladies, prospecting doesn't last longer than a few months on average. There is one certainty – if you cannot bring yourself to suffer through this period of prospecting, you will not make it into the club.

Never Compromise Your Values

Though everything I said in the previous section is true I must add this caveat for your well-being – know your limits and what you will (or won't) allow to happen to you. With that, I must tell you that at no time during any phase of your prospect period should you allow any person to cause you to compromise your self-worth or spiritual values for any reason. No one should ask you to break the law, perform sexual favors, invade your personal space or your body against your wishes, or perform any other acts that do not align with the values by which you live your life. It's OK to let them have their rags back and you go find some other SC for which you can prospect, if your self-respect is ever jeopardized.

Sexual Harassment

Sexual harassment is against the law! Never let anyone sexually harass you for any reason. In my time on the set, I once witnessed a brother club treat women in the SC as sexual flowers, from which any brother could pluck the loveliest petals at their desire. How this SC allowed themselves to get into this position, I will never know.

The situation deteriorated to the point that the sisters felt obligated to turn their unsuspecting young prospects over to these clowns, as a kind of rite of passage, in some sort of mass hypnosis, cult-like follow-the-leader behavior bullshit. I was so dumbfounded by how unhealthy the perversion of this the whole sick situation had become to the point that I made a mental note to remark about it should I ever author this book. Ladies, you can't be nobody's fool out here in these streets. Always be willing to tell a dirtbag to get lost! No one has control over your body but you. Don't let any sucker or any "would-be sister" talk you into anything you don't want to do.

Not Every Sister Who Wears the Patch Will Be Your Sister

I once overheard an MC president instruct a full patch sister of his sister SC to tell her prospect to meet him in the toolshed behind the clubhouse for a few minutes. "Just tell her that I just want to see "IT" and maybe touch on '"IT" a little bit." The full patch SC sister demurely nodded then walked over to her prospect and whispered to her that she should meet the president in toolshed as he quickly walked his married ass to the shed, hoping no one would notice him sneaking away. He slipped into the toolshed where he awaited the delivery of his prey. I saw the most surprised and confused look appear on the prospect's face as she fought internally before making her choice to follow her sponsor to the shed. It was obvious that she suddenly found herself in an uncomfortable position that she may not have known how to escape.

The ugliest part of that whole situation was that it didn't matter whether the prospect had said "Yes" or "No" in that toolshed, because the moment she walked in there she was already labeled an "EASY HO." You can't meet the president in the toolshed at a party and not expect everyone to see both of you walk in there. And it would be silly to believe that everyone didn't know the president's get-down because it surely wasn't his first time. So, the whispers and rumors would be swirling when she was being led to the door to be fed to that president. And what was so cold-blooded about it is that her full patch sponsor already knew that and had set her up for that cold-hearted shit.

Listen to me on this one, ladies! Just because someone wears a president's patch or appears to have some high rank within the MC or SC, doesn't mean that they are worth a damned as people or give a damned about you as a person! Some of them are on some really dark shit because they ain't worth a shit! Be ye not fooled for even an instant by these shenanigans, bullshit, and Tomfoolery. A club sister that would ask you to do some despicable shit like that is not your sister! She never was and she never will be! In that situation you would have been perfectly within your rights to tell that b*tch to kiss your motherfucking ass and promptly report her ass and that derelict MC president to your president. And if she didn't do something to punish that kind behavior, then you already know that would not be the SC for you! If a man wishes to talk to you let him step forward, speak his mind, convey his intentions and take his chances. As a prospect you are not to be delivered up like a lamb to the slaughter by a sister trying to curry favor at your disadvantage.

Never allow yourself to be somebody's toolshed circus attraction no matter what kind of peer pressure they try to apply. Tell that sister to go meet him in toolshed herself and let him touch her forbidden ecstasies because yours are reserved for gentlemen who have better sense than to ask for that kind of dumb shit to be delivered to you in some kind of disrespectful message from a full patch sister who is supposed to be looking out for your best interests instead of her own.

No Means No! Rape is Rape! Punish a Rapist with the Law!

There was a big MC in Atlanta that had a situation where a full patch brother slipped something in a sister's drink and raped her after a club party. On March 20, 2012, Atlanta's Channel 2's Erica Byfield spoke to the alleged rape victim. It turns out that she reported the crime to the president of the MC and the club had a council hearing about the matter. I don't know why the police were not called when the rape was initially reported, especially since the club president was a police sergeant and other members of the MC were also cops. Instead, according to the victim's statement during the interview, the club decided to put the accused rapist out of the club and allegedly promised to pay for the woman's medical bills and psychological counseling. The woman claimed that the club failed to pay for her counseling, so she went to the police and the news to report her assault. She intimated that she felt betrayed by the MC for not having her back while outside observers felt like the club had failed to protect a rape victim by not calling the authorities in the first place!

I am telling you this story to alert you to the fact that most clubs will move to protect their brothers first. The MC set is still a good-old-boy system where men slap themselves on the back and hide one another's bad or illegal behaviors. As a female on the set, you may find that your only protection and path to justice will come from you. Never wait on a male MC to do the right thing for you! If someone sexually or physically assaults you take it to the proper authorities immediately. If folks aren't getting you to a hospital or getting them damned laws called, they ain't got your best interest at heart! Rape needs to be handled in a court of law not in the "court of a damned MC" (or SC)!

Give Prospecting Your Best Effort

Only you know if you have what it takes to prospect. If you think you do, then give it your best effort. Prospecting is getting into the habit of participating. It takes a willing mind to put oneself in the service of servicing the SC. Well, that is what is called for when you begin your prospecting journey. Remember to have fun and enjoy the ride. If you accept this going in, you'll have a much better experience, I promise.

2 Conduct Yourself Responsibly

Any SC worth a damn is going to have rules, customs, and traditions based around how they carry themselves and how they are seen on the set. Most women in SCs do not tolerate irresponsible, silly, immature girls who don't know how to be grown and mature women on the set. How you carry yourself will determine how your SC is seen by the MCs with which it interacts. An SC will have little tolerance for women that do not carry themselves in a responsible manner. Being drunk and out of sorts and having to be carried to your car every time you go out because you cannot handle your liquor is the type of thing that will make a respectable SC get rid of your ass. These women aren't playing about this! You are expected to act in a responsible manner when representing your SC on the set. These women aren't playing about this! This is because they feel if you are thought of as a ho they will be thought of as hoes. So, no one is going to tolerate repetitive irresponsible behavior. Expect your prospectship to be terminated if your SC cannot trust you to conduct yourself responsibly.

3 Always Display a Positive Attitude

As I have told you before, the biker set is a fun place, but it can also be cliquish. Everyone will know you are "just a prospect," new to the set, when they see that prospect patch on your back or hanging around with no colors at all. As a new person you cannot have a negative attitude. And as a prospect you represent the SC. It is extremely possible for one negative sister to start trouble for the SC by displaying a piss poor/ bad attitude on the set. This is why your prospective sisters will expect you to display a positive attitude when out and about. You are a prospect —you don't have the right to have a bad attitude. If a brother greets you by telling you you're beautiful and you respond with a holier than thou attitude, you may bruise his fragile ego and now your SC has problems. Accept any compliments with class and kindness, not rudeness or disdain.

4 Participate as Much as You Think is Acceptable then Participate More

There are three things that make any organization great: Communication, Respect, and Participation. Your mastery of participation is paramount to your success in achieving your goal to be a full patch sister. By giving maximum participation over the next several months towards your SC, you will find yourself appreciated and respected beyond belief. This is because one of the hardest things to find in any organization is people who are willing to participate.

It seems like an easy proposition — if people love their SC (like they claim) there should be lines around the block with sisters volunteering to handle every need of the club. Unfortunately, for most clubs, this is not the case. Often it comes down to the willing few to get things done. By being a prospect that proves herself dependable early in the process by participating anyway you can, you will be amazed at how quickly your prospect time flies by when you are constantly awarded increased responsibilities. That is not to say that you need to forgo your other responsibilities. It is important to keep a consistent balance between work and family, but prospecting takes time and must be given as much priority as you possibly can. If you can give more, give more!

5 If You See a Club Sister You Haven't Met Take the Initiative to Introduce Yourself

In most SCs, to be voted in you must have 100% of the votes, which means you will have to get to know everyone to a greater or lesser extent because you will need everyone's vote if you want to succeed. You can't be shy about meeting, influencing, and getting to know any prospective sister that will be voting for you. Don't leave it up to a sister to come over and introduce herself to you. She's already in the club that you want to join. It's no skin off her nose if she never meets you because at the end of the day she is still in the club if you don't get her vote. Be proactive, get up and go introduce yourself! Just remember that during the introduction, you must present yourself as "prospect number" or "club name," never as your real name unless specifically asked.

6 Ask to Circulate and Greet Every Patch Holder

It is important to always have your best foot forward in front of prospective full patched sisters. Often, the best place to see them will be at events, parties, and gatherings. Keep in mind that some sisters don't make meetings or don't participate in everything, so get to know them whenever you can. When you find yourself at an event you will probably be very busy working for the club, but there will always be an opportunity to take a break. Instead of taking a break to catch a smoke, keep working towards your successful prospecting goals and use that time to go and meet sisters, especially ones that you've never met before or that you seldom see. Remember that you will also need their votes to successfully cross over from prospect to sister. Creating opportunities for them to get used to seeing you and taking the time to go out of your way to get to know them is absolutely in your best interest. Always be on the lookout at any event to find sisters that you've never seen, introduce yourself, and get to know them.

7 Anticipate Needs, Don't Wait to be Told

In this important lesson of prospecting, you must learn to be sort of a crystal ball when observing prospective sisters. While prospecting, functions are not your time to party and be chased by the men, you are there to serve and work for the SC. To be seen and not heard. You will see a huge difference in the treatment of the prospect with her head in the clouds—more concerned with the party than being of service to the SC and her sisters— than the prospect who is all about her responsibilities. Let the lazy prospect not be you! You don't want the negative attention she receives from her prospective sisters. Keep in mind that your time to party will come after you have achieved your primary goal and become a member of the club. Keep your eyes open and your mind sharp. Be anticipatory to see if you can predict the needs of your perspective club sisters, then get off your butt and go make yourself useful. It is always better to be working on something rather than to be sitting around waiting to be told to do something. The prospect who is always thought to be working and creating projects on our own will be thought to be resourceful and pragmatic. The one who always has to be told to do something, no matter how willing she is to be of use, will still be thought of as lazy and lackluster.

Anticipatory Observation Skills

For instance, if you see sister Harmony reach for a glass – consider how impressed she would be if you were handing her the glass before she could even grasp it in her hand? That's because you got yourself across that room fast enough to get it for her because you were watching.

Or if the president puts her glass down and turns her back to it to greet and speak with the president of an MC and you come behind her and put a napkin over the top of her glass and stand with it in your hand. How impressed is she when she turns around to get her drink only to find out it has been under your protection the whole time? The president is thinking, "Damn! That prospect really had my back tonight. I'm going to keep an eye on her to see if she is deserving of increased responsibilities." Sharpen your skills in anticipatory observations as they will help you to be at the right place at the right time.

8 Don't Get Overly Friendly with Any Non-Regular Acquaintance of the Club

One problem with being new is that you don't always know what someone is up to when they approach you to ask questions. Believe it or not, SCs have many enemies (they all do) and it may take you months before you can recognize them. For example, someone in another SC may want to see your club fail to take your sponsor MC because they can't get a sponsor MC and by removing your SC from the set, they can take your sponsor MC. Remember SCs can't operate on the MC set without a sponsor MC. In this scenario, if the enemy SC is digging for dirt and an underhanded witch spots you (the prospect) minding your business tending bar, what better person is there to ask a fucked-up question than the new girl who doesn't understand what's going on? Consequently, you get setup by a smiling face that is just about to bring you more misery than you ever thought possible because she was out for blood the moment, she spotted your innocent ass at that bar! You must be very careful about being overly friendly with someone so that you don't allow them access to information to which they are not entitled. One of the best ways to avoid this trap is to make it a practice to speak very little at functions and events on the set until you have spent enough time there to know what's going on. You don't have to be rude, after all prospects are not expected to speak very much anyway. If someone asks you a question it is perfectly OK to say, "I am a prospect and I'm not authorized to speak. Let me find you a full patch sister to answer your question." No one can take exception to that. It doesn't matter if it's a 1%, a brother of your sponsor MC, or a random person on the set. If your standard answer is, "Prospects can't talk," you can't say the wrong thing. If you pass along questions, you have no rank to answer, you can't get in trouble for answering the wrong question, or for putting information out you really don't know the answer to in the first place. It's called "covering your ass" (CYA). Having expertise at the CYA skill makes you a wise prospect and likely allows you to crossover quicker.

9 Sisters' Information Stays in the SC

Never, under any circumstance, should you give out a club sister's name, phone number, address, or any other personal information to anyone outside the SC! It is vital you learn this lesson first and foremost because it can protect your sisters' safety just as much as their privacy and anonymity. The SC is a private club that operates in very public venues. It is easy to be drawn into the idea that everybody is family because everybody is laughing, hugging, and smiling. But never forget there are predators all over the set and they seek prey for many different reasons. They are lurking looking to exploit every gap, miscommunication, weakness, or mistake. One of the worst mistakes a sister can make is to be caught slipping when it comes to another sister's safety. You can be duped into providing the information that gets one of your sisters hurt, kidnapped, raped, or murdered. And believe me, it can happen in an instant! The perpetrator can be anyone— a national president, regional officer, big-time local celebrity. Take, for example, actor and comedian Bill Cosby. He was found guilty and sent to prison for drugging and raping women. Though his sentences were eventually overturned, the mere fact that he admitted to some of the crimes took the entire world by surprise. Which solidifies my point — you can't trust anyone especially with your sisters' personal information! Don't fall for the president who comes up to you and says, "I can't remember sister Harmony's number and I lost it on my phone can you give it to me real quick?" Don't be taken in by the sister of another club who says, "I don't remember sister Harmony's address and I have to meet her first thing in the morning can you give it to me please out of your phone?" Consider the idea that, that sister may be mad at Harmony because she thinks she's sleeping with her man and she wants her address to go to her house to kill her, and you were the one that was duped into providing it. This kind of dumb shit happens. Do NOT be reason one of your sisters gets hurt.

I can remember when such a thing happened to me. Yes, many of the things that I tell you I am against are exactly the things that I have done. In this example, I gave out a brother's information because a very skilled woman was able to pry it from my lips. Let me set the scene … I was dating a woman and my chapter president decided that he would date her behind my back. The whole time she and I were together, I thought we shared a closeness. Little did I know she was sleeping with my club brother and chapter president. Now, I had known this club brother for about 25 years at that time and he had always been a womanizer, but we lost touch for some years. When we started hanging out again, he swore his womanizing days were over and he would never cheat on his new wife because of his newfound dedication to the Christian lifestyle. He claimed to be the paragon of loyalty and fidelity. He came across as the perfect family man.

One day when, the woman (let's call her "Tracy,") shocked me by saying, "Your president and I have been sleeping together for quite some time. I'm upset because he slapped me in the mouth the other day and called me a bitch." I just couldn't believe her! I got so angry at her I screamed, "Why would you tell those lies on that man? He's a Christian and he's a married man and he would have no reason on earth to sleep with you. That's my club brother and I cannot believe you would tell those kinds of lies on him and I no longer want to have any more dealings with you!"

Little did I know, I had just given her the magic potion that she sought. That tidbit of information I let slip from my lips, in a moment of rage, allowed her to know something that she had not known previously. You see he hadn't told her that he was married and learning this infuriated her. Revealing his marriage was not something I would have done to get revenge even though he was sleeping with her behind my back. Still, that's how it turned out.

"Loose Lips Sink Ships"

When I served in the submarine Navy, we used the saying "Loose lips sink ships!" And for me in this instance, my loose lips did indeed sink the ship of his marriage. Now armed with the fact that she knew he was married, "Tracy" began following him when he left her home and eventually, he led her to his home where she took the opportunity to show up on his front doorstep to tell his wife exactly who she was and exactly what they had been doing. I am not proud this all came from me! Expertly, she guided me to the revelation of his greatest secret, and I watched my club brother go through a divorce that occurred partly by my hand.

I say this from great experience —people are experts at manipulation and deceit, they are the kings and queens of subterfuge and espionage. "Tracy" could have shown up on the president's doorstep and killed his wife and family out of jealousy and outrage and that too would have been my fault. Be careful with the phone numbers, marital status, employment status, and any other personal information of your beloved sisters. Give out no one's information. The proper answer response to any request is, "Tell you what, give me your phone number and I will make sure that she gets it."

Never forget: "Loose lips sink ships and sinking ships kill people!"

10 SC's Information Stays in the SC

There is some specific information about your SC that you never give out to anyone. The thought behind it is that you would never tell anyone the exact size of your military defense unit, its capabilities, its logistics or its supply routes. Think of your SC the same way. You should never answer questions like, "How many members y'all got?" or "How many chapters y'all got?" or "Where do y'all hold y'all's meetings at?" As a prospect it is always okay to direct them to a full patch club sister who shouldn't be answering those questions either. It's also okay to simply say, "We never disclose the strength of our organization, it's locations or logistical statistics. Who would ever do such a silly thing?" Capiche?!

11 Stay Alert

As a woman on the set, you cannot afford to be naive to what is going on around you. Your survival depends on your street smarts and ability to observe and recognize danger when you see it. Your sisters' survival also depends on your alertness. If you are in an SC that is under an OMC, you must be even more vigilant as they often have way too much else going on to worry about your safety. The fact is most OMCs have conflicts going on with multiple clubs all the time. They fight amongst these enemies and even kill one another. Although this environment can be fun, exciting and adventurous, the situation can turn deadly in an instant. A gun battle could ensue when just a few seconds prior everyone was partying, dancing and having fun. You must have a good intuition about the set and almost "feel" when a situation is beginning to turn so you can grab your girls and get the hell out of there if need be. It's important to get to the point that you know the vibe of the set — such as who is beefing with whom. For instance, if you know two MCs are not getting along and you see them both arrive at an event you will automatically know it's time to get out of there because anything could occur between those two warring MCs. It will take you some time on the set before you are able to determine such things, but before you get to that level of awareness it shouldn't take you much time before you are able to understand when an atmosphere changes and it's time to alert your sisters that something isn't quite right. Your senior sisters will know what to do because you alerted them to a problem they might not have seen coming. As a prospect you won't know a lot about why things are going on but that shouldn't stop you from knowing or feeling that something isn't quite right.

11B. Listen to Your Somethings

There is an inner sense in everyone that tells them when they should be getting out of harm's way. Call it "intuition," "sixth sense," "premonitions," "gut feeling," or "something told you." I call it, "My somethings!" And I always listen to my somethings. Make sure you always listen to yours!

12 Conduct Yourself with the SC in Mind

When in public wearing your prospect colors always remember you represent your SC. No matter where you are or what you are doing the public sees you and by extension your SC. If you show your ass at a restaurant in your SC's colors, the public sees the entire SC showing its ass at the restaurant. A waitress you belittle may see one of your sisters in the restaurant later in the week and decide to spit in her food for the dumb shit you did just because she's wearing the same colors. If you are doing something illegal in the SC's colors, it's the same as the entire SC doing something illegal. When in public, everything you do represents the SC. If you start beef with another club, then the entire SC has started beef with another club. The SC has no place for selfishness and ego driven individualism. You are part of a hive and something you do to offend someone could cause trouble for a sister who is completely innocent of your transgression. You must always keep your mind on the fact that you represent something greater than yourself. Conduct yourself accordingly! The public never stops seeing you even when you think no one is looking.

13 Sisters Never Travel Alone on the Set

When you are with the SC, you arrive with the SC, and you leave with the SC. You never allow a prospect or prospective sister to go anywhere alone. Often younger prospects think the older full patch sisters are trying to be their mothers when they are told they aren't allowed to be anywhere on the set alone. But this is the farthest thing from the truth. There are plenty of predators on the set looking to exploit any situation where there is a breakdown in security or a display of weakness. These are evil people with evil intentions and there is no better target than a lone sister who isn't paying attention for just a moment in time. This is far less likely to occur if the SC forbids its sisters and prospects to ever be alone on the set for any reason. This means no one is ever allowed to walk off alone —not to get some "fresh air," not to go out to her car or bike to get something, not to make a quick call, not to powder her nose, NOT FOR ANY REASON! The best way to look at this is, "We came together, we stay together, we leave together, and we report in after we get home safely!"

14 Alert the SAA or Senior Sister to Negative Vibes

If you notice any negative vibes while at a function, alert the SAA or a senior sister. This rule is really an extension of rule eleven as it directs you who to report to when your alert mindedness detects a potential problem on the set. The club SAA is the first security officer and should always be reported to first, if possible, but a senior full patch sister is also an appropriate next step so that they can report to the brother club's SAA, and he will direct the family what to do next.

15 Keep your Eyes and Ears Open

You can't keep your eyes and ears open if you are so caught up in the party drinking, smoking, and having fun. Never put yourself in a position to become oblivious to the fact that you are on the set. The set is a place where the SC handles business, makes an appearance and moves on. You can party more comfortably back at the sponsor MC's clubhouse, which is home if your SC doesn't have its own clubhouse. On the set, stay vigilant and limit your time there.

16 You are a Prospect 24/7

Your association with the SC doesn't turn off when you take off your colors or aren't on the set. You are a prospect 24 hours a day, 7 days a week (24/7). You represent the SC even in your personal life. It is expected that the SC become part of your inner being such that you operate in the best interest of the SC in all of your dealings including professional, social and personal. Many SCs are so concerned with their public image they will regulate how their prospects and members conduct themselves even when they are not wearing the colors or participating in club events. Yes, being on Instagram or Facebook twerking may be an activity you are doing on your own time, but the SC may frown on that behavior enough to put you out over it. Take the time to understand the club culture and the social construct upon which the SC oversees the overall behavior of its sisters and be aware of the conduct that it expects from its members. Just like a church wouldn't want its head deaconess to be a stripper to make ends meet, the SC won't hear "your personal time is your own business." Make sure you understand the culture you are getting into before you get too deep. Ensure you are a good fit while prospecting for your SC because if you aren't you can easily become dissatisfied with them as much as they are with you. There are plenty of SCs on the set that are wilding out – go join one of them.

17 You Are Every Sister's Prospect

In most SCs you will need every member's vote to crossover into full patch sisterhood. You can ill afford to think that only pleasing your sponsor you be enough to get you into the family. Do whatever any full patch sister in good standing asks you to do with pride and a good attitude. Also, if you belong to a national club you will need to do whatever any full patch sister asks you in the nation (this rule might differ slightly in your club).

18 Never Wear Your Colors Out of Your Area Without Your Sponsor's Approval and Never Out of State Unless You are with Your SC

There are many rules associated with how and where an SC can travel or wear its patches. Often the SC must seek permission to fly in an area that is not their home. As a prospect, you will not be familiar with the rules of conduct on the set. You may want to proudly wear your colors but it's not always that simple. Never wear your colors outside of your area without your sponsor's approval and never out of state unless you are with your club sisters.

Let's say you decided to go back to Ohio to visit relatives and you want to wear your colors out on the Ohio set but your SC is not cleared to fly there. Or maybe your SC flies a support patch of an OMC and the area you are visiting is considered hostile territory for the OMC. In either of these scenarios, if you pop-up on the Ohio set wearing your colors, you inadvertently put yourself in a position to get jumped and even living the very negative experience of having your colors forcibly taken. This puts the whole extended family, including your SC, your brother MC, and your dominant OMC in a regional conflict that could conceivably get someone hurt or killed. All because you made the honest mistake of wearing your colors in the wrong area without permission. Although the scenario I just laid out is extreme it has happened. A less dangerous scenario, but just as serious, is that someone sees that you are wearing a prospect patch and decides to target you because you are alone without a knowledgeable sister around to head them off. As a prospect, being on the set alone is fraught with pitfalls and the potential for danger.

Never travel alone out of your area with your prospect colors without your club sponsor's approval, no matter how tempting the proposition.

19 Private Conversations Among Sisters

It is considered incredibly rude to interrupt two full patch sisters when they are having a private conversation. A prospect is expected to wait until their conversation is finished before approaching within earshot. This is true for both SCs and MCs. If you see two or more full patch members of any club such as a full patch sisters talking to a full patch member of another club do not interrupt. In a crisis or when an urgent situation arises that dictates you have no choice other than to interrupt, stand in a position of visibility, outside of earshot where you can ensure you are noticed. When there is an opportunity for them to pause their conversation, you will be recognized and called close enough to state your intent and purpose. You should profusely apologize for interrupting, state your business or ask your question, then quickly leave the area after receiving direction. If possible, get a full patch sister or your club sponsor to intervene on your behalf.

20 "Outlaw Club" Should Never Be Uttered on the Set

Terms like "outlaw," "biker gang," "gang," "outlaw motorcycle gang," and even "one percenter" can be inflammatory when used improperly or out of context on the MC set. As a prospect it is easy to misidentify a club's lane or authority, by giving them the wrong designation, you can cause some embarrassing or icy moments. It's best to refer to MCs by their name instead of any other description. If you don't know their names, you shouldn't be talking about them at all. Remember walls have ears on the biker clubs set. You never know who is looking, listening, watching, or reporting what you say so always keep it general, non-accusatory, and indiscriminate.

21 Never Lie to a Member of Another Club

There is a difference between lying and refusing to give up club information on the set. In one instance your club is thought of as liars and untrustworthy, in the other it is seen as tight-lipped and protective of its culture and business. The difference being that a lie was told when the words "none of your business" should have applied. Let's take the scenario where a member of another club asks you about the club or its membership. It is always acceptable to say, "That seems like club business, and I really can't talk about it." A prospect has every right to say, "I can get you a patch holder to answer your question as I am not permitted to talk about club business." This is much better than telling a lie that can put you and the club in a negative light.

22 Show Equal Respect to Full Patch Sisters of Any Club

Always show the same level of respect to full-patch sisters and officers of another SC or MC as you would your own SC. Although you only prospect for your SC and only full patch sisters of your SC may give you orders or expect you to complete tasks they request from you, it is always appropriate and expected for you to show respect to other SCs and MCs. It demonstrates to other clubs that your SC is training its prospects traditionally and with respect. For instance, if you are in the United States Submarine Navy walking down the pier in Turkey and you pass a senior Turkish officer of the Turkish Submarine Navy—you render a salute. Even though he's not in your chain of command, nor can he give you orders, you show respect to his military rank over yours. If your rank was senior, he would render a salute to you which you would respectfully return. Since MCs and SCs follow paramilitary structure, it is customary to show respect up and down the set.

23 Always Carry Pen, Paper, Watch, and Calendar

These are the tools of a prospect in most clubs on the MC set. There may be other tools prospects are required to carry in their prospect kit / prospect bag. No matter what your SC wants you to carry it is important to always have those items with you. In many clubs you may catch a fine or extra prospecting days if you are caught without your kit on your person.

24 Frequently Ask Full Patch Sisters How You Are Doing and if there's anything you Should be Doing Differently

By frequently asking full patch sisters how you are doing and inquiring about how you can improve or do things differently you avoid potential pitfalls that may hinder your ability to crossover. Some full patch sisters may hold a grudge against you for reasons you may never know. They don't intend to vote for you and never intend to tell you why. But by checking in with each full patch sister, you will disable her ability to hold up your crossover because she told you what she wanted you to change in enough time for you to change it before she could screw up your vote. Keep a running internal report card by asking frequently how you can be of greater service to the SC.

25 Never Ask When You may be getting Your Full Patch

One of the quickest ways to add time to your prospecting period is to ask when it will end. It is inappropriate to ask your sponsor or any full patch sister when you will be getting your full patch. You will receive your patch when your club sisters feel you are ready and not one moment before, so don't ask. Patch holders may become quite angry if you do and it's an excellent way to get a few months tacked on to your prospectship.

26 Never Call a Full Patch Your Sister

There are many SCs that feel prospects are not members until they crossover while others feel prospects are members under probation. Some won't allow you to call a full patch a "sister" until after you crossover, some will. Until you find out how it is in your SC it's best to err on the side of caution and call prospective sisters by their club names until after you've patched over.

27 Never Call a Full Patch or Prospect of another SC Sister

There is a long-held tradition on the MC set that only your club brothers are your brothers. No one outside the MC is allowed to call us "Brother" and we don't often refer to a member of another club as "Brother". This is especially true on the white MC set. On the Black MC set, however Black people have a history of calling each other brother and sister based on shared experiences of surviving in a hostile country that targets us for death because of the color of our skin, which makes this rule rather tricky. I rarely call anyone on the biker set that isn't my club brother, brother, but I take no offence if a Black man in another club calls me brother simply because that is our tradition as Black people in America. Similarly, I don't often call anyone outside of my club family "sister," but I don't take offence if a Black woman calls me brother to which I often return the sign of respect by referring to her as "sister" as well. Generally, in the SC world your sisters are considered to be the ladies who wear your same back patch. It is important that you know the general rule and why it was made, but I recommend you adhere to the guidelines set forth by your SC.

28 Patches are Earned Not Given

You must work for your patch. There are some who believe they have a birthright into the SC simply because their mother was the founder, they have some sort of a blood-rite into the SC without putting forth the effort of prospecting. Those women are sadly mistaken and will find out that there is no blood royalty in the SC or anywhere in the entire MC culture. Everyone must prospect to gain their patch. Patches are not purchasable, nor are they ever given (of course it happens but it shouldn't). This is the most basic tenet of this society.

29 Never Bring a Personal Friend or a Stranger into the Presence of your Prospective Sisterhood without asking Permission

As a prospect you do not have the right to bring guests before the sisterhood. Your prospective sisters are just getting to know and trust you, they are not going to accept strangers you bring before them, no matter your intent; especially if they are not expecting them. On the MC side, we tell prospects to leave your woman at home. You won't have time for her while you are working for the club, and you probably don't want her to see you in a subservient role as a prospect. Plus, you don't know the MC well enough yet to be trusting these strange men around your woman like that. It takes time to build relationships, trust, and loyalty. Take the time to learn your SC before bringing your man, family, or friends around. They don't really know you like that, and you don't really know them like that yet.

30 Never Turn your Back on a Patch Holder of Another MC

As a prospect, it is considered disrespectful and inappropriate to turn your back on a full patch member on the MC set. Naturally, this can be difficult if you are at an event with hundreds of people, obviously your back is going to be turned to someone. But the idea is to always remain respectful in your conduct on the set. It is better to back away from a full patch brother or sister than it is to turn your back and walk away.

31 Always Show Respect and Courtesy to Patch Holders of Other Clubs

As a prospect you should always show respect and courtesy to full patch members of any club. Remember you represent your SC on the set, and you should be the finest example of how your club should conduct itself. Although the set is fun, there are business aspects which require a level of professionalism. You are not there to be friends with members of other clubs, you are there to earn entry into your SC. Keep your encounters with outside club members short, polite, and professional then move on.

32 Keep Away from Men Associating with other SCs due to Pillow Talk

As I have said before, SC prospects on the MC set are seen as "fresh meat" by nearly every male on the set. Be mindful of any clubber you see bouncing from SC to SC seeking whomever he may devour. Let me remind you, these immature fools gossip worse than women and are not to be trusted.

"Me No Date Butterfly"

When I was in the Navy in the early 1980s, we used to sail the 7th fleet where we would often have ports of call in the Philippines. Back in those days it was customary to have a Filipina girlfriend when you pulled into port. She was your woman while in the Philippines and you were expected to have her and no other. There were many aspects about those relationships that fueled the Filipino economy because of the money that was spent on those relationships during those port of calls. At that time, the average Filipino salary was between $60USD and $300USD per year (The New York Times). A sailor could blow that amount of money on a girl in a weekend, which allowed her to support her entire family in a way her father couldn't. So, suffice it to say these relationships were often heavily based on financial support which allowed some sailors to use the situation as an opportunity to run through as many women as they could. These sailors were often referred to as "butterfly boys." Now, it was not a complement to be called a "butterfly boy" and you would often hear a Filipina say, "Me no date butterfly." This was an example of a Filipina taking control and exerting agency over herself and her body. She was not a whore to be run up in by some foolish sailor that wanted to butterfly himself from flower to flower across the land.

The Cambridge dictionary defines this phenomenon as, "A person who is not responsible or serious, and who is likely to change activities easily or only be interested in pleasure: He's such a social butterfly." You can learn a lesson from how those women protected themselves. Refuse to engage a clubber-butterfly. The whole "Me no date butterfly," is a policy that every SC woman should exercise. Shutting those fools down before they even get started can protect your heart and your reputation. Butterfly boys often run their mouths and whether they are spreading gossip on the pillow or spreading gossip on the set, they are toxic and not worthy of your time.

33 Prospects Never Partake in Consuming Alcoholic Beverages at any Open Function

Simply put, prospects do not drink or indulge in spirits of any kind on the set. Prospects should be working on the set not getting drunk. Your job is to earn your way into the sisterhood. There will be plenty of time for you to enjoy the party after you have crossed over.

34 Prospects Never Partake in any Unnatural Drug

Simply put, prospects should never get high on the set. Just like consuming spirits, prospects should be working on the set not getting high. Your job is to earn your way into the sisterhood. There will be plenty of time for you to enjoy the party after you have patched over. With that, you must also be aware of unnatural kinds of drugs circling on the set. Anyone could give you something synthetic that will ruin your life. Don't trust anyone with your life on the set.

35 Never Acknowledge a Prospective Sister's Husband or Boyfriend especially upon First Meeting Him

Keep away from full patch sisters' and fellow prospects' men. Do not be overly friendly or even open yourself up to the possibility of an accusation of too much interest in another woman's man. This is a grown-up world. Conduct yourself like a mature, grown-up woman at all times. Absolutely never be foolish enough to flirt with any full patch sister's significant other. It's a good way to never get voted into the SC. Just a word of advice to the wise.

36 Do not Touch or Sit on a Patch Holder's Motorcycle Unless Invited

In the biker club world, it is unacceptable to ever put your hands on or attempt to sit on a biker's motorcycle for any reason without asking permission or invitation. Breaking this rule could get you cursed out or physically assaulted. This rule goes for male and female bikers. Many on the MC set are over-the-top when it comes to their love of their machines. For them, motorcycles are given almost human-like attributes and their love for their bikes can exceed their love for humans. Of course, as a prospect you should never be away from the full patch sisters long enough for someone to ask you to sit on their bike or even to go for a ride, but it can happen and if does, never be so bold as to get on someone's bike without being asked.

Turning Your Cut Inside Out

There is also a rule on the MC set such that "nothing tops the cut of an MC," which means the MC's colors must always be distinctly seen and prominent when a brother is on his bike. This means if any

MC brother offers you a ride, do not be surprised if he asks you to take your colors off or turn your colors inside out. This is because your colors cannot top his while you are on the back of his bike. This occurs even if you are riding with a brother from your sponsoring MC. Familiarize yourself with your SC's policy before accepting any ride from a brother. Some SCs say, "Hell no! If I gotta take my cut off or wear it inside out, I don't want to ride on your damned bike," and so it may be the policy of your SC, whereas other SCs make no big deal about it and will remove their cuts or turn them inside out before getting on a clubber's bike. That policy is up to your SC. A lot of young brothers in today's MCs have no idea about the rules and don't know MC protocol well enough to even mention it. If they don't mention it, neither should you. Do not put yourself in a position to get into trouble while you are prospecting.

37 It's Not an Insult Not to be Acknowledged on the Set

If you see a sister from another SC you know personally while you are out on the set, don't be insulted if she doesn't particularly acknowledge you in an overly friendly way—as you might expect that she should. There are a lot of politics going on throughout the set so her club may not be on friendly terms with yours or there may be other reasons outside of your personal relationship that doesn't allow her to be friendly at that moment. If she is prospecting, there may be rules against her speaking while on the set, she may be trying to show loyalty to her sisters, or there are a myriad of other guidelines occurring which may prevent her ability to acknowledge you. Don't take any awkward interaction on the set personally. If it bothers you, get back to her off the set on a personal basis to discuss further.

The Social Clubs Bible
38 Learn Your Patch Parts and Colors

I cannot tell you how many clubbers I've met on the set that had no idea the meanings behind the colors they were wearing on their backs. Learn what each part of your patch represents and what the different color combinations of each club means. What a waste of your time prospecting if you don't even know what the color combinations of your patch mean. You must know what every thread on your patch represents if you are going to know what your SC (and in turn you as a member) stands for. What if you later discover that the blue in your patch meant your SC hates people who lived on the blue islands of the Pacific Ocean? Is that something you could champion? No, but here you were wearing that patch ignorantly the whole time.

Would you believe there are Black men in some Black MCs that wear swastikas on their cuts? Naturally, you'd think there had to be something wrong for a Black man to don a swastika given that most people equate the swastikas with Nazi racist culture and white supremacy. What would you think if his response to the question, "Hey man, why are you wearing that swastika on your cut and what does it mean," was "Heck, I don't know what it means but I liked the club and it was part of the uniform, so I wear it." You would look at him as the fool he was. But what if his response was, "The swastika has many different meanings in many parts of the world and even though the Nazi rendition of the swastika is perhaps one of the most recognized, it is not the only interpretation of the symbol. My club has chosen to recognize a different interpretation of this symbol that I am wholly in step with which is why I decided to wear this symbol despite what the popular interpretation of what it may be." Of course, you'd be blown away and your perception of this individual would change understanding that he knows what his club is about, what he is about, and the direction in which he is headed.

This is why you must know what your club's symbology is and what all your iconology means.

Knowing Other Club's Patches and Meanings

The more information you have the easier it will be to navigate smoothly on the set. Get to know as much about the other MCs in your area as you possibly can. Learn their colors, iconology, patterns, beliefs, mottos, and symbology. Learn why they do what they do because when you know them and what makes them tick, you will be in the best position to effect positive outcomes for your SC in the future when you become a leader. Let your prospectship time be the building blocks for your successful future SC career.

39 A Prospect must do Anything a Prospective Club Sister may ask

Of course, within reason and limits. Don't be anybody's fool after all your mamma didn't raise no idiot! Be prepared to let a mothafuka know they can take them patches and shove them up they mothafukin' ass! If need be.

40 Don't Touch another Club's Colors

The vest and colors are the walking billboard that expresses who and what a clubber is. They tell a history of where he has been, who he is now, and perhaps indicates where he is going. The colors also carry the standard of the MC as a back patch of between one and five pieces. It is considered highly disrespectful by some MCs to touch someone's colors, especially the back patch(es). It is also considered to be highly disrespectful to point to someone's patch, touch it, and ask why they got it or what it stands for. When you hug someone on the set it can be considered an insult to touch their back patch(es). Become adept at hugging without touching a person's back patch. Hug around the neck area perhaps with one hand on the left or right side, rather than wrapping them up with both arms around the back. Clubbers are known for aggressively educating the uninformed about this transgression. Of course, as with all rules on the MC set, this practice is not considered disrespectful by everyone and there are some clubs that do not care about it at all.

41 Prospects must show a Sincere Interest in the Club

If you are going to prospect, do it right because full patch sisters will be looking for you to display a keen interest in becoming a member of the SC. They know what they put into becoming a member so believe me when I tell you they are not going to have any sympathy for you not putting in the same, if not more effort. As I said before, start out like you can hold out.

42 Stealing is Not an Option

Thieves are not tolerated in most organizations or societies. The ironic thing about theft from your sisters, is that in most cases if you just ask almost anyone in your SC would give you what you thought you needed to steal. In most clubs stealing is automatic grounds for immediate termination. In others it is an immediate ass whooping too – at least in MCs, I don't know if SCs will actually beat your ass. I imagine it could happen though, but I've never personally witnessed that. Bottom line, don't steal because it will get you kicked out of your SC.

43 Do Not Sleep Around with Members of the Sponsor MC or Multiple Men on the Set

In most SCs there will be a strict prohibition against sleeping with the brothers of the sponsor MC for all the obvious reasons. It's hard to have a brother/sister relationship with someone you are screwing. It blurs the lines and when things go awry it ruins the ambience and atmosphere for everyone involved. When politics get involved, everything goes from bad to worse. Of course, people will break the rules, but don't be surprised if your SC shows your ass the door the minute you do.

Equally, most SCs you are not going to tolerate you being a "ho" on the set. As "T. Solo" clearly pointed out when she shared these 45 rules, "Ain't nobody going to walk up on me and touch my boobs because you've been letting them rub on yours. This causes problems, women want to swing on you for sleeping with [they] men, and when it comes to the men of our brother club—we don't do incest!" So, check your hormones at the door. If you want to belong to an SC of substance, you are going to be required to conduct yourself like a lady.

44. Your Colors Should Never Touch the Ground

Most SCs and MCs absolutely prohibit the mishandling of your colors. Your colors are the flag upon which your club is represented. No one is going to tolerate you slinging the colors around in a sloppy fashion, laying them on the ground, leaving them unattended in a chair, showing your ass while wearing them, breaking criminal laws in them, or letting another MC hold them. In many clubs such violations start with a 90-day suspension, a $200 dollar fine or both. Folks take these rags seriously and they will show you very quickly what happens when you disrespect them.

45 For Now, Just Follow the Rules

As you gain experience in the SC you will begin to see the importance of some of the points discussed in this chapter. You may not understand the reasons for every rule just yet — and no amount of writing can convey all you need to know the hope is that by learning and following these 45 rules of prospecting — you will at least have a basic understanding to get started on the right foot on your SC journey. Many SC prospects think the full patch sisters are trying to run them and be their mothers. Nothing could be further from the truth. These women are trying to use their wisdom to help you have the time of your life on the set while not having to relive the same bad experiences they endured.

BEST OF LUCK PROSPECT!

For more information on prospecting, be sure to get my number one best seller, "Prospect's Bible, How to Prospect for a Traditional Law Abiding MC" or my book "Prospect's Bible for Women's Motorcycle Clubs." Available on Amazon, Kindle, Audacity, and at www.blackdragonsgear.com where you can get an autographed copy.

CHAPTER Twelve
An SC Founder/Prez Speaks

When I decided to write this book, I figured I should spend time with some founders of SCs to ensure you ladies had a well-rounded perspective and educational experiences with this book spoken from the point of view of women who started SCs and made them successful. I mean, what would a women's book look like with only the perspective of a man? Balderdash! Therefore, chapters eleven and twelve are presented from interviews I've had with some magnificent women. Chapter eleven was spent with T. Solo of Simply Divas and Dames SC and in this chapter, we spent some time with 2 Extra of Dominant Beautiz SC. Some of the lessons of T. Solo's chapter eleven you will find repeated in 2 Extra's chapter twelve. This is because both of these presidents said many of the same things from different perspectives to achieve similar outcomes. I've decided to give you the benefit of reading it from both sides represented unfiltered, exactly how 2 Extra said it in this chapter and T. Solo said it in the last.

When I interviewed 2 Extra for this book, we spoke for four hours straight. She got going and never stopped. I've decided to present this chapter in her voice, like I heard it and she spoke it. So many of the things she said mirrored my research over the past ten chapters that I almost feel like you could read chapter twelve and throw the book away and you would have everything you need. This following chapter is exactly what she said to me:

I Keep my Prospects Quiet

One of the first rules I practice is that I keep my prospects quiet on the set. That's right, they are not allowed to speak. That's because they don't know anything to say anything so why should they be speaking? This is every bit for their protection and not to rule over them or treat them poorly. For the time being, they need to believe in me and their prospective sisters only! They need to listen to what we say, then do it. If they are talking then they are interacting with others, listening to others, and quite possibly believing others who do not have their best interests or their safety at heart. So, for now they need to be quiet and listen because you have to be quiet and learn before you can know anything. Prospecting time is the listening time.

Most prospects, new to the set, have no understanding that the excitement and fun of the set can change in an instant. The set is full of trouble and some very bad people. Under the façade of shimmering lights, fast motorcycles, and masculine men is a dark underbelly that you must know how to navigate if you are going to be safe, mentally sound, and emotionally well. If they aren't listening more than talking, then they are setting themselves up for trouble.

When the So-Called Experts and Bros Talk to Your Prospects

You also must be very careful about who is speaking to your prospects. I keep them quiet so that no one will want to come up and talk to them. The MCs will say that we are stuck-up because we shield our prospects from their sexual advances, games, and cheating men. We're not stuck up, we're controlled. If you keep your club controlled, you will be called a "trouble" president. But keeping your club controlled is not about causing trouble on the set. It's not about causing trouble with your brother MC. And it's not about causing trouble with the 1%ers. Keeping our SC controlled is about protecting our women. These women are my responsibility to protect. So, I am most careful about who they speak to and who "educates" them because if I'm not, all kinds of people with hidden agendas will try to position themselves to poison their minds, feed them false information, or try to turn them against the honest and true teachings of the SC. You have got to remember that your prospects don't know anything. They don't know MC protocol and they don't know SC protocol. They are just like babes in the woods waiting to be filled with anything good or bad someone wants to give them not knowing whom or what to avoid. And these men in these clubs will tell them anything. They will tell them things that are not MC protocol like they are MC protocol. There are people on the set that are just evil and out to hurt new girls. This is why we do not allow our women to go anywhere on the set alone. And we keep them controlled, and we keep them quiet, and we educate them ourselves. They don't need to be educated by outside clubs, brother clubs, or by anyone who may not have their best interest at heart.

A President Educates Her Girls

I educate my girls. I'll say something like, "Watch her, she came in her club the same time you came in with us. Look at her. She has already been patched and she is already looking tired. You can see it in her eyes. You can see the internal battle of unhappiness and you can see that she is thinking to herself, "I don't want to do this anymore. I'm not happy. It's not what I thought it was" This is because they have gotten to her. She has already been passed around and has already made a name for herself as being easy." You can see that president getting notoriety because she done fed that baby to those MCs. You have to watch those types of sharks. Because you've got these MCs teaching these SC presidents to bring these types of girls, get these types of girls and that's dumb. And we'll give you this and we're going to back you with this. And that's dumb.

Some SC Presidents and Founders will Sell Their Girls Out

Sometimes, Black Dragon, their own presidents and founders will turn these girls over to these men, in effect selling them out! The reasons are silly if you ask me, but they get made promises like they'll be given favor, or their SCs will be shown favor. This social club game has been turned into a numbers game. Presidents and founders are no longer taking the time to personally train their prospects or even spending the time to get to know them. Instead, they are trying to ante their numbers up as they are forced by these MCs to bring in as many girls as possible so that they can be added to the feeding trough. They've increased the number from 5, which is what is used to take to start an SC to 8 or 10. Now, these MC's will tell an SC you have such and such amount of time to bring in 8 girls or 10 girls or your SC will be kicked off the set. These presidents and founders have spent all of this money and all their valuable time building up a club only to have someone say it's going to be torn down and cast aside. It's almost too much for them to bear! They're thinking, "Hell, let me hurry up and throw some of these bitches in here to fill these ranks." It's a vicious cycle. The SC's have been forced to feed these MCs with these annoying girls who are excited to see the set and excited about the motorcycles and the culture without knowing what is lying in wait for them. They don't get to see the dark side until it is upon them and some of these SC presidents and founders want to be recognized, popular, and liked so much that they feed the ever-burning machine with new bodies.

If SC Presidents and Founders Knew Protocol

It's sad to see that's how some of these presidents and founders are thinking but, if you knew your education and what you can and cannot do, what is and what is not protocol, instead of jumping up under these MCs, just because you want to be up under this MC because of this and that, you would ask the right questions!

SC Presidents and Founders Don't Know What to Ask an MC

A lot of these ladies don't know what to ask an MC before you go up under them. For instance, what is your bylaws rule concerning fraternizing together? What is your rule? If any of these MCs' rules go against your bylaw's rules, that is not the MC for you! If you are already having conflict with your prospective sponsor MC's rules and bylaws before you even join together then that is not the MC for you!

Some MCs Don't Want to Play Fair If not, Don't Play

Another conflict is a lot of these MCs want to see your bylaws and rules, some of them even want to be in your chat, but they don't want to show you their bylaws, rules, and chat. If I'm going to be under you then why can't we see your bylaws and you see ours? A lot of these MCs will tell you that they are not allowed to show you their bylaws. But that was the number one question I asked! Can I see your bylaws!? Are we showing each other bylaws? This way you can't bullshit me when you are trying to give me a fine that may not exist because I never saw it in your bylaws. I need to see it in black and white so I can move accordingly. A lot of founders and presidents don't know that's a key thing you are supposed to do. The first meeting between you and that MC should be a meeting to compare bylaws. This way you can see if that MC will be able to support you, and you'll know how to move with them.

MCs Pitting One SC Against Another

Another thing these MCs like to do, especially if they have two or three SC's underneath them, is pit one SC against another. They like to play these games of who's my favorite. They convince these foolish women into playing the game of competing to see who can be liked the most. They will say, "We don't like your SC because y'all are stuck up and won't let us date your girls. Ya'll are a problem, and we are really sick of dealing with y'all. Look at this other SC, they are down but y'all are stuck up and not trying. Ya'll don't do as you're told. Y'all are hardheaded." And because you need to be attached to one of these MCs to be on the set, it becomes a cat and mouse game that only a strong SC president or founder can win.

Why are Women Competing against Women

There's so many of these silly women in these silly SCs but if they would just think for a minute and not compete with your sister against the enemy but stand with your sister, they wouldn't be able to get away with these amateur, silly games. If these women who had common sense would stand back and work together the MCs wouldn't be able to be on the bullshit. If you ladies would stop acting like you all are a threat to each other and not allow these MCs to say, "Such and such does this better so let us give her more attention," then SCs could stand together as an unbeatable force. But instead, these MCs sew division through these SCs, and make these SCs fight each other by planting seeds. But if these presidents of these SCs are educating these ladies and making sure they are confident and understood our meaning and why we are here this would not be the case!

Division Amongst SCs Because of Outside Influences

The division amongst SCs is also horrible. This SC doesn't want to deal with that SC, and that SC brings civilian shit on the inside of the set. Whatever you got going on, the outside needs to stay out there and not in this world. Civilian shit is another reason a lot of us are fighting amongst each other.

We are Not Fuck Buckets

Back to the MCs, they love issues between the ladies. If the ladies used open communication and learned how to talk, there would be no problems. Look and listen! These ladies don't know what an SC is for. We are not fuck buckets! This is a horrible term they use to classify us, especially the OMCs out here. The 1%ers have it bad calling us that.

A Few Rules Prospects Should Know About Dealing with MCs

1. Rule number one, you do not have sex with your brothers. In fact, Secret founder of "La Bella Crue SC out of Atlanta, GA told me to quote her as saying, "All Set dick is community that attracts only section eight pussy. And I don't deal with section eight pussy."
2. Rule number two, respect yourself at all times.
3. Rule number three, you are grown but if you decide to have initial grown time, you are going to go through two or three members or MCs in the same group. They are going to talk and you're going to be labeled. You're not going to hurt him by playing with him because they are going to have a brother bond. They already know what you are going to do.

This is Why We Keep our Prospects Quiet

So, we ensure that our ladies don't talk. We keep our prospects quiet. You can't have certain people teaching your girls and corrupting their minds. So that's why our prospects are silent on the set. They don't know nothing to talk. The time to talk is when you have learned something. By the time my ladies are crossed and put that patch on their backs they are wise and looking and listening. If you teach your prospects to pay attention, then they know what's going on as much as the full patch sisters. If your prospects are paying attention, they can alert the women.

Problems Associated with Having the Wrong Brother MC

Hooking up with the wrong brother MC can cause an SC more problems than you know. It can limit the community work you've been doing and prevent you from hanging out with MCs that have been long time friends. For instance, you might have been an SC that supported everyone, but the new MC has problems with other MCs on the set, and all of a sudden you can't visit everyone you used to know because you are up under this new MC. This is why you must choose a brother MC wisely.

You May Support the MC but does the MC Support You

Another thing. These brothers don't come out with the SC on the set at all. A lot of these SCs are on the set and you don't see none of their MC brothers which is dangerous. You've got five members of your SC out on an event you should have at least two brothers escorting. These MCs are charging you monthly membership fees, but they aren't doing anything to justify the expense. You are just giving them your money! If someone has a shooting, they aren't giving you protection or nothing! I can't roll like that!

MCs want to Govern SCs Bank Accounts

A lot of these MCs forcing the SCs to have a joint account is bogus. We've had to ask permission to spend our own money that we've sweated and hustled to make, only to watch it go right into their back pocket. Why would you have to ask any club's permission to spend your money for your patches? Or they will tell you what's necessary or important to spend your own money on. And if you challenge that then you are considered a troublemaker. You will be labeled as a problem. "We bought y'all's drinks and paid y'all's way in, so we need to get reimbursed." Make it make sense.

Pimping is Alive on the Set

The MC prez will say, "Look, we are fixing to go out of town, why don't you make sure we're good?" That's pimping. If you don't do it then you hear, "Ya'll don't know how to listen. Ya'll don't do as you're told…" You're labeled as trouble. "They won't listen. They gonna do what they wanna do…" I'm telling you ladies you really must choose an MC wisely.

Finding a Good MC is Nearly Impossible

I tell my ladies finding a good MC is like finding a good pair of walking shoes. You are going to have to wear a pair of shoes for a little time and they are either going to work or you're going to have to drop them and take them back.

Dropping an MC can be a Problem

So, when an SC drops a club it's a problem, but men jump from club to club all the time. The council will tell you that you can't change clubs even though they are grimy. They will always listen to the men first. That's why you better choose wisely.

Having a Controlled SC gets it Labeled as "Trouble"

If you've got your sister's back and something's going on and your sister is not coherent, to the MCs that's a no-no. We all know how the set life moves and changes in the blink of an eye. If you've got your sisters' backs, "Hey it's time for us to go!" The set life can turn without a moment's notice. So, you have to keep a controlled sisterhood.

If you are too controlled, this is what gets you labeled as "trouble" because you will speak your mind. If you keep your SC too controlled, then you get into trouble. "I'm not your wife, so why do I need to go and get your drink?" That's speaking your mind which means you are "trouble." You see?

Or, if I see an MC president moving grimy... you've slept with this sister, tried to talk to this sister, and now I see you easing up on another sister, and I put a stop to it. Then, according to that president, I'm a hater. No, I'm not a hater, I'm protecting mine because I see the pattern you going in. Then they say "Oh, you're being disrespectful to the club, I'm a president and no one can tell me what to do..." I can tell you what to do with mine! So, I say, "No, just because I speak like that I'm not speaking disrespectfully, I'm taking care of mine. They are my responsibility! She's in my sister circle. And as long as she's in my sister circle she's my responsibility and right now I'm protecting her." This gets me labeled as a "trouble" president because I know my shit! And what I don't know you can't just tell me anything. "Oh no brother let me go ask someone else this question." So, if you have a controlled club and these MCs cannot infiltrate, conquer, and divide, you are labeled as a "trouble club."

A Circle of Ladies who Define Themselves Empower Themselves

When a circle of ladies allows their ladies to make their own decisions, cause they are grown, they empower themselves. And I cannot play any games when it comes to that.

The SC is Responsible for its Members to their Families

I'm the one every lady is looking at to make the big decisions for our SC. When the family calls and wants to know where their missing family member is, guess where the heat is going to be? The heat is going to be with me. And I warn presidents that you and the SC can get sued, because she was with you. She was your member, which means she was your responsibility. You can get a wrongful death suit. People have tried.

So, I always know the emergency contact, updated every six months. I need to know your blood type in case we get in a wreck. I need to know what you're allergic to, But, if you don't have that type of control because you are growing numbers and not quality, then guess what, everybody is going to be on your back. That's why I have a controlled club. If we come together, we are going to leave together! We keeps a controlled club! We are all on the same GPS circle. A lot of times when you tell an MC that we are all on the same GPS they won't fuck with her. They won't try to follow her home because they know someone is checking up on her whereabouts.

So, if you've got a controlled club, you are labeled as a trouble club. You're stuck up. You ain't shit. "Y'all think y'all are better than everybody."

"BE" Mindful of these Niggas

BE mindful of these niggas. Even your club brothers must have a certain respect for you. These niggas are still putting shit in folk's drinks. If they really want you bad and they are sending drinks to your table, they will put something in your drink.

Creeper Niggas

Then you got what I call creepers. They just look at you. They stalk you and see what you are about and follow you. That's why your ladies should never be by themselves. They wait to see if you are capable of standing your ground. They look around to see where your sisters are at. They'll go and tell your "brothers" how you are moving so several of them can set you up. If you aren't careful, they'll get you. I know it's sad because we're all supposed to be family, but they'll get you.

Don't be Foolish Treat "Brothers" in Clubs with Caution

Now, I know these brothers are supposed to be family, like when you get with an MC. And everything is supposed to be family, but it isn't always so. You have to be cautious about these so-called "brothers" in the MC especially if you are a single female. For instance, if a brother is supposed to come over and pick up something and he's coming over to your house, you need to have a select area in your home that he can come into. A club brother doesn't need to have been all throughout your house. A club brother doesn't need to know everything that's moving around in your house because some of these club brothers will lie on their dicks. And when they lie on their dick it is to ruin your reputation and make you look bad and make them look good. So, maybe a club brother doesn't know how your inside of your house looks but rather knows how your porch looks. You're still a woman, you still must guard yourself, you still must guard your reputation! Guard yourself, your soul, your spirit, and your heart.

Learn to Cover Your Ass when dealing with the MC

Another thing is that these MCs will throw SC members up under the bus in a heartbeat. We're trying to sell bands and we ask, "Hey can we just sell these $25 bands for $15 to get rid of them? They'll say, "Yeah go ahead and do what you gotta do." But as soon as there's a problem with that the first thing you hear is, "I don't remember telling you that." Now you've been thrown up underneath the bus. And believe me they will take the MC's word over the SC's every time. So, you have to combat that. You have to cover your ass (CYA). You gotta practice CYA. I take down everything and put it in a text message and send that text message. That way when someone says, "I can't remember telling you that," you can say, "Oh well, yes you did, here's the text message, let me send it to you. Like why would I do that without asking my MC first?" But they find a way to throw you up underneath the bus. Because a lot of these brothers are grimy, cowardly, simple, and immature. They can't stand on their own two feet so they will throw a woman under the bus just to preserve their own access.

Know what Questions to Ask Everybody before joining an SC

For Heaven's sake and for your sake these are the questions that these people need to be asking when they are trying to come into this life. Women need to learn to ask when someone says, "Hey my friend, she has her own SC, and she wants us to come join." "Oh? What is her intent? Why does she want us to join? What's her history?" These are questions that women don't know to ask because they don't know the life, but you better know how to evaluate an SC well enough to know if you can trust them to teach you. Because when you go through this cycle of being passed around and that president or that founder has allowed it, the betrayal will break your heart and make you mad enough to want to hurt someone. That's when it's too late to ask the questions you should have asked in the beginning.

The Social Clubs Bible
CHAPTER Thirteen
The Way Forward

So, where do you go from here? First, it is important for you to know that you are a Goddess upon Earth and the mother of our race. Through great sacrifice in these lands, you have nurtured our spirits and uplifted our social condition while our path has been slippery and our climb to the summit fraught with disaster. Still, your important work is not done. So now is not the time to take your foot off the accelerator. You must revive the spirit of the Black woman's SCs movement and continue your mission.

You must not be hampered nor swayed by the impediments that would block you from the goals SCs established from the beginnings of slavery, when Black women sought to help their sisters and their families rise from the bondages of despair and hopelessness. Your mission must remain clear, and you must remain on course—focused, steely eyed, and determined. You have been our salvation and our hope. You Goddesses are more than we could ever deserve.

Black Men Don't Understand Your Purpose

Unfortunately, many of my Black brothers on the MC set have not yet begun to truly understand your purpose. As a consequence, they are ill-prepared and ill-equipped to lead you. Though you continually seek to put your direction in the hands of their flawed leadership they continually fall short while blaming you for our social condition. Their self-hate manifests in their destructive and unmanly behavior. They seek to turn your sacred sisterhoods into harems of harlots to be waded through like grape vineyards, picked clean of hearts, souls, and spirits. They erect barriers to your success instead of building bridges to facilitate your accension. Fear not, because in the absence of their leadership you must lead yourselves. But also, worry not for you are magnificent leaders.

TikTok Influencer DarkMatterGoddess

I want to close this book with part of a message I heard today from a TikTok Influencer named DarkMatterGoddess. She is a spiritual teacher, feminist, writer, shaman and dreamer. When she made this message, she was responding to a video civil rights Influencer and activist Dr. Umar made. In the video he told Black men to go home and cut the weaves and perms out of their wives' heads because the glues and perms were causing Black women to have more brain cancers. Needless to say, DarkMatterGoddess was livid at the thought that such an influential Black man would use his expansive platform to suggest that other Black men should go home and assault their wives by cutting their hair off without their permission. When I heard her words, it struck me that there was much in what she said that founders, presidents and members of SCs should take to heart when confronting ill-prepared Black male leaders in these MCs who attempt to force dominance over them. Below is my interpretation of DarkMatterGoddess' message:

A Broken Clock is Right Twice Per Day

"Melanated dominant people, sons and daughters [of] my ancient mother. Black women and Black men. I want you to [understand] this in our community; a broke clock is right twice a day.

Black women you are God! That's why I say, "Mind your mind [when] following men. Why? Because they come from a degenerated Y chromosome. Anybody that has an abnormality in a chromosome has some issues. So let me tell you the truth.

Why They Assault and Violate Black Women

Okay, think about it. When our hair was nappy, they made fun of us calling us "nappy headed" and gave us perms. When we permed our hair, they made fun of us and said we were trying to look like white women. And now you get a broke clock [Dr. Umar] assigning an assault on a Black woman, telling Black men to go home and assault their wives by cutting off their hair without their permission. This is a rape and a violation that this man used his platform to go against Black women! This [comes] from a degenerated Y chromosome [a man].

These Men are Jealously Obsessed with our Beauty

Ladies pay attention! [Men] are obsessed with our beauty. Why? Because of how we age, melanated dominant women. As we age, we age with beauty and grace and there is nothing that they can do about it. That's why they are obsessed with [figuring out] how they can destroy our beauty. They say, "She's beautiful nappy headed. Let me see your permed hair. Damn she's beautiful with permed hair, let me cut all of her damn hair off. She beautiful bald-headed. [Oh well,] make her take off the makeup. Damn she's beautiful without the makeup. Damn she's beautiful with the makeup!" They are obsessed with our beauty! Why? Because when they age, they get pot bellies, titties and they walk around looking like they're pregnant. Their big titties are bigger than mine. In the bed their testosterone has dropped so [the] only thing between their legs is a glorified clitoris! I said it, and I [speak] the truth [to] shame the devil.

Follow Yourselves Not Unfit Men

So, be careful with these men. I told y'all you're gonna need to stop following [them]. They're unfit to lead. Anything that comes from a degenerated Y chromosome is unfit to lead. [They are] completely narcissistic, yet the broke clock is right twice a day.

How can the Broken Clock be Right

I have seen the broke clock [Dr. Umar] say some of the most profound things, and I'm like, "Hey man!" But when I [hear that I also] understand that the clock is broke. Melanated dominant women I need you to look at [these] men and understand the clock is broke. And do not get confused, when they are right twice a day, [into thinking] that they are fit to lead. [Because] they are not!

Stand in Your Own Devine Power

Baby let me tell you something—you're gonna have to stand in your divine power. You gonna have to get over your, "Pick me," mind frame with these men. You gonna [have to] get [to the point that] every time you hear a man talk—[I] need you to condition your mind [that] you are talking to a broke clock from a degenerated Y chromosome! [So he might be right, twice per day].

Love the MC but Keep it in its Place

[You can] love them [men/the MC], and you ain't gonna never see me hitched up with no white boy. But let me tell you something, any man you see me with, I run it! Okay, no degenerated Y [chromosome] is running nothing over here. [You can believe that] he is in his rightful place. I'm sorry and [some of] you [men] ain't gonna like it. Unfollow me. [It makes] no difference but Black women you're gonna have to stand up and be God. You gotta stop letting this kind of mess run your life, your mind, and pollute our community.

Message to the Broken Clocks

Let [me say] something to the broke clock. I'm gonna say it how Sophia said it in *"The Color Purple."* "Honey, you wanna dead son-in-law? Keep on advising him like you do."

I love you melanated dominant people that's all I had to say."

Do You Require a Clearer Message

I wrote this book to convey a clear message that may illuminate a path to revive the spirit of the movement for which Black Woman's SCs were created in hopes that this movement will take hold on the Black biker set in ways that it has never before. It will require you to:

1. Stand in your divine feminine power.
2. Choose your own standards.
3. Refuse to be divided by jealous-hearted, inferior, unfit men in MCs.
4. Get rid of your "Pick me" attitudes of dependency.
5. Write your own bylaws and stand by them.
6. Stop fighting among one another's SCs. United you stand, divided you fall.
7. Open your own SC clubhouses. Your clubhouse YOUR RULES!
8. Support those who support you. If they don't want you on their set create your own set. It will be full of guests like you would never believe.
9. Refuse to be a fuck bucket. A goddess is too good for castoffs.
10. Trust but verify! Watch all with a jaundiced eye. Demand proof. Check backgrounds and resumes.
11. Know that not every woman who wears your patch is your sister.

12. Be wise enough to listen to those who have walked the path before you. Believe it or not they know WTF they are talking about.
13. Know your bylaws by memory. They are your only guarantee of equality.
14. Stop saying I, I, I, and start saying WE!
15. Expand community involvement, the children are needy.
16. Lift others as you climb.
17. Improve the condition of our race in the United States. You are a hero.
18. Backup your brother MCs and teach them the true meanings of honor, loyalty, trust, and respect.
19. Teach your sisters instead of hating and squabbling with them. Start with a sister you can't stand. This will teach you humility.
20. Have fun! Life is short!

Honorably yours

Black Dragon
Former National President
Former National Enforcer
Former East Coast Regional President
Founder Black Sabbath MC Goddesses of the Cross
Founder Black Sabbath MC Sisters of the Cross
Founder/President/Original 7 Atlanta Chapter
Lifer
Mighty Black Sabbath MC Nation
A Breed Apart
BSFFBS
Since 1974 and still strong..............///

The Social Clubs Bible
Appendix A:

Bibliography

AAREG. *https://aaregistry.org/story/josephine-ruffin-activist-philanthropist-and-newspaper-publisher/*. 2021. World Wide Web. 3 September 2021.

Above The law. *https://abovethelaw.com/2018/12/harvard-law-schools-first-african-american-graduate/*. 2021. World Wide Web. 3 September 2021.

Alabama Women's Hall of Fame State of Alabama. *Alabama Women's Hall of Fame "Inductees"*. 2005. World Wide WEB. 11 September 2021. <http://www.awhf.org/inductee.html>.

AmericanMotorcyclist.com. *American Motorcyclist Association*. 19 June 2023. worldwide web. 19 June 2023.

—. *AmericanMotorcyclist.com*. 18 June 2023. world wide web. 2023 June 2023.

Appleby, Joyce and Lynn Hunt & Margaret Jacob. *Telling the Truth about History*. W. W. Norton & Company, 1995. Print.

Appleby, Joyce, Eileen Chang and Neva Goodwin. *Encyclopedia of Women in American History*. Routledge, 2015.

Ball State University. *Ball State University Women's Club Records and Scrapbooks*. Ball State University, 2018. Print.

Bikerider Magazine. *brm.co.nz/brittan-morrow-the-queen-of-road-rash*. 3 July 2023. world wide web. 2023 July 2023.

Black Weomen's Suffrage. *https://blackwomenssuffrage.dp.la/key-figures/josephineStPierreRuffin*. n.d. World Wide Web. 3 September 2021.

BlackPast, B. *https://www.blackpast.org/african-american-history/1898-margaret-murray-washington-we-must-have-cleaner-social-morality/*. 29 January 2007. World Wide WEB. 10 September 2021. <https://www.blackpast.org/african-american-history/1898-margaret-murray-washington-we-must-have-cleaner-social-morality/>.

BMV. *Bureau of Motor Vehicles*. Indiana: Indiana Government Center North 4th Floor, 2016. 17 March 2016.

Boston Lieterary District. *http://bostonlitdistrict.org/venue/josephine-st-pierre-ruffin/*. 2021. World Wide Web. 3 September 2021.

Bowles, Nellie. *S.F. women's clubs aging, rolls declining*. SF Gate, 2011. 2017.

Britannica. *https://www.britannica.com/biography/Josephine-St-Pierre-Ruffin*. 27 August 2021. World Wide Web. 3 September 2021.

Britannica, Encyclopedia. *Motorcycle*. 2020. 29 August 2020.

Buechler, Stephen M. *The transformation of the Woman Sufferage Movement: The Case of Illinois 1850-1920*. Rutgers Univ Pr: 1st Edition, 1986. Print.

Burgess Wise, David. *Historic Motor Cycles*. Hamlyn Publishing Group Limited, 1973. 7 December 2023.

Bush, S. Gilbert. *History of The Montgromery City Federation of Women's Clubs, Inc 1939 - 2004*. 2004. World Wide WEB. 10 September 2021.

ChatGPT Artificial Intelligence. *ChatGPT AI*. 6 June 2023. Artificial Intelligence. 6 June 2023.

Comas, Martin E. "Women's clubs struggle to find new, younger members." *Orlando Sentinel* 1 March 2017. News Paper. 7 December 2023.

Congressionalist. "Color-Line in Women's Clubs." *Congressionalist* (1901 February 9): 6-86. Print.

—. "Race Discrimination." *Congressionalist* (1900 June 14): 24-85. Print.

Constitution Daily. *https://constitutioncenter.org/blog/dred-scott-decision-still-resonates-today-2*. 6 March 2021. World Wide WEB. 3 September 2021.

Cossalter, Vittore. *Motorcycle Dynamics*. Lulu ISBN 978-1-4303-0861-4, n.d.

Courier, Charleston News and. "Margaret Murray Washinton, "We Must Have a Clearner Social Morality,"." *Charleston News and Courier* 13 September 1898. News Paper.

Department of Justice. *Department of Justice*. n.d. World Wide Web. 12 December 2023. <https://www.justice.gov/criminal/criminal-ocgs/gallery/outlaw-motorcycle-gangs-omgs#:~:text=Outlaw%20Motorcycle%20Gangs%20(OMGs)%20are,weapons%20trafficking%2C%20and%20drug%20trafficking Sept. 2023>.

Dunbar, Erica Armstrong. *A Fragile Freedom: African American Women and Emancipation in the Antebellum City*. Yale University Press, 2008.

Emporia State University. *Faculty Wives Club Records*. Emporia State University, 2018. Print.

Encyclopedia Britannica. *Club Movement*. Encyclopedia Britannica, 1999. Print.

Ethics", "African American Reform. *African American Reform Ethics. National Women's History Museum*. National Women's History Museum, 2016.

Fiedler, David. *The Boneshaker - Invented by Michaux and lallement*. n.d. World Wide Web. 7 December 2023. <about.com>.

Flanagan, Maureen A. *Gender and Urban Political Reform: The City Club and the Woman's City Club of Chicago in the Progressive Era*. The American Historical Review, 1990. Print.

—. *Gender and Urban Political Reform: The City Club and the Woman's City Club of Chicago in the Progressive Era*. The American Historical Review, 1990. Print.

Foale, Tony. *Motorcycle Handling Chassis Design ISBN 978-84-933286-3-4*. Tony Foale Designs, 2006.

Gates, Henry Louis Jr.: Appiah, Kwame Anthony, eds. *Africana: The Encyclopedia of the African and African American Expeirence*. Oxford University Press, 2005.

Georgia.gov. *https://law.georgia.gov/press-releases/2023-06-05/carr-16-alleged-members-outcast-motorcycle-gang-indicted-bryan-county#:~:text=The%20Outcast%20Motorcycle%20Gang%20has,chapter%20was%20formed%20in%20Atlanta*. 6 June 2023. worldwide web. 6 June 2023.

GFWC.org. *GFWC.org*. 2021. World Wide Web. 2 September 2021.

Giddings, Paula J. "Ida: A Sword Among Lions: Ida B. Wells and the Campaign Against Lynching." Giddings, Paula J. *A Sword Among Lions*. Amistad Press, 2008. 28 November 2023.

GovInfo. "https://www.govinfo.gov/app/details/CFR-2010-title49-vol6/CFR-2010-title49-vol6-sec571-3/summary." 24 January 2023. *govInfo.gov Code of Federal Regulations, 49 CFR 57.3 Definitions.* 23 January 2023.

Hall, Peter Dobkin. *The Popularization of Voluntary Associations*. Harvard, 2017.

Hendricks, Wanda A. *Fannie Barrier Williams: Crossing the Borders of Region and Race*. Champaign: University of Illinois Press, 2013. Print.

Hilda A Davis, Patricia Bell-Scott, Darlene Clark, Elsa Barkley Brown and Rosalyn (eds) Terborg-Penn. *Black Women in Americfa; An Historical Encylopedia - ISBN 0-253-32774-1*. Indiana: Indiana University Press, 1994. Print.

History.com. *https://www.history.com/topics/black-history/dred-scott-case*. 26 August 2020. World Wide Web. 3 September 2021.

Jacqueline, Anne Rouse. *Out of the Shadow of Tuskegee: Margaret Murray Washington, Social Activism, and Race Vindication*. Association ofr the Stud of African American Life and HIstory, 1966. Print.

Kant, Immanuel and Hans Siegbert Reiss. *Kant Political Writings*. Cambridge England New York Cambridge University Press, 1991. Print.

Kent State. *Faculty Wives Club of Kent State University records*. Kent State, 2018. print.

Lerner, Gerda. *Early Community Work of Black Club Women*. The Journal of Negro History, 1974. Print.

Mah, Harold. *Enlightenment Phantasies: Culltural Identity in France and Germany, 1780-1914*. Cornell University, 2003. Print.

Massachusetts Hall of Black Achievement Josephine St. Pierre Ruffin. *https://vc.bridgew.edu/hoba/32/*. 2011. World Wide Web. 3 September 2021. <https://vc.bridgew.edu/hoba/32>.

Massachusetts Secretary of State. *https://www.sec.state.ma.us/mus/pdfs/16-Ruffin.pdf*. 2021. World Wide WEB. 3 September 2021.

Merriam-Webster. *Definition of a Motorcycle by Merriam-Webster*. Merriam-Webster, 2023.

Miles, Tiya. *TiyaMiles.com*. n.d. WorldWideWeb. 27 November 2023.

Mjagkij, Nona. *Organizing Black America*. Routledge, 2001.

Motorcycles, Motorcycle Timeline - Evolution of. *www.bicyclehistory.net*. n.d. World Wide Web. 7 December 2022.

Mount Auburn Cemetery. *https://mountauburn.org/josephine-st-pierre-ruffin-1842-1924/*. n.d. World Wide Web. 3 September 2021.

Movement, The Black Women's Club. *DeColonizing Our History*. The Black Women's Club Movement, 2017. Print. 6 December 2023.

National Geographic Society. *A History of Slavery in the United States*. National Geographic Society, 2016.

National Women's Hall of Fame. *https://www.womenofthehall.org/inductee/josephine-st-pierre-ruffin/*. 1995. World Wide Web. 3 September 2021.

National Women's History Museum. *African American Women During the Progressive Era*. National Women's History Museum, 2017. Print.

—. *Introduction to Clubwomen*. National Women's History Museum, 2017. Print.

Nugent, Walter. *Progressivism: A Very Short Introduction*. Oxford University Press, 2010. Print.

Oakland Wiki, LocalWiki Contributors. *https://localwiki.org/oakland/California_State_Association_of_Colored_Women%27s_Clubs*. 2021. World Wide WEB. 12 September 2021.

Oxford. *Progressivism in English*. Oxford English Dictionary, 2017. Print.

Perkins, Linda M. "Bound to Them by a Common Sorrow: African American Women, Higher Education and Collective Action Part 2." *JSTOR* 100.4 (2021): 721-747. World Wide WEB. 11 September 2021. <https://www.jstor.org/stable/10.5323/jafriamerhist.100.4.0721>.

Perry, Tonya Evette & Davis-Maye, Denise. *"Bein' Womanish: Womanist Efforts in Child Saving During the Progessive Era: The Founding of Mt. Meighs Reformatory*. Afillia, May 2007. Print.

Prezi.com. *https://prezi.com/2wf4w-glat5o/thunderguards/#:~:text=The%20Thunderguards%20Motorcycle%20Club%20originated,Charlie%2C%20Gordie%2*

C%20and%20Cuppie. 21 June 202. worldwide web. 21 June 2023.

Rabaka, Reiland. *Hip Hop's Amnesia: From Blues and the Black Women's Club Movement to Rap and the Hip Hop MOvement*. Lanham, Maryland: Lexington Book, 2012. 6 February 2023.

Roosevelt, Eleanor. *The Progressive Era (1890 - 1920) - The Elanor Roosevelt Papers Project*. Wayback Machine, 2014. Print.

Rouse, Jacqueline Ann. *Out of the Shadow of Tuskegee: Margaret Murry Washington, Social Activism, and Race Vindication*. Journal of Negro History, Winter 1996. Print.

Scott, Anne Firor. *Most Invisible of All: Black Women's Voluntary Associations*. Ed. JSTOR 2210662. The Journal of Southern History, n.d. December 2023.

Shaw, Stephanie J. In Mankiller, Wilma P., et al. *Black Clubwomn's Movement*. The Reader's Companion to U.S. Women's History Mairiner Books, n.d. Print.

Smith, Jessie Carney and Shirelle, eds. Jones, Mary Jane Richardson Phelps. *Notable Black American Women*. Vol. 3. Detroit: Gale Research, n.d.

Smith, Marian. *Women and Natrualization, Part 2*. Prologue Magazine, 1998. Magazine.

Smith, Mary Jane. "The Fight to Protect Race and Regional Identiy within the General Federation of Women's Clubs, 1895 - 1902." *Georgia Historical Quarterly* (2010): 479-513. Print.

The New York Times.
https://www.nytimes.com/1984/06/03/business/the-

philippines-uncertain-future.html. 3 June 1984. world wide web. 4 December 2023.

The Woman's Era. "Woman's Era Eminent Women Series." *Some Features of the Era Souvenir Program Number* June 1896: https://artsandculture.google.com/asset/the-woman-s-era/zwHDG1uXyP5lUA?ms=%7B%22x%22%3A0.5344420409158629%2C%22y%22%3A0.22097086912079622%2C%22z%22%3A9.70808888330695%2C%22size%22%3A%7B%22width%22%3A1.3648242602250014%2C%22height%22%3A0.4419417382415924%7. https://artsandculture.google.com/asset/the-woman-s-era/zwHDG1uXyP5lUA?ms=%7B%22x%22%3A0.5344420409158629%2C%22y%22%3A0.22097086912079622%2C%22z%22%3A9.70808888330695%2C%22size%22%3A%7B%22width%22%3A1.3648242602250014%2C%22height%22%3A0.4419417382415924%7.

Thomas, Mary Martha. *The New Woman in Alabama: Social Reforms and Suffrage, 1890-1920*. Tuscaloosa, Alabama: University of Alabama Press. ISBN 9780817360108, 1992. Print.

Timeline. *Women in Texas History*. Timeline, 2017. Print.

University of Washington. *University of Washington Faculty Auxiliary History*. University of Washington, n.d.

Vick, Estella M. *California State Association of Colored Women's Clubs*. 2018. World Wide WEB. 12 September 2021. <https://oakland.access.preservica.com/file/sdb:digitalFile%7C71e64792-437e-4e83-8037-0432f9ab3cc5/>.

Wada, Kayomi. *blackpast.org*. 11 February 2017. World Wide Web. 7 December 2023. <blackpast.org>.

Waluchow, Wil Azlta, Edward N. *The Stanford Encyclopedia of Philosophy*. Metaphysics Research Lab Stanford University via Stanford Encyclopedia of Philosophy, 2018. 17 August 2018.

Watson, Denise M. ""The Woman's Club of Norfolk Celebrates 100 Years of Reaching Back and Moving Forward." *The Virginian-Pilot* 6 June 2016. 6 December 2023.

Wiipedia Giddings Sword Amon Lions. *Wikipedia.com*. 2008. World Wide Web. 29 November 2023.

Wikipedia. *https://en.wikipedia.org/wiki/Hell%27s_Lovers_Motorcycle_Club#:~:text=Hell's%20Lovers%20Motorcycle%20Club%20(HLMC,founded%20in%20Chicago%20in%201967*. 21 June 2023. worldwide web. 21 June 2023.

Wikipedia.Org. *Alabama's Colored Women's Clubs*. n.d. World Wide Web. 27 Novemnber 2023.

Wikipedia.org. *General Federation of Women's Clubs*. 28 August 2021. World Wide Web. 2 September 2021.

—. *https://en.wikipedia.org/wiki/Margaret_Murray_Washington*. 18 April 2021. World Wide WEB. 11 September 2021.

Wikipedia-CSACWC. *https://en.wikipedia.org/wiki/California_State_Federation_of_Colored_Women%27s_Clubs*. 24 May 2021. World Wide WEB. 12 September 2021.

Wikipedia-Slowe. *Wikipedia*. 5 April 2021. World Wide WEB. 11 September 2021.

Wilson, Linda D. *Women's Club Movement*. 1 March 2009. World Wide Web. 7 December 2023.

The Social Clubs Bible
<https://web.archive.org/web/20170301092901/http://www.okhistory.org/publications/enc/entry.php?entry=WO002>.

Wright, Sharon D. Springer, Kimberly ed. *Still Lifting, Still Climbing: Contemporary African American Women's Activism*. New York: New York University Press, 1999. Print.

Yahn, M. Campbell. *Decolonizing Our History*. n.d. World Wide WEB. 9 September 2021.

Zackodnik, Teresa C., ed. *"We Must Be Up and Doing": A Reader in Early African American Feminisms*. Buffalo, New York: Broadview Press, 2010. Print.

These are bibliography QR codes for websites used. They are not guaranteed to work, especially several years after this book has been published as we do not manage the servers upon which they reside. These are the links to those sites as they exist as of the writing of this book.

Recommended Sources for further Research

Cooney, Jr. Robert P.J. Winning the Vote: The Triumph of the American Woman Suffrage Movement. American Graphic Press, 2005.

Frankel, Noralee and Nancy S. Dye, editors. Gender, Class, Race, and Reform in the Progressive Era. The University of Press of Kentucky, 1991.

Ginzberg, Lori D. Women and the Work of Benevolence: Morality, Politics, and Class in the Nineteenth-Century United States. Yale University Press, 1990.

Muncy, Robyn. Creating a Female Dominion in American Reform, 1890-1935. Oxford University Press, 1994.

Muncy, Robyn. "Julia Clifford Lathrop." Women Building Chicago 1790-1990: A Biographical Dictionary. Rima Lunin Schultz and Adele Hast, editors. Indiana University Press, 2001. 490-2.

Orleck, Annalise. Common Sense and a Little Fire: Women and Working-Class Politics in the United States, 1900-1965. University of North Carolina Press, 1995.

Open Collections Program: Working Women, 1800-1930. Harvard University Library. http://ocp.hul.harvard.edu/ww/

Rosenberg, Rosalind. Beyond Separate Spheres: Intellectual Roots of Modern Feminism. New Haven: Yale University Press, 1982.

Scott, Anne Firor. "Most Invisible of All: Black Women's Voluntary Associations." The Journal of Southern History. Vol. LVI, No. 1, February 1990.

Schneider, Dorothy and Carl J. Schneider. American Women in the Progressive Era, 1900-1920. Facts on File, Inc., 1993.

Sklar, Kathryn Kish. Florence Kelley and the Nation's Work: The Rise of Women's Political Culture, 1830-1900. Yale University Press, 1995.

Appendix B
Ida B Wells

Figure 7: Ida B. Wells, founder of the Alpha Suffrage Club Image original by Mary Garrity c. 1893 restored by Adam Cuerden based on image originally from NAEMVZELXQVsiw at Google Arts & Culture. Image public domain.

An American investigative journalist, educator, and early leader in the civil rights movement, Ida Bell Wells-Barnett was one of the founders of the NAACP. She spent her lifetime combatting racism, toiling for African American equality, and battling for equal opportunities for women. She was instrumental in founding several women's social clubs campaigning for prominent issues for African Americans of the day.

She endangered her life daily to write investigative articles detailing the evils of lynching after the lynching of a close friend named Thomas Henry Moss and two of his employees William Stewart and Calvin R. McDowell in 1892. Their lynching came to be known as "The lynching at the curve in Memphis" and occurred because a white store owner (Barrett) was angry with the direct competition his store faced (Barrett's Grocery) when Moss opened his store across the street (People's Grocery). They were hung by a mob of 75 angry white men instigated by Barrett. Just before he was killed Moss said to the mob: "Tell my people to go west, there is no justice here." (Giddings)

These events caused Wells to become incredibly focused and active in anti-lynching campaigns where she used her writing talents to speak out in activism. Her lectures were fierce and in demand worldwide. She was invited to speak in England, Scotland, and Wales where her speeches eventually caused boycotts of southern plantations by European textiles traders, until plantation owners publicly came out against lynchings.

Her Free Speech newspaper was destroyed by a white mob in 1892 causing her to flee Birmingham not to return for twenty years. She had been pressing the issue that white men were using lynching to stop Black men from competing with them in business, rather than for actually attacking and raping white women, or for committing murders as many of them had been charged before they were lynched. White newspaper publishers were so angry they demanded that she be punished and had she not been on vacation in the Hamptons when her newspaper was burned—she would have almost certainly been murdered or lynched.

Wells took up residence in Chicago in the late 19th century and became regularly active in the national Women's club movement. In 1893, she organized the Women's Era Club. In 1896, she took part in the meeting in Washington, D.C., which founded the National Association of Colored Women's Clubs. She fought against school segregation in Chicago and for women's suffrage. She started the Alpha Suffrage Club focusing on obtaining the right for women, especially Black women to vote.

Wells was not always well-liked by the Black academia or intelligentsia of the day even with all her success. Being a woman hampered her even among her own male contemporaries who were fighting the same battles she was. She was often seen as too radical. For example, there are differing accounts of why Wells' name was excluded from the original list of founders of the NAACP. In his autobiography Dusk of Dawn, W.E.B. Du Bois implied that Wells chose not to be included. However, in her autobiography, Wells stated that Du Bois deliberately excluded her from the list (Wiipedia Giddings Sword Amon Lions). Wells simply became too controversial a figure among local and national women's clubs despite her pioneering the movement. This was evident in 1899 when the National Association of Colored Women's Clubs intended to meet in Chicago. Writing to the president of the association, Mary Terrel, Chicago organizers of the event stated that they would not cooperate in the meeting if it included Wells. When Wells learned that Terrell had agreed to exclude her, she called it "a staggering blow." (Wiipedia Giddings Sword Amon Lions)

History has given her the everlasting final say, however, as it has recorded her great contributions and recognized her for them. She was even inducted into the National Women's Hall of Fame in 1988, and the Chicago Women's Hall of Fame in that same year.

Ida B. Wells died of kidney disease on March 25, 1931.

Appendix C:
Alabama Colored Women's Clubs

Alabama's Colored Women's Club refers to any member of the Alabama Federation of Colored Women's Club, including the Ten Times One is Ten Club, the Tuskegee Women's Club, and the Anna M. Duncan Club of Montgomery. These earliest clubs united and created the Alabama Federation of Colored Women's Club in 1899. By 1904, there were more than 26 clubs throughout Alabama. The most active ones were in Birmingham, Selma, Mobile, Tuskegee, Tuscaloosa, Eufaula, Greensboro, and Mt. Megis (Wikipedia.Org).

The first African American women's club in Alabama, the Ten Times One is Ten Club, was established in Montgomery, Alabama in 1888 (Perry 211-212) (Bush). Laura Coleman, the founder, wanted to create a club to both improve the lives of the members and the community (Bush). It was followed by the Anna M. Duncan Club of Montgomery, established in 1897 (Bush). Duncan funded the educational and civic club and during her lifetime it was known as the Twentieth Century Club (Bush). The Duncan Club would continue its tradition of social service to the community into the twenty-first century (Bush).

Under the leadership of Margaret Murray Washington, the Tuskegee Women's Club was formed by female faculty and the wives of male faculty members of the Tuskegee Institute (Thomas). Thirteen women attended the first meeting of the club in 1895, which was meant to enlighten the members in both intellectual and moral ways (Thomas). Meetings were held twice a month and new teachers were encouraged to join (Thomas). Since the members were part of the academic arena, the services were related to learning and education. The Tuskegee Women's Club also helped to form new communities and construct social services (Thomas). One of its pioneer actions was to provide educational and social services to the poor inhabitants of plantation settlements (Thomas).

Appendix D:
Margaret James Murry Washington

Figure 8: Margaret James Murry Washington 1915 Image public domain.

Margaret Murray Washington (March 9, 1865 - June 4, 1925) was an American educator who was the principal of the Tuskegee Normal and Industrial Institute, which later became Tuskegee University. She was the third wife of Booker T. Washington and was inducted into the Alabama Women's Hall of Fame in 1972 (Alabama Women's Hall of Fame State of Alabama).

In 1890, Murray was hired as Lady Principal of Tuskegee Institute. In this role, she was responsible for supervising women students and supporting women on Tuskegee's faculty. She established the women's division curriculum for the lower and post-graduate division in sewing, laundering, millinery, soap-making, table-setting, cooking, and broom-making (Wikipedia.org) (Perkins).

In 1895 a large group of Black women formed the National Federation of Afro-American Women to which Margaret Murray was elected the president (Wikipedia.org).This organization did an array of jobs from helping women in the south that were trying to buy a house to opening day care giving women an opportunity to go to work. The union of the NFAA and the Washington Colored League formed the National Federation of Afro-American Women. Washington was a firm believer that many racial issues could be fixed through interracial cooperation. She believed that not everyone was out to harm people of color.

Black Women Rising to Power

The Washingtons gave twin lectures at Old Bethel A.M.E. Church in Charleston, South Carolina on September 12, 1898. Booker T. Washington addressed audiences in the morning and evening. Margaret Washington spoke to African American women in the church that afternoon. She used the occasion to describe the disproportionate infant mortality, the problem of unwanted pregnancy and the high death rate among African Americans. She also called on the largely middle-class women in her audience to engage in "moral uplift" and community service to address these problems. Her speech appears below:

> *"I want to say in the beginning that I do not come before you to criticize or find fault especially, but you know that a great deal of harm has been done us as a race by those who have told us of our strong points,*

of our wonderful advancement, and have neglected to tell us at the same time of our weak points, of our lack of taking hold of the opportunities about us. Praise a child always and he soon gets to the point where he thinks it impossible for him to make mistakes. If we wish to help each other let us not only praise ourselves, but also criticize.

Plain talk will not hurt us. It will lead each woman to study her own condition, that of her own family and so that of her neighbor's family. If I can do anything to hasten this study, I shall feel repaid for any effort I may put forth. In consenting to come before you women today I am influenced by this thought more than anything else: We need, as a race, a good, strong public sentiment in favor of a sounder, healthier body, and a cleaner and higher-toned morality. There is no use arguing; we do not think enough of these two conditions; we are too indifferent; too ready to say: 'O, well, I keep well, my girls and boys behave themselves, and I have nothing to do with the rest of the race!'

No nation or race has ever come up by entirely overlooking its members who are less fortunate, less ambitious, less sound in body and hence in soul, and we cannot do it. We must not do it. There are too many of us down. The condition of our race, brought about by slavery, the ignorance, poverty, intemperance, ought to make us women know that in half a century we cannot afford to lose sight of the large majority of the race who have not, as yet, thrown off the badge of the evils which I have just mentioned.

You are not, I know, surprised to hear me say that the women, young and older, among us, who most need to take caution in the matter of health and character, are the last to take any personal hold. It is no longer a compliment to a girl or woman to be of a frail and delicate mold. It is no longer an indication of refinement in woman to possess a weak and fastidious stomach. It was the great French Emperor who declared that the greatest need of France was mothers. And today all who are willing to study facts with reference to our growth and strength in this country declare also that the most serious drawback to the race is its lack of a careful, moral, and healthy motherhood. You have already noticed that I speak of health, then morals; morals, then health; my sisters, these two things go hand in hand, they are interdependent. They must go thus. They must be studied together at this time. They must be corrected at the same time.

To be a stronger race physically we have got to be a more moral one. We do not want to lose our tempers when we discuss these conditions either. Now that, as women, we may be able to make a move in the direction of improving the race, we have got to take certain facts regarding our health and morals. They are not all from the standpoint of the Southern white man, either, nor are they all from the Northern white man with a Southern soul. You know that we often feel that every white man and woman south of the Mason and Dixon line is a real devil. It is pretty bad down here, I will admit, but there are many very fine and noble Southern white people, women as well as men. It is a Southern man, an Alabama man, at that, who, in part at least, makes it possible for us to be here together today to study our own shortcomings and to try to find a way out of them. I say it is not Southern whites alone who have felt that we should make a move upward, who feel that we are weak in these directions; nor is it the white man alone at all, but our own medical men, our own educators, who also feel and know that there is too great a laxity amongst us.

It is not an easy thing to secure accurate data with reference to the race in these particulars, for, in making up the statistics, especially in Southern localities, the health boards have entirely ignored us; of course, many places in the South have had health boards only recently. However, we have evidence sufficient on each of these subjects to condemn us, to make us feel that something must be done; that some step, and that quick, must be made to stay the awful death rate and the alarmingly increasing illegitimate birth rate among our women and girls. This may not apply to a single woman under the sound of my voice, but it does apply to the race, and so far, it comes home to you and to me. We cannot separate ourselves from our people, no matter how much we try; for one, I have no desire to do so.

I do not mean to tell you, or leave the impression, that all of the disease and immorality in the race are confined to what we are pleased to call our poorer classes or second-class folks. There is too much in our higher classes, especially in the case of too many men who as fathers of the girls and boys who, in their turn, will be fathers and mothers of other girls and boys. And does hereditary influence count for nothing? Study your own family as far back as your great grandparents and you will agree with me when I say hereditary influence is a mighty power in the formation of character, physical, as well as moral.

I give you now these facts for five of our large Southern cities: these relate especially to the death rate of colored people in excess of white people: Rate per thousand in city No. 1, colored 36, white 19; city No. 2, colored 36, white 22; city No. 3, colored 37, white 22; city No. 4, colored 32, white 18; city No. 5, colored 35, white 17. This gives us a decrease in race by death rate in these five cities, in excess of the white people, who already so far outnumber us, respectively 100, of a fraction, 68 and over, 77 and over, and 106 per cent. In one of the large Western cities, and this is not Chicago, either the death rate of colored people is more than twice that of the white people. Pneumonia and consumption are our most deadly foes. They are not standing still but are on the increase in every city I have mentioned. In one Northern city alone, in one year, out of ten thousand, there was an excess of deaths, caused by pneumonia and consumption, of 135 percent of colored people over whites; colored dying, 225, and whites, 126.

The death rate of our children is something to make us tremble. As long as it is so high, we cannot hope for much. Numbers count for a great deal in this country. For five years, in one of our largest Southern cities alone, the excess in death rate among colored children under 5 years of age was 163 per cent, while that of the whites was only 32 per cent and a fraction over. In another large Southern city, the death rate per cent in excess for colored children over whites is 883.4 per cent. The diseases which are undermining the life of our babies and robbing the race of its future men and women are, cholera infantum, convulsions and still born. There is an excess in this last disease, still born, of colored infants over white of 149 per cent per thousand. What a terrible tribute to our womanhood and to our motherhood this is. In another Southern city, not a thousand miles from here, over half the colored children die before they are 12 months old.

We are very often inclined to treat this subject lightly by saying that we are a great reducing race, but I have no patience with this indifference, for it is simply impossible for any race to balance any such loss at this. And now, more than this, women, we are not so productive as we used to be. I do not know why I wish I did. I would count no sacrifice too great to bring about a change in this respect. My grandmother had thirteen sons and daughters, every one of whom lived to rear large families. My mother had ten, most of whom have lived long enough, but they have no children. In the whole ten of us, all grown, there are only two children, and they are the children of the youngest girl, who is now 27 years of age, and there has never been more than these, and what is worse, there never will be. Study this race question, this phase of it, and you will find what I say to be true.

We have got to change this state of things. Our educated women will not or do not become mothers and our less intelligent mothers let their little ones die, and thus our numbers are each year growing less and less. In every city in the country where you observe it you find that we are losing by death more than we are gaining by birth. Immorality, as well as poverty and ignorance, bears its share of the blame for this low state of vitality. It makes us susceptible to all forms of disease and death. We must have a cleaner 'social morality.' A man who has given thought to the moral life of the race claims that over 25 per cent of the colored children born in one city alone are admittedly illegitimate. In a certain locality, in a certain State, another man states that there were during one year 300 marriage licenses taken out by white men. According to the population 1,200 licenses should have been bought by colored men. How many do you suppose were in reality taken out? Twelve hundred should have been secured and only 3 per cent were taken out. Twelve hundred colored men and women, for whom there is no excuse, living immoral lives, handing down to their offspring disease and crime, and only three living in such a way as to advance the race. No spectacle can be more appalling.

In a certain Northern city only 2 per cent of the people are colored, yet we furnish 16 per cent of male prisoners and 34 per cent [of] female criminals. In another Northern or Northwestern city, we make up 1 1/3 per cent of the whole city, and yet 10 per cent of the arrests fall on us. Immorality is directly responsible for these crimes, and hence punishment.

Immorality is also directly responsible for physical inability to resist crime.

Go North or South, East, or West, and the numbers of the dens of abandoned women, of profligate men is too large. These are the breeders of disease and the millstone of the race. You say there are causes for all these, causes for which we are not responsible. I admit this much, but there are also causes for which we are responsible. And the fact that there are causes ought to make us hopeful, because we have it in our power to remove these causes. It will take time, however, and it will take wise and consecrated women to effect a change along these lines. Not only are poverty, ignorance, and intemperance the cause[s] of all this misery, but downright negligence, too, plays a large part in these matters. Colored men drive, cut wood, unload ships, etc., all day in the pouring rain, at night they throw themselves onto a bed and sleep without removing their wet clothes. Our women are little or no better. What is a better feeder for pneumonia and all forms of tuberculosis? The men clean streets, sweep and dust great buildings, with no effort to keep the throat clear of dust and dirt.

The majority of cases of consumption are not inherent but are contracted through lack of thought and interest in one's own self. How many of our women during their pregnancy make nothing of lifting from one bench to another heavy tubs of clothes, drawing buckets of water, lift great sticks of wood, run up and down stairs, and a dozen other similar things entirely against them. They do not know the laws of health, and they will not learn them. No, I do not say do not work during the months of unborn motherhood; work, even hard work, is good for one, but the manner in which labor is performed is what I criticize. As women can we not do something to correct our condition physically and morally? I think we can.

The average-colored person dislikes water, and he won't keep himself clean. He bathes, if at all, once a week [on] Saturday night and changes his clothes in the same indifferent way. He seldom uses a toothbrush. He often even neglects to comb his hair, except on Sunday. There is no excuse for this. Bathe at least twice a week, and change the clothes as often, and be sure to clean the teeth at least once a day, and do not forget to comb the hair each day.

We eat too little or too poor food. We are ready to buy showy clothing, but we stint our stomachs too often. They call us great eaters. Let us eat more and better food. There is very little vitality in grits and gravy. Get fresh women, but to their offspring. Keep regular hours. Do not stay in church till 12 and 1 o'clock at night. Go to bed at 10, especially if you labor through the day. When you get up in the mornings air the bedding, open up things for a while and let the sunshine in. When the little child comes, do not have an ignorant granny, secure a good physician in addition to at least a clean nurse. Apply your lessons of bathing, feeding, sleeping to these little ones, remembering, of course, their age. Teach the boys as well as the girls respect for the marriage tie and home.

Be companions for your sons and daughters if you would stop the tide of immorality. A young girl has no business out to a party or church or picnic without some older member of her family or woman friend. Teach the boys to come home at night. Teach them the sin of ruining some man's daughter. These lessons can be taught around the fireside at night, from the pulpit, in the school room, in mothers' meetings; and there should be a mothers' meeting in every community. They can be instilled in many ways. Help secure a minister and teacher who will take an interest in the physical and moral improvement of our families, and together with what we women can do and our ministers and teachers, we shall be able to make some progress in the coming ten or fifteen years which will prove to our enemies that our condition physically and morally is nothing inherent or peculiar to race, but rather the outcome of circumstances over which we can and will become masters. In this way and only in this way will [we] satisfy the men and women, both North and South, who still have faith in us. Let us teach our boys and girls some useful occupations, let us insist upon an intelligent and moral ministry, let us employ teachers only who are above reproach, and above all let those of us who have had an opportunity, who have educational advantages, modify our cause lines stoop down now and then and lift up others (BlackPast) (Courier).

Activist for Anti-lynching

- In 1920 a National Association of Colored Women Conference was held in Tuskegee, Alabama. The main topic on the agenda was lynching. Many of the recently founded anti-lynching organizations in attendance expressed their support in a bill that defined lynching as an act of "murder", and that the killer had to suffer repercussions for their actions. Two important white women in attendance, Carrie Parks Johnson, and Sara Estelle Haskins, from the Southern Methodist Women's Committee, were invited to Washington's home. Both women were surprised at the huge number of highly educated Black middle-class women there (Wikipedia.org) (Jacqueline)

Appendix E:
Association of Deans of Women and Advisers to Girls in Negro Schools

Figure 9: Lucy Diggs Slowe founder Alpha Kappa Alpha. Image public domain.

Lucy Diggs Slowe (July 4, 1885 – October 21, 1937) was an American educator, athlete, and first Black woman to serve as Dean of Women at any American university. She was a founder of Alpha Kappa Alpha sorority, the first sorority founded by African American women.

Slowe was also a tennis champion, winning the national title of the American Tennis Association's first tournament in 1917, the first African American woman to win a major sports title (Wikipedia-Slowe). In 1922, Slowe was appointed as the first Dean of Women at Howard University where she continued for 15 years until her death in 1937. In addition, Slowe created and led two professional associations to support college administrators.

Established in 1929, the Association of Deans of Women and Advisers to Girls in Negro Schools (NAWDACS) was an advocacy group for Black women within colleges and universities in the United States, lasted for twenty-five years until 1954, when it merged with the National Association of Personnel Deans and Advisers of Men in Negro Institutions (Hilda A Davis, Brown and Terborg-Penn).

Through this organization, Lucy Slowe identified five problems that needed to be addressed:

1. Black women were under-represented on trustee boards and college administrations.
2. Properly qualified and salaried deans and advisers to girls were needed.
3. Female college students needed adequately equipped housing.
4. Female students needed properly planned extracurricular activity.

Girls attending high school on college campuses needed separate housing and treatment.

Appendix F: California State Federation of Colored Women's Clubs

Figure 10: California State Federation of Colored Women's Clubs. Image by Unknown author, public domain

The California State Federation of Colored Women's Clubs Inc. (CSACWC) was formed in 1906 by Mrs. Eliza Warner. In adherence to its motto *"Deeds Not Words,"* the club served to improve the welfare of African Americans and of providing service to the African American community. The CSACWC developed different areas of service, including International Peace and World Affairs, Forestry, and Prison & Parole. The CSACWC also created district associations to oversee the local associates, for example the Northern District included the clubs in the Bay Area of California. In 1908 the club joined the **National Association of Colored Women's Clubs (NACWC)** (Oakland Wiki, LocalWiki Contributors) (Vick).

Appendix G:
Joesphine Silone Yates

Figure 11: Joesphine Silone Yates November 15, 1859 - September 3, 1912. Image public domain.

Josephine Silone Yates (November 15, 1859 – September 3, 1912) was a professor, writer, public speaker, and activist. She trained in chemistry and became one of the first Black professors hired at Lincoln University in Jefferson City, Missouri. Upon her promotion, she became the first Black woman to head a college science department and may have been the first Black woman to hold a full professorship at any U.S. college or university. Yates also made significant contributions to journalism (sometimes under the pseudonym Mrs. R. K. Potter) and the overall social mobility of Black women. For example, she was a correspondent for the Woman's Era (the first monthly magazine published by Black women in the United States). She wrote for other newspapers and magazines including Omaha, Nebraska's Enterprise. Yates was a major figure in the African American women's club movement and was instrumental in establishing women's clubs for African Americans.

In 1852, at 11 she moved from her birthplace, Mattituck on Long Island, New York to Philadelphia, Pennsylvania to live with her Uncle Rev. J.B. Reeve, in hopes of finding greater educational opportunities. While in Philadelphia, she attended the Institute of Colored Youth run by Fannie Jackson Coppin. She was the only African American student in her class and first to graduate from Roger's High School in Newport, Rhode Island—as class valedictorian. She went on to attend the Rhode Island Normal School and again was the only African American student to graduate.

Yates was involved in clubs and organizations that fought for racial and social change. She helped to organize the Kansas City Women's League and was its first president in 1893. After the NACW was established in 1896, she became one of its most dedicated supporters, serving as treasurer from 1897 to 1901 and president from 1901 to 1905.

Appendix H:
Georgia Mabel DeBaptiste

Figure 12: Georgia Mabel DeBaptiste. Image public domain.

Georgia Mabel DeBaptiste (November 24, 1867 – April 20, 1951) was a journalist, teacher, and social worker from Chicago. After completing her education, she taught at various notable Black schools before becoming the first woman of African descent to be employed at the Chicago Post Office.

Born in Chicago, Georgia was the youngest child and only daughter of Georgianna Brischo and Richard H. DeBaptiste. Her mother died when she was six, leaving her to be raised by her father, a noted writer and preacher. Following her family's move to Evanston, DeBaptiste began writing for The Baptist Herald, The Baptist Headlight, The African Mission, and a regular contributor to Our Women and Children.

DeBaptiste's career in education began as a personal assistant to William J. Simmons at the State University in Louisville, Kentucky, after which went on to teach music at universities in Alabama and Missouri. She eventually returned to Chicago, where she worked as the first African American woman clerk of the Chicago Post Office.

In 1902, DeBaptiste and her husband, Dr. Henry Clay Faulkner, were sent to Liberia by the Baptist Foreign Missions Board, where DeBaptiste worked as an instructor at Liberia College. Following the death of her husband in 1907, DeBaptiste returned to the United States with her son, Frederick Faulkner, in 1908, moving in with her brother in Brooklyn, New York where she continued her work in the settlement house, music and lecturing. With her marriage to Walter R. Ashburn in 1915, she relocated to Virginia, but returned to Chicago in 1917 following their separation. In 1917, DeBaptiste was elected as the Women's Auxiliary president, and she served as a social worker and organizer in the Butler Community and served as superintendent of the Home for Business and Working Young. She supervised the Youth Conservation Council and the School's education department, was very active in clubs and organizations, and was president of the District Teacher's Association of Chicago and the Mother's Union. She was involved with the NAACP, the Urban League, the YWCA, and the World's Fellowship of Faiths, as well as serving as president of the exclusive Old Settler's Club.

Appendix I:
Benefit Societies

Black women founded mutual benefit societies, settlement houses, and schools. Some Black female workers, particularly laundresses in the South, made efforts to unionize and undertook strikes. Black women in the North also worked to provide services for Black women recently arrived from the South. The National League for the Protection of Colored Women, which later merged with other organizations to form the National Urban League, and "colored chapters" of the YWCA offered services to female migrants. Black women were involved in the formation of the National Association for the Advancement of Colored People (NAACP) and performed much of the local work.

Notable Black women reformers include Mary McLeod Bethune, who founded the National Council of Negro Women, the Southeastern Federation of Colored Women's Clubs, and the Bethune-Cookman Institute; Nannie Helen Burroughs, who founded the National Training School for Women and Girls in Washington, DC; and Maggie Lena Walker, the first American woman bank president, who was also head of one of the largest and most successful Black mutual benefit societies.

Figure 13: 5 female Negro officers of Women's League, Newport, R.I. Reportedly displayed as part of the American Negro exhibit at the Paris Exposition of 1900. Image public domain.

Figure 14: Eartha White (center, first row) is pictured with delegates at the State Meeting of the City Federation of Colored Women's Clubs of Jacksonville, at Palatka, Florida – May 16, 1915. Image public domain.

Figure 15: First Convention of the Montana Federation of Negro Women's Clubs, Butte, Montana, August 3, 1921, Image by Zubick Art Studio public domain.

Figure 16: Delegates representing South Carolina women's clubs in Detroit in 1958. Image by South Carolina Federation of Colored Women. Image public domain.

Figure 17: Phyllis Wheatly Club of Buffalo, New York 1905. Image public domain.

Figure 18: Mary Church Terrell Image credit Library of Congress. Image public domain.

Appendix J:
4 African American Women's Clubs That Helped Write History

"When the history of the nineteenth century comes to be written, women will appear as organizers, and leaders of great organized movements among their own sex for the first time in the history of the world," Great words written by journalist Jane Cunningham Croly in her book *"The History of the Women's Club Movement in America"* circa-1898. But Croly was referring to the white woman's club movement and their rapid expansion at the time, the emerging African American woman's club movement would offer testament that African American women would achieve remarkable success for their race through women's clubs as well (https://savingplaces.org/stories/4-african-american-womens-clubs-that-helped-write-history).

Throughout the 1890s, Ida B. Wells traversed the United States speaking out against lynching and in many cases, establishing the first African American women's clubs in some of the cities she visited. Following her lead, Black women across the United States started building local clubs of their own, creating what became a national movement. These women's clubs sought to secure women's suffrage, empower women in their communities, and combat racism, which was a key impediment given the days of Jim Crow laws. Many clubs joined together in 1896 to create the National Association of Colored Women's Clubs (NACWC), the oldest secular African American organization still in existence.

Not all clubs targeted the same issues. Some, like Los Angeles' Wilfandel Club, provided a space for female Black community members to gather and celebrate , while others chose to champion specific issues, such as improving methods of waste disposal. Here are four more African American women's clubs that helped write the history books:

1. Phyllis Wheatley YWCA—Washington, D.C.

Figure 19: Phylis Wheatly YWCA By APK - Own work, CC BY-SA 3.0. Image public domain.

The oldest YWCA (Young Women's Christian Association) building in the nation's capital sits just a few blocks south of Howard University. Washington's chapter of the YWCA was organized in 1905 by several African American women who shared membership in a booklover's club. They held their first meetings in the old Miner Institution Building before their present Colonial Revival-style headquarters could be constructed in 1920, financed in part with funds appropriated by the national YWCA's War Work Council.

Since then, the chapter has been a powerful, positive force in the city despite receiving much less financial support from its parent organization in its earliest years than white

YWCAs. Its members provided shelter and food for African American women newly arrived in Washington from the South seeking employment. In 1923, it protested a U.S. Senate-approved statue that would have glorified the "Mammy" caricature of enslaved African Americans and helped prevent its construction. Later, it functioned as a recreational and entertainment space during World War II for African American soldiers barred from entering United Service Organizations locations.

2. Fanny Jackson Coppin Club—Oakland, California

Figure 20: Fannie Jackson by Unknown author - Fanny Jackson Coppin, Reminiscences of School Life, and Hints on Teaching. Image public domain.

Named in honor of the first African American woman to become a school principal, the Fanny Jackson Coppin Club was founded in 1899 by members of the Beth Eden Baptist Church. Its priority was to provide African American travelers who could not stay at segregated hotels welcoming places to spend a night (a kindred spirit with Victor Hugo Green, author of the Negro Motorist Green Book which included 60 YWCA's). But in keeping with its motto— "Not failure, but low aim is the crime"—and its namesake's impact as an educator, the club introduced services that benefitted more members of the community, such as tutoring for students and musical performances featuring artists like world-renowned tenor Roland Hayes.

Figure 21: Beth Eden Baptist Church, the oldest African American religious establishment in Oakland, established 1889. Image public domain.

As author and academic historian Shirley Ann Wilson Moore writes, the club was "part of the ongoing African American struggle to address an array of social and economic community needs and to challenge the barriers of segregation and sexism." It helped spur the development of African American women's clubs across California in the ensuing years and remains an influential local organization today.

Figure 22: Fannie Jackson Coppin Club. Image public domain.

3. Detroit Study Club—Detroit

The Detroit Study Club began modestly in 1898, when six learned African American women gathered at the home of music teacher Gabrielle Pelham to read works by British poet Robert Browning and further educate themselves on cultural and social issues of the time. These friends were Fannie Anderson, Sarah Warsaw, J. Pauline Smith, Mrs. Wil Anderson, and Mrs. Tomlison. Pauline Smith served as the club's first President (Miles). Upon their meeting, the new association that would later be called The Detroit Study Club was born. Soon the scope of the club's meetings expanded, and not just in terms of its reading list.

Together, the members of the Detroit Study Club created an organization motivated by a desire for self-betterment and to improve their community. They engaged nationally prominent speakers and brought some of them to Detroit to share their thoughts on how African American interests could best be advanced. This included Booker T. Washington, perhaps the country's most significant African American leader at the time, whose speaking engagement drew 22 other women's organizations to attend. Detroit Study Club members also helped fund the educations of underprivileged youth, created the Phyllis Wheatley Home for Aged Colored Ladies (unrelated to the Phyllis Wheatley YWCA), and worked to preserve Frederick Douglass' home and estate—now the Frederick Douglass National Historic Site.

Club members of the 1890s were well educated and economically privileged women whose families had often been generations removed from slavery. The families of founding members were intimately tied to the Black Underground Railroad activist network and the later Black professional class of Detroit, both as wives and children of prominent men, and more rarely, as professionals in their own right. Descendants of Asher and Catherine Aray, such as their granddaughter, Mrs. John A. Loomis, and descendants of William Ferguson, continue to serve as officeholders and active members in the Detroit Study Club in the present day (https://tiyamiles.com/detroit-study-club/) (Miles).

As Midwest members of a nation-wide Black women's club movement, the Detroit Study Club women had interest not only in matching the cultured refinement of white women in the city, but also in furthering the progress of the Black race. They sought to do the latter by hosting influential thinkers and reformers working toward racial uplift. On Thursday, April 14th, 1910, the club hosted a "Celebration of Reciprocity Day" tea in honor of the towering African American educator and orator, Booker T. Washington. Washington was to lecture and then respond to questions, promoting general conversation among attendees. Twenty-seven women's clubs and organizations in the state were invited to the formal event and twenty-two happily accepted. Washington's commitment to Black education dovetailed with the primary focus of the Detroit Study Club, and their interest in hearing from him reflects a support of his views shared by many Black club women around the country. Proceeds from the event went toward the education of underprivileged students to increase their opportunities to attend and succeed in school (tiyamiles.com/Detroit-study-club/) (Miles).

4. The Grand Old Lady—Washington, D.C. Image public domain.

As the first permanent headquarters of the NACWC, the five-story "Grand Old Lady" is both a guardian of the past and a steward of the future for a storied organization. It was constructed in 1910 and served the Knights of Columbus before the NACWC's purchase in 1954. Today it houses records, artifacts, and more that document the NACWC's history since its establishment in 1896, while also maintaining its use as administrative offices and meeting spaces.

◊◊◊

The Social Clubs Bible
Appendix K: Biker Set Readiness Test

You should have a firm knowledge of the MC Biker Set. Test your knowledge with the following test. This test is by no means all-inclusive, but you can use it as a guide to begin your research:

1. In what city, state, and year was your SC founded?
2. In what neighborhood was your SC founded?
3. How many members comprised the founding mothers of your SC?
4. What were the names and occupations of the founding mothers of your SC?
5. What is the motto of your SC and what does it mean?
6. What is the birthday celebration of your SC?
7. What is the mascot of your SC?
8. Describe your SC's colors and explain the meanings, origins, and symbols of all the elements of the patch.
9. What was the name of the first sister killed on a motorcycle in your SC? What year did she die, and how was she killed?
10. What is the history of the first split in your SC and what happened to the members who split off?
11. How many years must you be in the SC before you are authorized to wear the SC's medallion or ring?
12. What are the names of the Presidents of all the chapters within your SC?
13. When did the President of your local chapter join your SC? What are the telephone numbers and contact names for all of the chapters within your SC?
14. How often are club meetings generally held throughout your SC and when?
15. How many members are necessary to hold a quorum in your SC?
16. What is the order procedure for how church is conducted in your SC?

17. What are the real names, phone numbers, email addresses and emergency contact numbers for every member in your chapter?
18. What are the steps to becoming a Prospect in your SC?
19. Who can be a Prospect sponsor within your SC?
20. What are a sponsor's responsibilities?
21. When does a chapter President vote on a motion?
22. What are the main responsibilities of the Road Captain in your SC?
23. What is the responsibility of a Road Captain in an MC?
24. What are all the award patches you can earn in your SC?
25. If an SC member suspects that a brother is too drunk to ride what is her obligation to that drunken member according to your SC's bylaws or policies?
26. What is the SC's procedure for one member borrowing money from another member?
27. What is the procedure for solving a physical altercation between two members in your SC?
28. What member of your SC is allowed to physically strike another other member?
29. What members can actually fine other members?
30. What members can actually fine the chapter President?
31. Under what specific circumstances may your colors be taken from you for an infraction against the bylaws?
32. If a president requests your colors what must be done before the president can keep your colors forever?
33. Who comprises your SC's governing Council?
34. What can your significant other wear to support the SC?
35. What is the status of men associated with your SC?
36. Does your SC have a First Sir/Man that is the spouse of the President?
37. What is the definition of a member in good standing?
38. What are the main responsibilities of a Prospect?
39. What are the basic rules of conduct for a Prospect?

40. Where are required patches to be worn on the vest of a Prospect and full patched sisters?
41. What is the quickest way to tell if you are dealing with a 1% outlaw MC Nation member if you greet him face to face and have not seen the back of his vest?
42. How can you distinguish outlaw colors from the back?
43. What is the definition of an Outlaw MC?
44. What is a 99%er MC?
45. What is a 1% MC?
46. Is there a difference between an outlaw MC and a 1% MC and if so, what is that difference?
47. Where did the term 1% come from?
48. What is the philosophical definition that sets 1% MCs apart from traditional MCs?
49. Who was the first sister to lose her life in the SC?
50. What criminal or civil actions, if any, have been brought against your SC by city, local, or national law enforcement agencies in an attempt to shut down, prosecute, and/or fine your SC during its history, and what were the outcomes of those charges?
51. To whom do the colors, insignia, designs, patches, logos, and other paraphernalia of your SC belong?
52. What is a club flip or patchover in the MC world?
53. Does your SC wear support patches for a 1% MC Nation? If so, which one?
54. If your SC wears a support patch for a 1% MC Nation, who are their enemies?
55. If your SC wears support patches what areas of town, cities, or states is it unsafe for you to go in your colors without being in the company of your brothers?
56. Why is it important to always remember that you are representing every SC member when you are operating out in public?
57. What is your SC's consequence to you if you rip your patch

off of your vest disrespectfully?
58. What is the consequence for striking another sister of your SC?
59. What are the consequences for stealing from your SC?
60. What are the consequences for discussing SC business outside of the SC?
61. What are the consequences for posting SC business on social media?
62. What are the consequences for cyber-banging on social media?
63. What are the consequences for losing your colors?
64. What are the consequences for disrespecting your colors?
65. Should your colors ever touch the ground?
66. Should you ever let anyone outside of your SC hold your colors?
67. What is another term for the vest used to hold your colors?
68. What does the term backyard mean?
69. What is the 80/20 rule in the MC world?
70. What is the AMA?
71. What is ABATE?
72. What are broken wings?
73. Why is it against protocol to show out at an MC's clubhouse?
74. What is a cage?
75. What does attending church mean in the MC world?
76. What does the term "Club Hopping" mean?
77. If your President wants to Prospect a hang-around who was first a member of another SC, what is the proper protocol to accomplish this?
78. What is the proper hand signal flashed to the pack when a cop/highway patrol vehicle is spotted?
79. What is the proper hand signal flashed to the pack when debris is in the road on the left side of the bike?
80. What is the proper foot signal flashed to the pack when

debris is in the road on the right side of the bike?
81. What is the proper hand signal flashed when the Road Captain wants the pack to assume a single file formation?
82. What is the proper hand signal flashed when the Road Captain wants the pack to assume a staggered formation?
83. What is the proper hand signal flashed when the Road Captain wants the pack to assume the suicide (two abreast) formation?
84. When the Road Captain lifts his hand up to indicate a left or right turn what does the rest of the pack do?
85. What is the proper hand signal flashed when the Road Captain wants the pack to slow down?
86. What is the proper hand signal flashed when the Road Captain wants the pack to continue while he drops out of the pack to view it for safety?
87. What is the proper hand signal flashed when the Road Captain wishes to change places with the Assistant Road Captain in the back of the pack?
88. What is the best way for a motorcycle to cross railroad tracks in an intersection?
89. During a rainstorm when is the road the slickest for a motorcycle?
90. Why does the front brake have more braking power than the rear brake on a motorcycle?
91. According to distribution of impact locations on motorcycle helmets during collision studies conducted by Dietmar Otte, Medizinische Hochschule Hannover, and Abteilung Verkehrsunfallforschung in Germany, where are most head injuries concentrated for motorcyclists?
92. What does DOT stand for and why is it important when purchasing a motorcycle helmet?
93. What is a freedom fighter?
94. What does FTW mean?
95. What does KTRSD mean?

96. What does LE/LEO mean?
97. What is an OMC?
98. What is an OMG?
99. Are cell phones allowed in your church meetings?
100. What is the consequence for secretly taping your church meetings?
101. What is an MRO?
102. What does the term "On Ground" mean?
103. What does the term "On Two" mean?
104. What does the term "Patch Over" mean?
105. What does the term "Flipping" mean?
106. What is a PRO?
107. What is a probie?
108. What are the major differences between an RC and an MC?
109. What is the RICO act?
110. What is a rocker?
111. What is a run?
112. What is a gypsy run?
113. What is special about a mandatory run?
114. What is a tail gunner?
115. What does the diamond "13" mean?
116. What is the significance of the three-piece patch?
117. What is the significance of turning your back on another MC or patched person?
118. What does (X)FF(X) mean?
119. What does DILLIGAF mean?
120. What is a boneyard?
121. What is a 5%er?
122. What is a 3%er?
123. What is a lick and stick?
124. What does the term "Running 66" mean?
125. What is a vested pedestrian?
126. What is a hang-around?

The Social Clubs Bible

127. What is a civilian?
128. What is a "Property of"?
129. What is a House Mamma?
130. What is an ink slinger?
131. How often should the financial report be given at your SC's church?
132. Where must your SC's colors be purchased?
133. What are your rights if you ever face your SC's disciplinary committee?
134. What is necessary for you to be found guilty of a charge in your SC?
135. Who are the closest SCs to yours that can be considered to love your SC like sisters and where your SC will always have a home away from home (allies)?
136. What is a dominant MC?
137. Is there a such thing as a dominant SC?
138. It is possible for someone to Prospect for an MC without owning a motorcycle?
139. If you don't like the direction the pack is going you can simply leave the pack, take a shortcut, and catch up to the pack later? Y/N
140. Folks can join your SC without prospecting? T/F
141. It is okay for a brother in an MC to pop a wheelie in the pack? T/F
142. It is okay to leave a sister in trouble? T/F
143. It is okay to screw a sister's old man or husband? T/F
144. Can the Road Captain fine a member without a trial for infractions committed in the pack?
145. When can the Road Captain of an MC order a member not to ride their bike?
146. Does the Road Captain have the right to see a member's license, registration, and insurance in your SC?
147. When is it okay to give out personal information about an SC member to someone outside of the SC?

The Social Clubs Bible

148. It is okay for an MC President to attend a function thrown by your SC without being searched for a weapon if everyone else is being searched?
149. What is the ranking order for the way your SC drives in formation?
150. Who was the first Godmother of your SC, and what was her contribution to the SC?
151. Who is the Godmother of your SC today?
152. When is the Road Captain considered the President of the SC?
153. What is required to take a leave of absence from your SC?
154. When are you allowed to retire from your SC?
155. Where are standard business cards ordered for your SC?
156. How do you get a SC email address?
157. What duties must a Prospect perform daily in your SC?
158. What is the name of the most honored member within your SC?
159. Does your SC have a National President?
160. How many MCs operate in your town and what are the names of twenty-five of them?
161. What is the C.O.C.?
162. What is meant by the term "Top 5" when talking about MCs?
163. Name the OMCs in every state surrounding yours.
164. What is a support MC?
165. It is okay to walk into a MC representing your SC without wearing your colors?
166. Should you have a Set of colors with you no matter where you travel?
167. What is the mission statement of your SC Nation?
168. Does handling a problem internally within the SC relieve you of your legal responsibility to call law enforcement if you think a crime has been committed?
169. What are the rules for all members to stand duty at the

clubhouse should your SC have a clubhouse?
170. What are your SC's local website URLs?
171. What is the phone number and password used for your SC's conference calls?
172. How do you jump start a motorcycle?
173. When would you jump start a motorcycle?
174. Can you use a car to jump start a motorcycle safely?
175. How do you push start a motorcycle?
176. How do you pick up a motorcycle if it falls over?
177. Do your MC brothers ride in formation—staggered or suicide?
178. Where is lane splitting legal in the United States?
179. When encountering a tornado on the open road should you take refuge under a bridge? Why or why not? (Refer to http://www.srh.noaa.gov/oun/?n=safety-overpass, especially slide 22 – this may save your life!)
180. What should be done to avoid tornadoes in open country?
181. If on the open highway and you encounter sudden heavy fog, how should you seek to protect yourself?
182. When riding on the back of a motorcycle cross country in extreme heat (100° F or higher) degrees what is one of the greatest mechanical concerns?
183. When riding on the back of a motorcycle cross country in extreme heat (100° F or higher) degrees how can you quickly cool off if you feel overwhelmed by the heat?
184. When traveling cross country through various OMC territories what should your SC do before entering their territory in patches?
185. If riding on the back of a motorcycle cross country what auto parts store will always carry motorcycle batteries?
186. How does the AAA club motorcycle towing package' differ from your motorcycle insurance coverage towing plan?
187. When riding on the back of an MC member's bike could you be asked to remove your colors or turn them inside out, and if

so—why?

188. If your SC is national what is your local chapter's responsibility to your SC Nation?
189. If your SC chapter needs a bank account, is it okay for a member to put that account in her name alone?
190. Why do you want to be a member of your SC?
191. What do you bring to your SC?
192. What do you want from your SC?
193. What can you give to your SC?

For answers to this test send an email to blackdragon@blacksabbathmc.com. Put "SC Test Answers" in the subject. Also, in that email you can let me know how you like the book, or suggestions you may have for additional subjects, corrections, or grammar issues. Thank you.

◊◊◊

The Social Clubs Bible
Appendix L:
Brief History of the
Mighty Black Sabbath Motorcycle Club Nation

Mighty Black Sabbath Motorcycle Club Nation

The Mighty Black Sabbath Motorcycle Club Nation is a national, traditional MC whose members ride all makes of street legal motorcycles (cruisers at least 750cc and sport bikes at least 600cc). The Mighty Black Sabbath Motorcycle Club Nation does not belong to any governing organizations like the AMA. It is an independent MC nation that does not wear support patches or coalition support insignia. The Black Sabbath MC derived its name from the Original Seven African American male founders who rode on Sundays after church. When the Original Seven were looking for a name to call themselves—they said, "We are seven Black men who ride on the Sabbath after worship, so let us call ourselves Black Sabbath MC!"

Though we have been asked many times throughout the decades our founders had never heard of the band named Black Sabbath when they started the MC.

History

The Original Seven founding fathers of the Mighty Black Sabbath Motorcycle Club Nation taught themselves to ride on one Honda 305 Scrambler in the hills of a neighborhood called Mount Hope in San Diego, California in 1972. That bike, given to father 'Pep' by a close friend, was shared between them. The founding fathers mostly worked at the San Diego Gas and Electric Company or were enlisted in the US Navy, some were merchant marines. They practiced evenings and weekends on the Honda 305 Scrambler, until they eventually learned how to ride, and each eventually bought a motorcycle.

Faithfully, they gathered at each other's garages after church on Sundays to ride, tell tall tales, and drink beers. By 1974, their wives united and revolted, demanding that no more club meetings be held in their garages on Sundays because the neighbors kept complaining and the wives felt threatened by the strength of the brotherhood. Undaunted, the founding fathers rented an abandoned bar at 4280 Market Street; where they remained one of the most dominant, influential, and successful MCs on the African American Biker Set since 1974 (nearly fifty years at the time of this writing).

Founding Fathers

The seven original founding fathers were:
- First Rider: Robert D. Hubbard 'Sir Hub' (SDG&E Electrician)
- VP: William Charles Sanders 'Couchie' (SDG&E Electrician)
- Sgt-at-Arms Alvin Ray 'Stretch'
- Road Capt.: Paul Perry 'Pep' (SDG&E Meter Reader)
- Asst Road Capt.: Solomon 'Sol'
- Secretary: John Kearny 'Black'
- Clayton Mitchell "Mitch" (Designer of our colors)

The Social Clubs Bible

Note: Originally the leader of the BSMC was called "First Rider." We did not adopt the term "President" for many years later.

Racing roots

The Black Sabbath MC was not complicated in its mission during the early years. It was comprised simply of seven men who loved to ride, mostly on Sundays, who were similarly possessed with an insatiable appetite for custom building "Choppers" and unbeatable drag race bikes. This is still true today. All bike styles are welcomed, and racers are still most cherished in the Mighty Black Sabbath Motorcycle Club Nation.

Battle cry "I came to race"

The MC's battle cry was fathered by Black Sabbath MC legend-fabled racer, Allen 'Sugar Man' Brooks, who once wrecked Pep's motorcycle (early 1970's), on the way to the Salton Sea bike run/race event, without a helmet at over one hundred ten mph. Pep had warned Sugar Man that his bike was not operating properly and was excessively vibrating when it got to one hundred mph—so he told him not to exceed one hundred mph on the bike. Sugar Man still insisted that Pep let him test it. Needless to say, he exceeded one hundred mph and the bike went into a high-speed wobble. He crashed and destroyed Pep's bike. After the accident, Sugar Man was forbidden to compete as the MC deemed that he was too injured to race. The President threatened to take his colors if he attempted to compete in the drag racing the next day. Sugar Man said, "You can take these damned colors if you will, but I came to race!" Sugar Man consequently won the drag racing competition despite his injuries; thereby etching himself into the Black Sabbath MC's history books. His battle cry has been echoed by Black Sabbath racers from that time until now; "I came to race!"

San Diego Mother Chapter

The Mighty Black Sabbath Motorcycle Club Nation's mother chapter clubhouse stood at 4280 Market Street on the corner for forty-three years. During most of that time the MC reined dominant as the most successful MC in San Diego and is the oldest surviving MC on the Black biker set there. For decades, the Black Sabbath MC clubhouse was the only clubhouse on the Black biker set in the city. During that time, all San Diego and Los Angeles MCs came to San Diego to celebrate the Black Sabbath MC's yearly anniversary, which grew to be called "The First Run of the Year." Even to this day, West Coast MCs gather in San Diego for the first run which generally happens around the second or third weekend in February. These days Mighty Black Sabbath MC Nation chapters around the country send their riders on this great pilgrimage across the United States braving freezing winters to get to this annual celebration. This run was named by Black Dragon as "The Cold Ass Run to The Mother Chapter." Brothers who make this ride are awarded the Snow Bear Disciples patch.

Nationwide chapters

The Mighty Black Sabbath Motorcycle Club Nation has chapters across the United States from coast to coast. Growth was initially slow as the MC never envisioned itself a national MC from its inception in San Diego in 1974. The Black Sabbath MC is also the oldest surviving MC born in San Diego. The second charter was not given until 1989 some fifteen years after the MC started. Club racing legend, Allen 'Sugar Man' Brooks, took the colors to Wichita, Kansas where Knight Rider and Lady Magic (previously members of the Penguins MC) developed the chapter; subsequently becoming the oldest surviving MC on the Black biker set in Wichita.

In 1999, then National President Pep, launched the Denver, Colorado chapter. Not long after, he assigned veteran member, Leonard Mack, to head up the Minneapolis, Minnesota chapter. Two years later, Pep ordered Dirty Red to launch the St. Paul, Minnesota chapter. In 2004, Pep launched the Little Rock, Arkansas chapter with his nephew, Lewis 'Doc' Perry, who became the first East Coast Regional President. Once again, two years later Doc launched the Oklahoma City, Oklahoma chapter with his high school buddy, James 'JB' Baker, as President. In 2008 former mother chapter President, Dewey 'Jazz' Johnson, launched the Phoenix, Arizona chapter. By then, the Wichita, Kansas chapter was all but dead with only a few active members.

Exponential growth was not seen until 2009 when then National Enforcer John E. 'Black Dragon' Bunch II was given the mandate by Father Pep to build the club into a national powerhouse. Pep's dream, as intimated to Dragon, all the way back in 1997, was to construct a legendary national MC known worldwide for hard riding on iron that could one day become a household name. Black Dragon accepted the assignment. His first move was to convince Sugar Man to come out of retirement and together they launched the Tulsa, Oklahoma chapter. Black Dragon then rebuilt the Wichita, Kansas chapter over the next three years, but despite his best efforts it could not sustain the re-launch until Lady Magic tapped her son, 'Pull-it', and grandson, Chris 'Chill' Hill. With the addition of those two brothers the Wichita chapter again soared. Black Dragon simultaneously re-launched the Atlanta, Georgia chapter with former Oklahoma City member, Pappy, who had also grown up with Doc Perry. Later, in 2009, Black Dragon launched the Houston, Texas chapter with Bernard 'Krow' Augustus who became the first Mid-Central USA Regional President.

In 2010, the Atlanta, Georgia chapter (originally launched in 2000 by Dragon) was taken over by Black Dragon's former submarine shipmate, Leon 'Eight Ball' Richardson, who also became the second East Coast Regional President. Black Dragon became National President in 2010, and patched over the Macon, Georgia chapter under Curtis 'Ride or Die' Hill from the Zulus MC Nation under a negotiation with 'Wolverine' then the Zulu National President. 'Ride or Die' became the third East Coast Regional President and eventually rose to become the fourth National President of the Mighty Black Sabbath MC Nation. Black Dragon then patched-over Sic Wit' It MC in Rome, Georgia under President G Man to make Black Sabbath MC among the few clubs to achieve three chapters in Georgia at that time.

Sugar Man's first cousin, Jamel 'Huggy Bear' Brooks, launched the San Antonio, Texas chapter by the end of 2010, and became the first West Coast Regional President assuming command of the Phoenix, Arizona chapter later. Black Dragon instructed then National Vice President Tommy 'Hog Man' Lewis and Huggy Bear to patch over the Inland Empire, California chapter under the leadership of former Regulator MC President 'Big Dale' in 2011. Big Dale eventually became the second West Coast Regional President. In 2012, National Vice President Tommy 'Hog Man' Lewis received a blessing from the Chosen Few MC to open the Las Vegas, Nevada chapter with then West Coast Regional President Huggy Bear, but this chapter never actually materialized. In 2012, Black Dragon launched the Jacksonville, Florida chapter under President 'Prime'. In 2014, Black Dragon instructed West Coast Regional President Big Dale to patch over a former 1%er club that had been shut down due to west coast external conflicts. It launched in Riverside, California as the Riverside chapter under President Bob 'Bob O' Rinaldi. In 2015, Black Dragon opened the Hutchinson, Kansas chapter under President Dizzle. External problems with local 1%ers caused them to have to fly "West Wichita" colors for nearly three years, but eventually, through continued negotiations the Hutchinson chapter finally flew their rightful city once again. In 2015 Black Dragon launched the Colorado Springs, Colorado chapter under President 'G-Ride' which flies under the Olympic City flag today. In 2016 Black Dragon opened the Topeka, Kansas chapter under President Cliff 'Big Red Dog'. Consequently, the chapter bounced up and down for nearly four years and never fully opened until about late 2019. In 2017 Black Dragon launched the Beaufort, South Carolina chapter under President Homesick after nearly three years of negotiations with local 1%ers. In 2017 Black Dragon gave President Jason 'Ol' Skool' Monds the mandate to open the Pensacola, Florida chapter but it took until 2019 to secure all necessary agreements to bring it online. Also in 2017, after nearly four years of work Black Dragon opened the Fort Worth, Texas chapter under President Big Mixx who was the second longest prospecting member of the Mighty

Black Sabbath MC Nation. In late 2017 early 2018 Black Dragon launched the RONIN chapter of the Mighty Black Sabbath MC Nation which was the Nation's first nomad chapter. Shortly after that he stepped down from the position of National President. In 2020 Black Dragon consulted with President Big Mixx to open the West Fort Worth chapter and in 2021 Black Dragon launched the North Shore Louisiana chapter under President Cuban and the Frederick Maryland chapter under President Devil. In April 2021 Black Dragon began prospecting the Lagos Nigeria chapter, his third attempt to forge into Africa but he failed to bring it to fruition once again. Black Dragon came out of retirement in 2022 to become the fifth East Coast Regional President and began the patch-over of the Shadow Riders RC to the Columbus chapter. He also approved the introduction of the new Savannah chapter. During his retirement the Orlando (started by Hardcorps and Bones), Wisconsin (started by Loki and Goose), Kansas City (started by), and Spring Texas (started by Miles) chapters were born. Mid-central Regional President Miles also began to re-establish the Oklahoma City, Oklahoma chapter. Hail to the forefathers of the Mighty Black Sabbath Motorcycle Club Nation! We hope they are proud of what their dreams have become. Amen.

Membership

A prospective member is allowed into the Black Sabbath Motorcycle Club as a "hang-around," indicating that the individual is invited to some MC events or to meet MC members at known gathering places. This period could last several months to several years. It is the time for the hang-around to evaluate the MC, as well as for the MC to evaluate the hang-around. If the hang-around is interested, and the Black Sabbath Motorcycle Club likes the hang-around; he can request to be voted in as a Prospect. The hang-around must win a majority vote to be designated a Prospect. If he is successful, he will be given a sponsor and his prospectship begins. The prospectship will be no less than ninety days, but could last for years, depending upon the attitude and resourcefulness of the

Prospect. Former National President Black Dragon prospected for nearly five years before he crossed over. The Prospect will participate in some MC activities and serve the MC in whatever capacity the full patched brothers may deem appropriate. A Prospect will never be asked to commit any illegal act, any act against nature, or any physically humiliating or demeaning act. The Black Sabbath Motorcycle Club never hazes Prospects. A Prospect will not have voting privileges while he is evaluated for suitability as a full member but does pay MC dues.

The last phase, and highest membership status, is "Full Membership" or "Full-Patch". The term "Full-Patch" refers to the complete one-piece patch. Prospects are allowed to wear only a small thirteen-inch patch with the letters of the local chapter (i.e., BSSD) and the black cross on it. To become a full patched brother the Prospect must be presented by his sponsor before the MC and win a one hundred percent affirmative vote from the full patched brothers. Prior to votes being cast, a Prospect usually travels to every chapter in the sponsoring chapter's geographic region (state/province/territory) and introduces himself to every full patched brother. This process allows all regional chapter members to become familiar with the Prospect. Some form of formal induction follows, wherein the Prospect affirms his loyalty to the MC and its members. Often the Prospect's sponsor may require him to make a nomadic journey on his motorcycle before crossing over, sometimes as far as 1,000 miles that must be completed within twenty-four hours to ensure that the Prospect understands the Black Sabbath Motorcycle Club is a riding motorcycle club. The final logo patch is then awarded at his swearing in and initiation ceremony. The step of attaining full membership can be referred to as "being patched", "patching in" or "crossing over."

Command Structure
- National President
- National Vice President

- High Council President
- High Council
- National Business Manager
- National Ambassador
- Regional President
- President
- Vice President
- Secretary
- Sgt-at-Arms
- Road Captain
- Treasurer
- Business Manager
- Public Relations Officer
- Media/Web Design Officer
- Full Patch Member
- First Lady S.O.T.C.
- Full Patch S.O.T.C.
- Head Goddess
- Full Patch Goddess
- Support Crew
- Prospect
- S.O.T.C. Prospect
- Goddess Prospect
- Hang Around
- Special officers include Disaster Chief, Nomad/Ronin, National Sgt-at-Arms, Enforcer, Support Crew Chief, Father, Godfather, and Godmother.

Colors

The Black Sabbath Motorcycle Club patch is called the "Turtle Shell". The colors are set out on a white background inside a black circle, inside a black crested shield, with the words Black Sabbath MC encircling the riding man. The crested shield on the sixteen-inch back patch gives the appearance of a turtle's shell when worn as it covers most members' entire back. The MC's colors are white, yellow, black, and blue.

In the fifty-year history of the MC the colors have remained untouched except for the addition of the shield in 1975 and the enlargement of the patch to nineteen inches by sixteen inches in 2009. The adherence to the original patch mirrors their adherence to the core values of the Original Seven founding forefathers.

Racial Policies

Because the Black Sabbath Motorcycle Club was started by African Americans and its membership is primarily African American (90%) it is considered to be on the 'Black biker set" by biker clubs across America. However, the Black Sabbath Motorcycle Club states that even though it was started by seven African American men who rode on Sundays, today it is a multi-racial organization that is accepting of all religions, ilk, creed, class, caste, social status, or financial standing in members, with chapters across the United States from coast to coast. The Mighty Black Sabbath Motorcycle Club Nation is a brotherhood based on a unified lifestyle centered on riding motorcycles, living the biker lifestyle, and embracing one another as extended family- as close as any blood relatives.

Neutrality

The Mighty Black Sabbath Motorcycle Club Nation has followed all MC protocol in setting up its chapters nationwide. To that end, it has secured negotiations to operate by dominants in every area in which it has chapters. As a neutral elite traditional motorcycle-enthusiast riding MC the Mighty Black Sabbath Motorcycle Club Nation wears no support patches as it takes no political sides and does not align itself with OMC politics.

Women in the Black Sabbath MC Nation

A male dominated organization, the Mighty Black Sabbath Motorcycle Club Nation men belong to the brotherhood of the cross. Women fall into two unique categories. Women who do not ride motorcycles belong to our female social club known as

"Goddesses of the Mighty Black Sabbath Motorcycle Club Nation". Women who ride motorcycles belong to the "Sisters of the Cross MC of the Mighty Black Sabbath Motorcycle Club Nation".

Sisters of the Cross MC

The Sisters of the Cross MC of the Mighty Black Sabbath Motorcycle Club Nation (SOTC) is a female motorcycle club that rides under the protection of the full patched brothers of the Black Sabbath Motorcycle Club. The SOTC was established in 2011 by then National President, Black Dragon. SOTC Prospects must be eighteen years old, own a motorcycle and have a motorcycle driver's license. The SOTC are called the "First Ladies of the Black Sabbath Motorcycle Club", and the ranking SOTC is called First Lady. The SOTC MC was created to recognize the achievements of many of the Goddesses of the Black Sabbath Motorcycle Club who were buying, learning how to ride, and getting licenses for motorcycles at an incredible rate. The Mighty Black Sabbath Motorcycle Club Nation sought to reward the hard work and passion to ride these women displayed by giving them their own MC under the auspices of the Mighty Black Sabbath Motorcycle Club Nation.

Goddesses of the Cross

The "Goddesses of the Cross" of the Mighty Black Sabbath Motorcycle Club Nation is the social club auxiliary that supports the MC. Goddess Prospects must be eighteen years old, be of exceptional character and devoted to serve the best interests of the Mighty Black Sabbath Motorcycle Club. The GOTC was created by then National President Black Dragon in 2010.

Mission Statement

1. "To become the greatest riding motorcycle club in the world by pounding down great distances on two wheels, bonding on the highways and byways as family, camping out while riding to biker events or cross country, enjoying the wilderness, racing, competing, winning, and experiencing

our extended family by tenderly loving each other more and more each day!
2. To become the greatest motorcycle club family in the world by encouraging diversity within our MC, building strong, lasting friendships among members, instilling a sense of love, pride, and togetherness within our communities, helping those in need through volunteerism, and cultivating a mindset of moral and social responsibility amongst our members; also, by inspiring our youth to achieve beyond all limitations which will leave a legacy of hope and boundless dreams for future generations of the Mighty Black Sabbath Motorcycle Club Nation to come."

National President
The office of the National President was created by Tommy 'Hog Man' Lewis then President of the mother chapter and former mother chapter President Dewey 'Jazz' Johnson in the summer of 2000. Paul 'Pep' Perry, the last original founding member left in the chapter, was elected the first National President. Curtis 'Mad Mitch' Mitchell was appointed first National Vice President one year later. Pep also created the office of National Ambassador to which he assigned Jazz. The National Vice President position was eventually terminated. In 2010, Godfather Washington of the Mighty Black Sabbath Motorcycle Club Nation died, and Pep retired to become Godfather. National Enforcer and President of the Atlanta chapter, Black Dragon, was summoned to the mother chapter in San Diego and was elected as the second National President of the Mighty Black Sabbath Motorcycle Club Nation during the February mother chapter annual dance. Black Dragon recreated the National Vice President office and recruited then retired former San Diego President Hog Man for the position. Black Dragon created the High Council President office to which he assigned Sabbath racing legend Sugar Man. He also created the High Council which consists of the President and Vice President of every chapter. Black Dragon also created the National Sgt-at-Arms, National Business Manager,

Nomad/Ronin, Disaster Chief, Support Chief, and Public Relations Officers (PRO) offices.

Riding Awards and Designations

In order to challenge his MC members to ride harder and to distinguish the Mighty Black Sabbath Motorcycle Club Nation as a superior elite motorcycle-enthusiast riding MC, Black Dragon created the Nomad Rider program. In an article written in the Black Sabbath Magazine, Black Dragon stated, "A historic traditional MC Nation is nothing if its members do not ride!" The Nomad Rider program recognizes and awards Black Sabbath Motorcycle Club nomad riders for their achievements. Some of the awards include:

- Nomad Rider = 1,000 miles one-way (N1)
- 1 K in 1 Day Nomad = 1,000 miles one-way ridden in twenty-four hours or less (N124)
- Nomad Traveler = 2,000 miles one-way (N2)
- Nomad Warrior = 3,000 miles one-way (N3)
- Nomad Adventurer = 4,000 miles one-way (N4)
- Nomad Wanderer = 5,000 miles one-way (N5)
- Snow Bear Disciple Nomad = one hundred miles traveled in sleet, snow, or 18° F (SBN)
- Poseidon's Disciples Nomad = traveling through three states during continuous driving rain (PSN)
- Great Plains Nomad = riding across the Oklahoma or Kansas great plains (GPN)
- Panhandle Nomad = riding across the great state of Texas (TPN)
- Great Winds Nomad = riding through fifty mph windstorm (GWN)
- 1,000-mile bull's horn = eleven-inch bull's blowing horn, awarded to all Nomad Riders
- 2,000-mile Kudu's horn shofar = twenty-three-inch Kudu antelope's blowing horn, awarded to all Nomad Travelers
- 3,000-mile Kudu's horn shofar = thirty-three-inch Kudu or

Blesbok antelope's blowing horn, awarded to all Nomad Warriors
- 4,000-mile horn shofar = forty-inch Kudu, Blesbok or Impala antelope's blowing horn, awarded to all Nomad Adventurers; can be Kudu, Blesbok or Impala
- 5,000-mile horn shofar = fifty-inch antelope's blowing horn, awarded to all Nomad Wanderers; can be any horned cloven-footed animal.

Violence
Violent incidents have occurred in and around nationwide clubhouses.

- In 2002, President 'Bull' of the Zodiacs MC was killed after he pulled a gun on his former Prospect, who was partying at the mother chapter with a new MC in which he was interested. The former Prospect slashed Bull's throat with a knife when he looked away during the confrontation. This was the first killing ever committed at a Black Sabbath MC clubhouse and brought the city of San Diego down on the club. The City Attorney initiated a campaign to shut down the clubhouse nearly finishing the Black Sabbath MC. The clubhouse was subsequently firebombed in retaliation for Bull's killing.
- In February 2010, the mother chapter at 4280 Market Street was again targeted by arsonists who attempted to burn it to the ground right before the 2010 annual. They were unsuccessful.
- In 2010, a man was fatally shot in a hail of gunfire near the Phoenix chapter of the Black Sabbath MC clubhouse during an altercation over a woman. He died a block away while fleeing the scene. This incident caused the closing of the Phoenix chapter clubhouse.
- On 11 May 2012, San Diego mother chapter President, 'Wild Dogg', was murdered in front of the Black Sabbath Motorcycle Club clubhouse at 4280 Market Street during a drive by assassination. The case is still unsolved and open.

Epilogue

"Everything that I stand so firmly against today, I once was! It is only through experience, pain, suffering, and being blessed to learn life's lessons that I have evolved to whom I've become. I've been the very worst as an MC brother. I hope to live long enough to develop into the very best!"

                      John E. Bunch II
                      Black Dragon
                      Lifer
                      East Coast Regional President
                      Mighty Black Sabbath MC Nation

◊◊◊

Glossary

1%er: Initially a description falsely attributed to the AMA to describe some of the MCs that attended Rolling Gypsy race meets. It was alleged that the AMA stated that 99% of the people at their events were God fearing and family oriented. The other 1% were hoodlums, thugs, and outlaws. Non-AMA sanctioned MCs, thus being seen as outlaws, adopted the 1%er moniker and embraced it as an identity. Over time the 1%er designation became exclusively associated with OMGs, criminal biker syndicates, and some OMCs. Though not all 1%ers are criminals it is certain that the 1% diamond designation attracts law enforcement scrutiny like no other symbol on a biker's cut.

5%er: A member of an MRO. Only five percent of motorcyclists are involved with MROs that are dedicated to protecting the rights of the other ninety-five percent of bikers by spending money, dedicating time, and championing pro-biker legislation.

80/20 Rule: A requirement held by some MC councils requiring all blessed MCs within a council's region to demonstrate, via a bike count, that 80% of the MC's members have operational motorcycles at all times.

AMA: American Motorcyclist Association

ABATE: An organization started by Easy Rider Magazine to fight against discrimination toward motorcyclists, mostly helmet laws originally. Once called "A Brotherhood Against Totalitarian Enactments" or "American Bikers Against Totalitarian Enactments", ABATE now has many other names including "American Brotherhood (or Bikers) Aimed Toward Education." ABATE fights for biker rights and champions many issues well beyond helmet laws. Members often help charities. Membership comes with yearly dues and officers are elected from the active membership.

Ape Hangers: Tall handlebars that place a biker's hands at or above his shoulder height.

Backyard: Where you ride often—never defecate there.

Baffle: Sound deadening material inside a muffler that quiets the exhaust noises.

Bike Count: To stem the tide of the so called "popup clubs" some councils require a minimum number of motorcycles to be in a MC before they will allow it to start up in their region. MC numbers are proven when the MC undergoes a bike count of its members; usually with all members present on their bikes.

Black Ball List: A list enacted by an MC coalition or council. It is directed at non-compliant MCs that serve to notify other MCs not to support the "black-balled" chapter nor allow it to participate in any coalition authorized Set functions.

Blockhead: The V-twin engine Harley, 1984 – 2000.

Boneyard: Salvage yard for used bikes and parts.

Brain Bucket: Small, beanie-style helmet (usually not Department of Transportation (DOT) approved).

Broad: A female entertainer for the MC. She may be a dancer or at times a prostitute.

Broken Wings: A patch meaning the rider has been in a crash.

BS: bullshit: NONESENSE usually vulgar: to talk foolishly, boastfully, or idly: to engage in a discursive discussion.

Burnout: Spinning the rear wheel while holding the front brake. (Conducting burnouts while visiting another MC's clubhouse is disrespectful as it brings complaints from the neighborhood and invites unwanted police attention. Make trouble in your own neighborhood and be respectful with noise and other commotion while visiting others.)

Cage: Any vehicle of four or more wheels, specifically not a motorcycle.

Cager: Driver of a cage. (Usually, cagers are thought of as dangerous to bikers because they do not pay attention to the road.)

Chopper: A bike with the front end raked or extended out.

Chromeitis: A disease associated with a biker that cannot seem to buy enough aftermarket accessories (especially chrome).

Church: Clubhouse ("Having church" or "going to church" is referred to as the club meeting at the clubhouse).

CLAP: Chrome, Leather, Accessories, Performance

Clone: A motorcycle built to resemble and function like a Harley-Davidson motorcycle without actually being a Harley-Davidson motorcycle.

Club Name: Also known as a handle. A name given to a MC member by his brothers most often based upon his character, routine, quirks, and/or a noteworthy event that happened in the MC of which that member played a part. This is usually a name of honor and often indicates the personality one might expect when encountering that member. This name is generally accepted with great pride by the member and is a handle he will adopt for a lifetime. For instance, I once became annoyed with a member of the Black Sabbath Atlanta chapter for giving me a hard time when I needed him to break into my house and get the keys to my trailer so he could rescue me from the side of the road in Little Rock, AR nine hours away. He gave me so much grief about my trailer registration, working condition of my signal lights, and notifying authorities before he would break in my place that I frustratingly named him "By-the-Book", instantly changing his name from "Glock." By-the-Book so loved his new name that when he later departed the Mighty Black Sabbath M.C. Nation, he took his name with him and is still called By-the-Book to this very day. It is an honor for the MC to name you and quite improper for you to name yourself.

Club Hopping: The frowned upon practice of switching memberships from one MC to another. Traditional MCs have low tolerance for bikers who "club hop" as this phenomenon breaks down good order and discipline in MCs. In fact, this was seldom done in the early days. Most coalitions and councils regulate club hopping and enact vigorous laws against it. Often, OMCs refuse to allow former members to wear another MC's colors after serving in their OMC. An MC should generally ensure that a club hopper waits at least six months before allowing them to prospect for their MC unless the former President sanctions the move.

Colors: Unique motorcycle club back patch or patches.

Crash Bar: Engine guard that protects the engine if the bike crashes.

CreditGlide: A RUB's Motorcycle.

Crotch Rocket / Rice Burner: A sport bike.

Counter Steering: Turning the bike's handlebars in one direction and having it go in the opposite direction. All bikers should learn this maneuver for safety.

Custom: A custom-built motorcycle.

Cut: Vest containing the MC colors. The name comes from the practice of cutting the sleeves off of blue denim jackets.

DILLIGAF: "Do I Look Like I Give A Fuck?"

DOT: Department of Transportation.

Drag Bars: Low, flat, straight handlebars.

Evo /Evolution®: Evolution engine (V-Twin, 1984 – 2000).

Fathead: Twin-Cam engine (V-Twin, 1999 – Present).

Fender / Fender Fluff: A female passenger who is not an Old Lady but simply a lady a biker has invited for a ride.

Flathead: The Flathead engine (V-Twin, 1929 – 1972).

Flash Patch: Generic patch sold at meets and bike shops.

Flip: Occurs when an OMC takes over a less powerful OMC or 99%er. This can occur against that MC's will and could be violent. The less powerful MC will flip from their colors to the dominant MC's colors.

Flying Low: Speeding.

Forward Controls: Front pegs, shifter, and rear brake control moved forward (often to the highway pegs).

Freedom Fighter: An MRO member dedicated to preserving or gaining biker's rights and freedoms.

FTA: "Fuck Them All."

FTW: "Fuck the World" or "Forever Two Wheels."

Get-Back-Whip: A two-to-three-foot leather braid with an easy release hard metal clip that can be attached to the front brake handle or the clutch handle. Often it contains a lead weight at the bottom of the braid with tassels that just barely drag the ground when the bike is standing still. This ornamental decoration can quickly be released to make a formidable weapon to be used to slap against offending cages that invade a biker's road space (to include breaking out the cager's windows). Either end can be used in an offensive or defensive situation. The Get-Back-Whip is illegal in MANY states.

Hard Tail: A motorcycle frame with no rear suspension.

Hang Around: The designation of a person who has indicated that he formally wants to get to know a MC so he can begin prospecting for them.

HOG: Harley Owners Group.

Independent: A biker who is not a member of a MC, but is normally a well-known, accepted individual of local Biker Set (of a higher order than a hang-around).

Ink: Tattoo.

Ink-Slinger: Tattoo Artist.

KTRSD: "Keep the Rubber Side Down" Riding safely and keeping both tires on the road instead of up in the air—as in having a wreck.

Knuck/Knucklehead: The Knucklehead engine (V-Twin 1936 – 1947).

LE/LEO: Law Enforcement Officer/Official.

Lick and Stick: A temporary pillion back seat placed on the fender through the use of suction cups.

MC: Motorcycle Club.

MM: Motorcycle Ministry (Also known as 5%ers).

Moonlight Mile: A short adventure with a lady friend away from camp.

MRO: Motorcycle Rights Organization. These organizations seek to protect the rights and freedoms of bikers (i.e., ABATE, BOLT, Motorcycle Riders Foundation, American Motorcycle Association, MAG, etc.).

MSF: Motorcycle Safety Foundation.

OEM: Original Equipment Manufacturer.

Old / Ole Lady: Girlfriend or wife of a biker, definitely off limits!

OMC: Outlaw Motorcycle Club.

OMG: Outlaw Motorcycle Gang.

On Ground: Refers to showing up on or riding a motorcycle instead of showing up in or driving a cage.

On Two: Refers to showing up on or riding a motorcycle instead of showing up in or driving a cage.

Pan/Pan Head: The Pan Head engine (V-Twin, 1948 – 1965).

Patch: The back patch is the colors of a MC.

Patch-Over: Like club flipping a patch-over occurs when a MC changes patches from one MC to another. This is acceptable and not looked upon unfavorably in most cases. 99%er MCs patch-over MCs they acquire instead of "flipping" them because 99%ers do not enforce territory. This will be a peaceful gentlemen's agreement that happens unremarkably and without incident. 1%ers flip MCs.

Pillion Pad: Passenger Seat.

Pipes: Exhaust System.

PRO: Public Relations Officer.

Probate/Probie/Probationary: A member serving a period of probation until he is voted into full patched (full membership) status.

Probation: The period of time a Probie must serve before full membership is bestowed. This is the time distinguished from being a hang-around because the member is voted into the Probie status and is permitted to wear some form of the MCs colors. The Probie is also responsible to follow the MC's bylaws.

Prospect: A member serving a prospectship until he is voted into full patched (full membership) status.

Prospectship: The period of time a Prospect must serve before a vote for full membership is held. This is the time distinguished from being a hang-around because the prospective member is voted into the Prospect status and permitted to wear some form of the MCs colors. The Prospect is also responsible to follow the MC's bylaws.

Rags: Club colors or a Cut.

Rat Bike: A bike that has not been maintained or loved.

RC: Riding Club. A group that rides for enjoyment (perhaps under a patch), but members do not incur the responsibility of brotherhood to the level of traditional MCs, modern MCs, or OMCs. Members generally purchase their patches and do not often Prospect/Probie to become members. Rides and runs are generally voluntary and there is no mandatory participation. RCs are still required to follow MC protocol when operating on the MC Set and would do well to know the MC laws and respect them so as not to wind up in any kinds of altercations.

Revolution™: The Revolution engine, Harley-Davidson's first water-cooled engine (V-Twin, 2002 – Present)

RICO Act: Racketeer Influenced and Corrupt Organizations. Initially, these laws were passed for law enforcement to combat organized crime such as the mafia. They were quickly used to prosecute OMGs, OMCs, and some 99%er MCs.

Riding Bitch: Riding as the passenger on the back of a bike.

Road Name: Also known as a Handle. A name given to a MC member by his brothers and is most often based upon his character, routine, quirks, or a noteworthy event that happened in the MC of which that member played a part. This is usually a name of great honor and often indicates the personality one might expect when encountering that member. This name is generally accepted with great pride by the member and is a handle he will adopt for a lifetime.

Rocker: Bottom part of MC colors which usually designates geographic location or territory, though other information may be contained there such as the word "Nomad."

RUB: Rich Urban Biker.

Rubber: Tire.

Rubber Side Down: Riding safely and keeping both tires on the road instead of up in the air—as in having a wreck.

Run: Road trip "on two" with your brothers.

Running 66: Though rare it is sometimes necessary to ride without the MC's colors showing (also known as "riding incognito").

Shovel/Shovel Head: The Shovel Head engine (V-Twin, 1966 – 1984)

Shower Head: The new Harley-Davidson V-Rod motorcycle motor.

Sissy Bar Passenger Backrest.

Slab: Interstate.

Sled: Motorcycle.

Softail®: A motorcycle frame whose suspension is hidden, making it resemble a hard tail.

SMRO: State Motorcycle Rights Organization. Same as an MRO except defined by the state in which they operate, (i.e., ABATE of Oklahoma, MAG of Georgia, etc.).

Straight Pipes: An exhaust system with no Baffles.

Tats: Tattoos.

Tail Gunner: The last rider in the pack.

The Motorcyclist Memorial Wall: A biker's memorial wall located in Hopedale Ohio where the names of fallen riders are engraved for a nominal fee (www.motorcyclistmemorial.com). Memorial bricks may also be purchased to lie at the beautiful site.

The Motorcycle Memorial Foundation: The foundation that operates the Motorcyclist Memorial Wall. P.O. Box 2573 Wintersville, Ohio 43953.

Thirteen ("13") Diamond Patch: This is a patch commonly worn by some Outlaw MC Nations. The "13" symbol can have several meanings referencing the thirteenth letter of the alphabet, "M," standing for Marijuana, Methamphetamines, Motorcycle, or the original Mother Chapter of a MC. In Hispanic gang culture, "13" can represent "La Eme" (Mexican Mafia).

Three-Piece Patch: Generally thought of as being OMC colors consisting of a top rocker (name of MC), middle insignia (MC's symbol) and bottom rocker (name of state or territory MC claims). Not only OMCs wear three-piece patches, but new 99%er MCs should stay away from this design and stick to a one-piece patch.

Turn your back: A show of ultimate disrespect is to turn your back on someone.

Twisties: Section of road with a lot of increasing, distal, radial turns.

Vested Pedestrian: Is a person who is in a MC and wearing colors but does not own a motorcycle. Often thought of as a person who has never had a motorcycle, rather than someone who may be between bikes for a short period of time (i.e., a month or two).

Wannabe: Someone that tries to pretend to be a part of the biker lifestyle.

Wrench: Mechanic.

XXF-FXX/XXFOREVER – FOREVERXX: Patch worn by MC members to represent their total commitment to the MC and every other member of that MC. XX stands for the name of the MC (i.e., Black Sabbath Forever Forever Black Sabbath).

Thank you for reading my book Social Clubs Bible Revival of the Women's Social Clubs, "Lifting As We Ride!"

John E. Bunch II

About the Author

John E. Bunch II 'Black Dragon' rode on the back of a Honda Trail 50cc for the first time when he was six years old. Instantly, he was hooked! His mother could not afford to buy him a motorcycle so he borrowed anyone's bike that would let him ride- on the back roads and farms all over Oklahoma where he grew up. When he was fourteen his mother bought him a Yamaha 125 Enduro, cashing in the US Savings Bonds his father had given him. By the time he was seventeen, his stepfather, J.W. Oliver, gave him a Honda CX500. He was known throughout the neighborhood as the kid who always rode wheelies up the block (16th street and Classen), and as the kid who always rode wheelies with his sisters, Thea, and Lori, hanging off the back. He took his first long distance road trip at seventeen riding from Oklahoma City to Wichita, Kansas to visit his aunt and uncle. He knew then that he was born to distance ride! The nomadic call of the open road in the wind, rain, cold, heat—under the stars were home to him.

In the late 1980s, he found himself a young submarine sailor stationed in San Diego, California. He got into trouble on the base with a Senior Chief who gave him and his best friend an order they refused to follow. The white Senior Chief did not want to see the young Black man's career ended over insubordination, so he did Bunch an extreme favor. He sent him and his insolent friend, Keith (Alcatraz) Corley, who was similarly in trouble; to see African American, then Senior Chief, George G. Clark III, instead of to a Courts Martial. Senior Chief Clark threatened Bunch and Corley with physical violence if they did not obey the white Senior Chief and worked out a solution that saved both of their careers. Later, Clark invited them to 4280 Market Street when he discovered Bunch had a love for motorcycles. Bunch walked into the mother chapter and was blown away to learn that Senior Chief Clark was also known as 'Magic', former President of the Black Sabbath Motorcycle Club Mother Chapter. His insubordinate ways were not quite behind him, so it took Bunch several years to actually cross over as a full patch brother known as 'Black Dragon' in the Black Sabbath Motorcycle Club Mother Chapter.

In 2000, Black Dragon began advising writer/filmmaker Reggie Rock Bythewood, who co-wrote and directed the Dream Works movie Biker Boyz. Black Dragon went to Hollywood and worked as the Technical Adviser on the film. Biker Boyz has often been credited with re-birthing the African American MC movement in the United States.

In 2000 Black Dragon brought the Black Sabbath Motorcycle Club to Atlanta, GA and was blessed by President Skull of the Outcast MC Nation to start the chapter but the Atlanta chapter never really gained steam until he got serious about it in 2009. He suffered his first setback in Atlanta during a coup d'é·tat that cost him the Presidency of the Atlanta chapter in December 2010. In February 2011, he was elected to the Office of National President and began his nationwide march to spread the Black Sabbath Motorcycle Club from coast to coast. By 2011, the Black Sabbath Motorcycle Club became the Mighty Black Sabbath Motorcycle Club Nation with chapters from the West coast to the East coast.

2002 to 2013 Black Dragon has published several biker magazines including: *Urban Biker Cycle News, Black Iron Motorcycle Magazine, Black Sabbath Motorcycle Newsletter,* and the popular blog *www.blacksabbathmagazine.com.*

In 2013, Black Dragon wrote the first MC phone app, *"Black Sabbath Motorcycle Club."*

In 2014 Black Dragon wrote "Prospect's Bible" which has become required reading for over 3,000 MCs worldwide.

In 2015 Black Dragon wrote "MC Public Relations Officer's Bible" and "Prospect's Bible for Women's MCs."

In 2016 Black Dragon started the wildly popular YouTube channel "Black Dragon National President" which eventually became "Black Dragon Biker TV." It quickly rose to become the number 1 MC protocol and biker news channel in the country. He also created the online news magazine www.bikerliberty.com.

In 2017 Black Dragon wrote "Sergeant at Arms Bible" and was the keynote speaker at the PROC one of the largest MC education conferences in the United States.

In 2018 Black Dragon was again invited to speak at the PROC.

In 2019 Black Dragon created the podcast "The Dragon's Lair Motorcycle Chaos" on the Spreaker podcasting platform.

In 2021 Black Dragon wrote "President's Bible Chronicle 1, Principles of Motorcycle Club Leadership."

In 2023 Black Dragon launched "BlackDragonBikerTV" TikTok and went to 83 thousand subscribers in six months.

In 2023 November 6th Black Dragon was honored to be invited to participate in the rap unification song … by Taa Shon 1%er (Thunderguards MC) and Pipeline 1%er (Outcast MC). This rap song announced a truce between all major 1% Black and mixed-race MC nations operating on the Black biker set. Black Dragon had a cameo appearance in the music video which can be found at https://www.youtube.com/watch?v=4eZBEUbLar0. In this video members from Outcast MC, Thunderguards MC, Chosen Few MC, and Wheels of Soul MC can be seen.

In 2023 Black Dragon was honored to be included on the El Domino song "Diamond on my Heart (Outlaw Biker Anthem) featuring Big Buzz and Black Dragon on the El Domino comeback album, "The Preacher The Gangster The Outlaw" featuring Snoop Dogg, Three 6 Mafia, Akon, T-Pain, The Game, Baby Bash and Mr. Criminal. The music video "Diamond on my Heart" was produced by three-time Emmy award winning director Joshua Coombs. Black Dragon did the voiceover in the music video quoting former South African President Nelson Mandella, "A wise man once said, when a man is denied the right to live the life he believes in, he has no choice but to become an outlaw."

In 2023 December 10th, Black Dragon wrote "Social Clubs Bible Revival of the Black Women's Social Clubs Movement Lifting as We Climb!"

Today Black Dragon is looking ahead to see where he can be of service to motorcycle clubs, riding clubs, social clubs, and biker organizations worldwide. Black Dragon is currently a senior lifer and East Coast Regional President in the Mighty Black Sabbath Motorcycle Club Nation.

    Black Sabbath Forever Black Sabbath
    A Breed Apart
    Since 1974

    www.blacksabbathmc.com

◊◊◊

A NOTE FROM BLACK DRAGON

Now what? You have read the book, and you know the power of the information held within. I want you to know that you can help other Social Club prospects and members navigate their way through the murky waters of having a successful club life in their beloved social clubs on the Black biker set.

If you were helped, educated, or informed by this book there are a couple of simple things you can do to join me in remaking the MC/SC world through knowledge, experience, education, and love:

> 1. If you believe the Social Clubs Bible has helped you then I ask that you spread the word by buying a copy for someone you think should have one.
>
> 2. Setup a reading group to discuss how this book applies to helping to better your SC. You can also write an honest review on social media, your blog, website, or on your favorite bookseller's website. There are countless ways you can help others by spreading this word. Social Clubs Bible is not just a book worth reading, it is a vision and a plan worth following for every member to contribute positively to their SC. It is a vision worth sharing.
>
> 3. Enrich other SCs and MCs by buying this book for your brother and sister MCs/SCs on the set with whom you share alliances. Imagine if sister SCs could have the benefit of the knowledge you have attained.
>
> **Thank you for your support!** Send me an email anytime with questions, improvements, or your best SC tales! blackdragon@blacksabbathmc.com

About the Cover

"Lifting As We Climb"
Commissioned by: Black Dragon Created by: Holly Joseph

Figure 23: Cover by Holly Joseph assisted by Artificial Intelligence software.

The picture in this book was created by Artificial Intelligence (AI) under the expert prompting work of Holly Joseph. Her concept is sisters standing together in unity within the circle of a motorcycle tire. They represent the spokes in the tire which is the rigid frame that provides the strength upon which the motorcycle rides. In the bottom right corner, you will see the rolling hills of the highway or the curves of the woman's body lying down.

I wanted this work to be created by a Black woman. I searched hi and low and all initial attempts failed. When I called my project manager, Holly, to discuss the outline, we started talking about other aspects of the book and I mentioned that I didn't have a cover. I told her that I was thinking of an SC member dressed in 1800s period clothing reaching back to guide the SC sisters of today suggesting the theme, "Lifting as we Climb." I didn't even know that she was really listening, but it seemed that almost as fast as we hung up (maybe an hour or two later) Holly submitted several designs, to my surprise and delight. This is the one I chose.

Who is Holly Joseph:
Writing – Communications – Project and Relationship Management
Instructional Designer, Book Author Consultant
MS, Instructional Design and Technology Georgia State University
MA, Applied Linguistics Georgia State University.

Thank you so much Holly for coaching me and helping me write the outline for this book. I know it's incredibly longer than any book you would allow to be written! Perhaps we can trim it down together for the second printing. And thank you for developing my cover in less than an hour, saving me once again from floundering!

If anyone is writing a book and you need professional coaching, oversight, and project management, I highly recommend my friend of nearly 20 years, Holly Joseph.

hjoseph.works@gmail.com

The Social Clubs Bible

I am currently writing the Social Club Encyclopedia which will attempt to list the names and history of every social club in the United States. If you want your club to be included, please send me an email to blackdragon@blacksabbathmc.com. Volume 1 will be published near October 2024 so please do not hesitate to contact me and get your Social Club included.

JBII

Buy Prospect's Bible

More from John E. "**Black Dragon**" Bunch II

Bunch Media Group LLC.

Prospect's Bible
Amazon #1 Best Seller

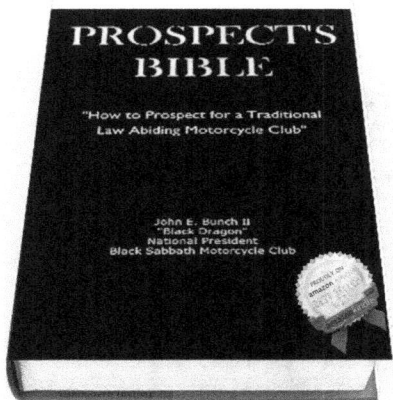

Learn how to prospect for
a traditional MC!
Order 24 hours per day
www.blackdragonsgear.com
Available from Kindle, Amazon.com, Audible, and retail bookstores.

The Social Clubs Bible

Buy Sergeant-at-Arms Bible

More from John E. "**Black Dragon**" Bunch II

Bunch Media Group

Sergeant at Arms Bible
Amazon #1 Best Seller

Learn how to be the Sergeant-at-Arms for
a traditional MC!
Order 24 hours per day
www.blackdragonsgear.com
Available from Kindle, Amazon.com, Audible, and retail bookstores.

Buy Public Relations Officer's Bible

More from John E. **"Black Dragon"** Bunch II

Bunch Media Group

Motorcycle Clubs Public Relations Officer's Bible
Amazon #1 Best Seller

Learn how to be the Sergeant-at-Arms for
a traditional MC!
Order 24 hours per day
www.blackdragonsgear.com
Available from Kindle, Amazon.com, Audible, and retail bookstores.

Buy President's Bible Chronicle I
Principles of Motorcycle Club Leadership

More from John E. "**Black Dragon**" Bunch II
Bunch Media Group Amazon #1 Best Seller

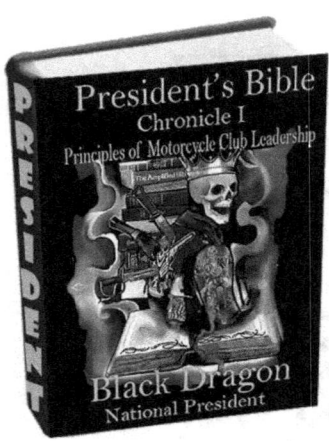

Learn the 17 scientific principles of motorcycle club leadership! Get this number one best-selling book now!

Order 24 hours per day

www.blackdragonsgear.com

Available from Kindle, Amazon.com, Audible, and retail bookstores.

www.ingramcontent.com/pod-product-compliance
Lightning Source LLC
Chambersburg PA
CBHW071234290426
44108CB00013B/1404